MEMOIRS

— OF A —

SHOP TEACHER

STANLEY SIPKA

BALBOA.PRESS

A DIVISION OF HAY HOUSE

Balboa Press books may be ordered through booksellers or by contacting:

Balboa Press
A Division of Hay House
1663 Liberty Drive
Bloomington, IN 47403
www.balboapress.com
844-682-1282

ISBN: 978-1-9822-5375-2 (sc)
ISBN: 978-1-9822-5376-9 (e)

Print information available on the last page.

Balboa Press rev. date: 10/13/2020

THIS BOOK IS DEDICATED TO

JOANNE C. SIPKA

Joanne died on October 11, 2019

TRIBUTE TO JOANNE

Joanne C, Sipka, my wife of 61 years

Everything I have is the result of meeting Joanne on a blind date in the spring of 1955. My first thrill was seeing her as she opened the door to greet me and Steve, who arranged the date. Silently I said, Wow! She's pretty!". We played miniature golf and did not care what our scores were. As the night ended, I walked her into her house and leaned over and gave her a kiss. I backed away, looked at her, and she said: "I don't let guys kiss me on the first date." I replied, 'There's always a first time for everything!". That was not the last kiss.

She attended Akron University and then worked for a doctor. We talked about marriage, but I had a six-year military obligation. I volunteered for the draft because we didn't want to be married and separated. We were married on June 28, 1958, a beautiful sunshiny day. I completed my Army responsibility, and we lived with her parents. She encouraged me to obtain more education, even though I attended Hower Vocational High School and lacked confidence in my academic background. She worked long hours while I attended Kent State University, and I worked part-time. In 1961, Joanne gave birth to Christine, Cathleen, in 1963 and Carol in 1965. She had difficult and painful pregnancies, but after she enjoyed happiness with her three beautiful daughters.

She enjoyed watching her daughters and grandchildren participate in sporting events and school activities, and, in later years, encouraged me to return to playing baseball with the old "bad news bears."

Her most rewarding accomplishment was she and I moved in with her mother, Julia, after her Dad died. Joanne mothered her mother and allowed her mother to enjoy life to the age of 103.

Joanne was always concerned about me, the three daughters, eight grandkids, and everyone else. All of us are who we are because of her.

Thank You, Joanne, I want to see you again and give you a kiss like the first one.

EPIGRAPH

"It is the way you presented the math!"

"It's the way you presented the math!" was said by Rocky, a student who said he was as dumb as a rock and can not learn anything as he started the class. At the end of the year, he was helping everyone, and they would ask him for help. He could recite all the trig formulas by heart and how or when to use them. I told him, "I taught trig to a rock."

From the beginning of 1966 to 2000, the presentations were different because I found more assignments that added to the ease of understanding. I learned what helped the students.

"Stan, don't worry. Together we'll make it work."

With Joanne's words and help, together, we made it work for 61 years. That is the way Joanne lived every day of her life with me. That is why it's hard to plan things myself with no discussion from her. My three daughters and grandkids help, but it is not the same when there is a decision to be made, I imagine what she would say. This way, it is both of us making the decision.

CONTENTS

PART 3 – YOU HAVE HOMEWORK

CLASSROOM RELATED INFORMATION

SPECIAL INSERT - METRIC AND INCHES

PART 3 – YOU HAVE HOMEWORK!

BLUEPRINT READING

PART II – TEACHING WAS AN EDUCATION

Part two is titled TEACHING WAS AN EDUCATION, and it was. It is mentioned thought out the book and not a list if separate sections. I would say, "I learned something about that experience."

When taking classes in my master's program, I became interested in student development. Dr. Mark Savickas was the professor and instilled a desire to understand more of how my students learned and strive for more learning. My strategies changed with students; it's wasn't one size fits all. Communicate with the individual to obtain results. The math that developed over time brought out smiles to faces when they saw the successful completion of problems. What seems tough wasn't so tough.

There are assignments, many made by me, to show how I wanted to guide the person to work a problem easily. How to work formulas, eliminate the oversupply of formulas to the basic few; how to sequence steps and write them down so they can be viewed, if needed.

In the shop, it was quality first, then quantity. Thousands of an inch was the standard with senior year jobs. Parts had to fit and work together. Machine operations were common to the industry. Surface finishes were stressed. We used the saying it has to be so smooth, "if a fly lands on it, he would slip off and break a leg."

PART III – YOU GOT HOMEWORK

NOTE – The last part contains copies of assignments given to classes from high school, adults to middle school students. The one comment, "it's the way you presented it." Should be reflected in my samples of work presented. I'm sure some will attempt to work the examples and find fought with my work. Yes! There are some mistakes but no intentional, except those mentioned.

Included are pictures of jobs the students made and kept. Not every student made all those shown. The vise was the final project, and many were completed. Some students didn't complete the vise because they gained employment through the co-op program before they graduated.

PART IV – THE LAST PART

We are arriving at placing the last period in the work of 20 years of writing on different types of paper and places and time. I have to quit reading what has been written because I keep adding and subtracting stories. My family and I remember Joanne and her help, and I can see and hear her telling me to finish this because she thinks it is good.

EPILOGUE

PREFACE

I tell stories about my different stages of life, from an early age through grade school, high school, army, marriage, family, teaching, and now retirement, every chance I get. I retired in 1997 and became a driver for my grandkids, a full-time husband, assistant baseball coach, and even returned to playing baseball myself and two heart attacks. The free time allowed me to work with wood, stain glass, talk, and write. It was just write anything; soon, one story followed another, and words began to add up in the tablets. Then the idea was, "why not a book!' even if it's just for my pleasure. After watching the movie "Bucket List," I started my list with several items and added, "Write a Book." Individual stories were added when the ideas presented themself. There was a need to present the stories in a continuous order. I had no trouble following my story from start to finish. Being retired, I was in charge of my time; and plans and ideas appeared and disappeared. There was no routine and commitment, just an easy way of life. That's why it has taken me 20 years to complete this project. Since my wife Joanne, passed away, my daily routine is more serious because Joanne is not taking care of me. I have to do this by myself. The transition is not easy because we did things together, but the daily look or touch is missing, and sometimes a loud reminder about some household issues. The routine is much the same daily working in the machining industry. You have control of the equipment (house) and know where the on-off switch is located, and the emergency stops switch (cell phone). The various products (keeping the family together) you work on are your sense of pride and thrill. Your audience is your fellow workers (family). You are by yourself and engrossed in a job (helping the family).

Teaching is not the same. The interactions between students and teachers can change quickly. Your exhaustion comes from the constant interaction between students and others in the school. There's no stop switch to use. You also want to be proud of the finished product.

ACKNOWLEDGMENT

To my wife, family, friends, company owners, and students for their encouragement to continue this project.

My grandchildren also helped by reading and making suggestions. The additions of pictures and documents were made easy by Julia Sincel. Melissa Sincel and Corey Spicer.

There is a special acknowledgment to our local Machining companies who helped with student employment and their scrap materials.

Thanks to the faculty of Cuyahoga Falls School Systems - High School, Sill and Bolich Middle Schools, The Akron Machining Institute, and Kent State University undergraduate and Master's programs

INTRODUCTION

"SHOP TEACHER"

"SHOP TEACHER" describes my position in the Cuyahoga Falls School system from 1964 to 1997. Keys hung from my side and had a shirt pocket protector with pencils and rulers. The shop was away from the main campus. You would see lathes, vertical and horizontal milling machines, surface grinders, drill presses, stock racks, and tool room. The room had a unique aroma of oil, grease, and tar. The floor was wood with a coating of tar, which caused problems in the homes of students and teachers. The students changed clothes because the machines and materials used would dirty their clothes. There were aprons, shop coats with rags in the pockets along, safety glasses worn by the teacher, and students. There were brooms, dustpans, and barrels used by the students when they had to clean the shop. Every student learned "to be humble" when sweeping because shop teachers believed "a clean shop is a happy shop." (A humble sweeper is one that is bent over with one hand near the bottom the broom and the other high on the broom. The bristles are bent from pressure, and the floor is clean)

My classroom was at the end of the building. When girls delivered messages from the office, many didn't like to enter the room because the students looked funny wearing those safety glasses. The room, in the beginning, was too small; picture a one-car garage with three cars end to end. In 1970 the new room was spacious, two stories high with a balcony with lockers, restroom, and wash area.

Every day I worked with students providing opportunities for them to acquire machining skills. Entering the building and shop each day, I would wonder what will happen today. Would it be a good day or a bad day? After 5973 school days (33years x 181 school days per year), I realized what I've experienced as a teacher. Retired in 1997, and after 32 plus years, I want to present with words, good and bad experiences, and to emphasize, I learned something from each occurrence.

The idea "TEACHING WAS AN EDUCATION" wasn't present when I started in 1964. Every day was a learning experience. It wasn't just in the classroom or shop (the term now is lab). I was sure of my skills in the shop, but the daily contact with young individuals and how to handle this interaction was the question I couldn't answer. Every day the different face to face encounters showed me teaching each student was stressful. Safety for the individual, fellow students, equipment, how to work machines, read drawings, plan the sequence of steps to complete the job, and math-related to the trade, was expected of me. The unexpected experiences resulted from being in the class and other parts of the school during the school day. These unique encounters were the learning that wasn't thought of as I started my teaching career.

The third part of the title "YOU GOT HOMEWORK!" shows assignments presented to students in the machine trades in high school, adult programs, and middle school students. These are the problems that "Rocky" learned because these concepts "were presented differently" from his days in school ("Rocky's" quote). (Rocky was an adult in the apprenticeship program at Akron Machining Institute, and his experience will be in a later section). These examples evolved to make learning the concepts and evaluating the returned assignment. The students in the early years didn't experience the reworked assignments. The introduction of calculators allowed more learning in the late 1970s.

Remember, the work presented was from the mid-1960s to the 2000 period. The advance in electronics and automation would make my examples outdated. This change is called "PROGRESS!"

Included are pictures of projects assigned to help the students gain the skills needed to gain employment. The students kept what they made.

PROLOGUE

"THE THRILL OF VICTORY AND
THE AGONY OF DEFEAT"

That was heard at the beginning of the TV program "Wide World of Sports" from April 1961 to January 1998, hosted by Jim McKay and others. You would see a winning team celebrating, and another scene shows a ski jumper falling off the edge of the jump ramp instead of landing far below. For me, "The Thrill of Victory" encompassed my life; it's the thrill of success instead of victory, and the agony is not being successful. It's not just sports; I have experienced success in the last 85 years. I was successful in driving my tricycle when I was four years old, drunk and not pedaling off the sidewalk onto the street or four years ago, age 81, successfully catching a line drive, inches from my face. I remember seeing the back of my hand as the baseball smashed into the glove. Yes! From age 10 to 85, the thrill was constant from baseball and learned to like it. I realized I wouldn't become a professional baseball player and wanted success in what was to follow. It was "The thrill of doing what makes me and others happy." My routes to the thrill of success took many paths. One path was becoming a shop teacher

THE END OR BEGINNING? IT'S BOTH

June 1997, Bolich Middle School in Cuyahoga Falls, Ohio, the bell rings, the students run out, this was the last day of school for the 1996-1997 school year. It's the start of the summer break for them and me. It's a happy and sad moment because today is the end of my last year of teaching full time and the beginning of my retirement. Even though I thought about this day, I can't imagine the feeling and wonder what lies ahead? As the noise of the kids fades away, you know there are things to do for the last time. You get busy looking for the forms that I had to fill out at the end of a school year.

Mr. John Brilla, the other shop teacher, walks in and informs me that Mrs. Green, School Principal, wants me to attend a conference with her and a parent regarding a discipline given to her son by me. I told John I was done with students because I'm "retired," and he should go for me. He told me it would be a short meeting, and don't get all worked up about it. As we walked to the meeting, I kept saying I'm retired, and this meeting is on my retirement time. We walked to the room, me still complaining, I went in, saw my Wife and Daughter, Christine, and many faculty members, a table with a "HAPPY RETIREMENT" sign and a cake to celebrate my last day.

The story about the discipline meeting was to make the party a surprise, and it was! I started to cry (because I'm like that) and looked at John and said: "You got me!!!

That was the last day for students, but teachers have another day to finish the year-end reports, inventory, order supplies, and list equipment in need of repair for next year. For shop teachers, ordering supplies was a time-consuming process because we needed many items for the following year. But, because this class would be eliminated, no supplies were ordered. The year was 1997; the logical program to start was computer "tech" classes.

FIRST DAY OF RETIREMENT

In the world of work, the first day of retirement is the next day you would have worked but didn't and stayed home. In teaching, that first day is when the kids return to school in late August. My wife worked as a teacher's aide as she prepared to drive to school; I was up helping her with breakfast, finding her keys, or staying out of her way. When she drove off "THAT'S" when I realized I was retired. What do I do with all this time? I was planning to work with wood, make things, and have fun! I found an oak door someone was throwing away weeks before and decided to remove some of the trim. This door was carried from my garage to a table on my garage porch. I removed the oak trim from one side and prepared to work on the other side. As I grabbed and turned the door, I felt something strange and warm in my left arm. My elbow looked different. There was an indentation by my elbow that wasn't there before. I stopped what I was doing and went inside. Boy! What a way to start my retirement!!! I went to the doctor then to the hospital and a day later had surgery on my torn ligament. When I turned that door over a ligament tore loose, rolled up my arm like a window shade rolling up. So, the first month, I had my left arm in a sling and a scar to remind me about my retirement. I hope no one's first day of retirement was like mine.

THE EARLY YEARS 1935 – 1948
DAY 1 - JANUARY 23, 1935

My birth occurred at home at 1074 Avon Street in Akron, Ohio; the time was 9:31 in the morning. On my 75th birthday in 2015, I visited that house and met the lady living there. I gave her a picture of my mom holding me on the porch steps with the numbers on the porch post.

My Dad, born in 1901, grew up in the Akron area and was a bus driver for the Akron Transportation Company until the Second World War when he worked for the Firestone Tire and Rubber Company. He was the oldest of six children. His parents were born in Poland and arrived in America in 1897.

My Mom, born in 1908, grew up in Rome, New York, and while visiting her Uncle in Akron, she met my Dad as a passenger on his bus. We would comment at times, what would have happened if our mom caught a different bus. My Mom's family (3 sisters and six brothers) all lived in Rome, and we would visit nearly every year. The seven of us, mom, dad, four sisters - Rita, Betty, Arlene, Helene, and I would spend the 10 hours traveling the 400 miles to Rome N.Y. My family now talks about how we survive seven in one car without any electronic devices and air condition. I think the five of us started the famous sayings "are we there yet!" and "how many more minutes?" During World War II years, we took the train to Rome.

What were some of the earliest moments I can remember? I remember sitting on my dad's shoulders, watching and listening to Franklin D. Roosevelt speak from the end of a train at a station off Market Street in 1939. Had to be four and a half years old, He was campaigning for the 1940 election. That location was visible from the second-floor room window of Joanne's hospital room last year, but the station was removed years ago. I remember the big crowd.

The Rubber Bowl opened in Akron about 1939. It was a WPA (Worker Public Act), and my dad drove a special bus to transport local officials to the official opening.

In 1939, I viewed the remains of the doodlebug train burned-out shell after the horrible train crash in Cuyahoga Falls, Ohio, at the intersection of Front Street and Hudson Drive. Those railroad tracks aren't used today, but the tracks across Hudson Drive are still there as a reminder of the accident. There is a park on Front Street that commemorates that tragedy.

MY GRANDMOTHER SAVED ME!

On one visit to Rome, when I was 4 or 5 years old, my Mom and Aunts bought me a pair of shiny black patent leather shoes and was proud of my new shoes and would show everyone to hear their comments. My grandfather was sitting outside on the porch, reading his paper. I walked up and asked him to look at my shiny shoes. He looked over the rocking chair rail, made a sound from his mouth, moved his head down, and appeared to spit on my new shoes. I looked down, realized what I thought he did, and bit him on his arm so hard I left teeth marks on his arm. In seconds, he screamed loud enough to make my grandmother run out of the door, just a few feet away. He wanted to grab me; I ran behind her, keeping her between him and me. He was livid and showed my grandmother the teeth marks on his arm and wants to get to me. My grandmother asks me why I bit Grandpa. I pointed to my shoes and said he spit on my shoes! Well, Grandma yelled at grandpa and was sure the neighbors could hear her telling him he deserves the bite. I stayed close to my grandma for a few days and watched out for my grandpa. Later I found out the words my grandpa was yelling were Polish cuss words.

DRUNK AT THE AGE OF 5

During my time working with senior boys in the age range of 15-19, I was asked if I was ever drunk or "smashed." I would tell them I had to give up drinking when I was 4 or 5 years old. I almost fell off my tricycle and nearly drove off the sidewalk on the way home from a beer joint - drunk. We were again visiting my Mom's Mother in New York. My parents and grandma wanted to go shopping and didn't want me along because I was a pain in the neck. My mom's two brothers took me to the corner beer joint, and I drove my tricycle there and parked it in the room where I could see it. We were there for a couple of hours and had chips, pop and things to eat. They let me drink the beer that remained in the glasses for the 2 hours; I know they didn't drink every last drop. I guess being 4 or 5, it doesn't take much to get light-headed. Of course, my young uncles had a good time entertaining me. It was time to leave, as I pedaled home on my "wheels," my parents and grandma returned and could see my uncles and me coming home. As I drove my tricycle, I (using my acting skills and facial expressions with the students) was not moving in a straight line it was left then right back and forth and almost dropped off the sidewalk to the street. My uncles were behind me laughing as was my dad, but my Mom and Grandma were furious and ready to kill her sons and brothers. I stopped drinking because I had flashbacks about falling off the sidewalk into the busy street. Of course, the guys shake their heads, walk away, and make comments about my "drinking problem." I included a picture of my spiffy tricycle. It's obvious why I was proud of my wheels.

WORKING WITH METAL THE FIRST TIME

My very first experience with metals was when I was 6 or 7 years old. I watched and helped my dad use a hack saw to saw thin slices of metal off a bar of steel locked in a vise. These slices were filed down and used as slugs in slot machines. Yes! These slugs were illegal. I can imagine the headline in the paper where a father and son (me) were going to jail for making slugs. One day a neighbor lady came over, sees these slugs on the table, and asked my dad what they were? My dad told her they were slugs for slot machines. She got excited and wanted a couple to use in the slot machines at her husband's Afro-American Social Club on Howard St. in Akron, Ohio. My dad said, "OK." as she left, with several slugs, she said she would "split her winnings with him." A couple of days later, she came back, drops down several coins on the table, and tells my dad these are his share of her winnings. She also stressed her husband not be told she used slugs because he came home that evening announcing in an angry, upset voice that some "no-good so and so" put slugs in his slot machines, and he's going to wring his neck when he finds out who did that!! It was his wife.

THE SWINGING BRIDGE

Photo courtesy of the Akron Beacon Journal and Mark Price. This appeared March 11, 2011

I was 7 or 8 years old when I did this that nearly cost my life on the swinging bridge. We lived a couple of hundred feet from the swinging bridge over the Cuyahoga River, and I had crossed that bridge many times. Every time I had to be careful because there was no side protection on the right side, and a single cable to hold on to on the left side (a picture illustrates this unique bridge.) When we had rain, the river level would rise and become unsafe while it flowed toward Cleveland. Several older kids would take advantage of the increased flow by standing on the bridge with fishnets attached to poles catching balls as they flow toward Cleveland. These balls were lost on streets in Akron. All the rainwater would enter the river and pass under this bridge. The guys would toss the balls to those watching. I was told not to go on the bridge because it was too dangerous for my size. Well, as you can imagine, I also wanted to do that. This particular day we had a rainstorm, and I thought it was my chance to pluck balls from the river. I took my mom's clothes line pole, tied her kitchen strainer to the end, and walked to the bridge. No one else was there, just me. The water level was high and rushing by quickly. I positioned myself on the bridge looking up the river for a ball, here comes one! I shove the pole in the water. It's pulled out of my hands, in the water, under the bridge, and moving down the river. I looked around and watched the pole disappear, and thought I could be in the water going north toward Cleveland with little chance of living. NO ONE knew I was on the bridge. I walked off and thought I was lucky. I never told anyone that experience, especially my mom; I felt I was under the care of my guardian angel.

Weeks later, during the warm days of spring, my mom, like most mothers, would hang clothes outside to dry. She asked my dad if he did anything with her clothes pole. "No," he replied. So, the pole just disappeared, gone. I could travel along the banks of the river, maybe find it, but how could I explain to my mom how her clothes pole was a half a mile down the river. I never did tell her or anyone until now.

The 1933 photo shows an unnamed boy on the bridge. I lived in the house on the corner and beyond the trees. Otto Street runs to the right, and Border Street runs to the left. As you look at this construction marvel, you wonder if any individuals fell the 6 + feet in the river. The water was normally only a foot or so deep, but after heavy rains, the water level would be rushing down a few feet to a few inches below the low part of the bridge. I can imagine many viewing this for the first time would also say they would not cross the bridge.

Mark Price, a reporter from The Akron Beacon Journal, wrote a story because he thought this "construction marvel" was a part of Akron's uniqueness in the early years. I received approval from Mr. Price to use the picture. It appeared on March 10, 2011.

PROVIDING WATER TO THE WORKERS

During the hot summer months of 1940, men were digging deep trenches in Otto Street for sewer lines. I would sit and watch the guys digging by hand with no heavy machinery to help. One day I asked my mom if we could give these guys some ice water because they were working hard, and the day was hot. She said that was a good idea; we gave the workers water for several days. One day one guy gave me a nickel or a few pennies, which was big money those days. I'm sure I bought a lot of candy with that large amount of money.

The year is now 2016, and here again, guys are working in the street, different street, and cities, like 1940. This time almost no one is using shovels, just machines shoving pipe into the ground, traveling up and down the road. I watch like I did back then and wanted to provide some water to these hard-working sweating guys. This time I have several bottles of ice water and handed the bottles out to the few guys in front of the house. They thanked me, and I tell them the story about 1940 and how the guys gave me a few pennies, I wanted to share my experience and didn't expect any money. One guy reaches in his pocket and hands me about 7 pennies. He then tells me not to spend the money in one place. I said, "thank you, and I have to go to the store to buy some candy."

ST. HEDWIG'S GRADE SCHOOL
THE ONE HALL SCHOOLHOUSE!

My parents selected my elementary school for three reasons. First, we were Catholic, and St. Hedwigs Catholic School had grades 1 - 8. Second, I would have two older students walk me to school and back to learn the routine of the mile-long walk until they moved to the high school. Third, finally, I then walked with my first sister, Rita, then my second sister, Betty. My other two sisters, Arlene and Helene, had Rita and Betty helping them because I was in High School.

The school was one long hallway. The three classrooms and a storage room were on the right. On the left, two rooms were for the four nums who lived there – three teachers and one cook-housekeeper. The last two rooms were made into one large area used for the cafeteria, gym, and assemblies.

The school was above the church, small, with three classrooms for the eighth grades. One room had the first, second, and third grades; the next class had the fourth, fifth, and sixth grades and last, was the seventh and eighth grades. The number of students in each grade was usually less than ten, so the nuns had time for each student. When I was in the seventh and eighth grades, I was the only boy with five girls; the other grade had 7 or 8 students too. These small classes helped me later in high school and college.

The walk to St Hedwigs was dangerous because we had to cross Cuyahoga Street and Howard Street (which was dangerous). The crossing of Howard St. was on the long steep hill where it crossed Glenwood St. My sisters and I remembered how we had to cross Howard St. a few times during the winter months on all fours because of the ice. We didn't have to worry about cars because drivers knew the danger. Imagine standing in the street and sliding down the road because of ice.

My sisters and I had to behave at St Hedwig's because these Nuns knew our aunt, Sister Benilda, who was also a nun in the same order.

I am in the eighth grade; it's early September 1948, the Cleveland Indians are tied for first place with the Boston Red Sox for the America league championship. There would be a one-game tie breaker game in Boston at 1:00 pm on Monday to determine who will play in the World Series. I asked the nun if we could listen to some of the game; she rants and raved about this disturbance. *I was in school to learn and not to be engaging in baseball*. I sat there upset because this nun didn't realize I was Cleveland's "Good Luck Piece"; when I listen, they win. After school, I RAN home and just heard the last out, and Cleveland won. If Cleveland had lost, I would not have talked to that nun again!

Walking to and back from St. Hedwig's, I passed a house where a young girl lived until her family moved to Cuyahoga Falls, Ohio. That little girl, Joanne, became my wife in 1958.

Imagine being in the eighth grade with five other girls. In retrospect, it was like a one-to-one classroom experience with five eighth-graders and six seventh graders. In the seventh grade, I would watch the nun working with the eighth grade on the right side wall black board. (the seventh-grade blackboard was in the front of the class). They were learning the steps to extract the square root from a number. She asked what would be the next step. No one answered for a short time, so I yelled the answer. She yelled back; I should do my seventh-grade assignment. I turned my head and got busy. The individuals in those classes received a quality education. It was only later in life I realize the benefit of my early education at St. Hedwigs.

The nuns had some unique forms of discipline that I couldn't use today. If I used them, I would be in trouble with the law. I know for sure the nun, who taught the 7th and 8th grades used a ruler to smack the knuckles and or pull your hair pass one's ear to get one's attention. It safe to say these "attention getters" were mostly for the boys, and yes! I had a few of those attention getters.

WORLD WAR II

Sunday, December 7, 1941, my parents, sister, Rita, and I were at my Aunt and Uncle's house, keeping busy while the adults played cards. The radio was on, and we heard President Franklin D. Roosevelt speak about the attack on Pearl Harbor by the Japanese. I watched the faces of the adults, and they looked troubled. On the way home, I asked questions about this happening; my parents answered the best they could and seem concerned. One word I remembered spoken by the President was "Infamy." At school the next day, the nuns kept us focused on our subjects, but they too were concerned.

The years 1941 – 1945, all Americans young and old were geared to winning the war. Everyone had to sacrifice items like gasoline, cigarettes, tires, food, appliances, new cars, nylons, and more. Included is a picture of books for the rationing of food and gas. Joanne's name is on a book.

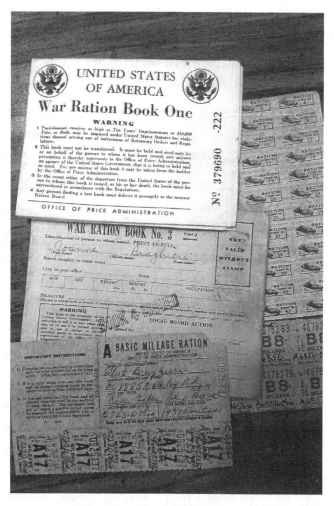

Photo by Stan Sipka

Women had to do without nylons but had a colored liquid; they could wipe on their legs to look like they were wearing nylons. Being 7 through 10 years of age, I didn't have to sacrifice too many items. I learned how to plant a garden or at least dig the ground for the plants, weed, and take care of chickens, which helped with eggs and drum sticks every so often. I would go to two dumps looking for scrap metal to sell to a man who would come by with his horse and wagon. This 5 to 10 cents helped out. I acquired sheets of silhouettes of Japanese airplanes so I could spot one if it flew in Ohio. None were detected. We did see daily the Navy plane F4U Corsair, a beautiful powerful fighter plane made in Akron, with their distinct engine sound flying being ready for combat. These planes had different wings shape that put fear in the enemy during the war. If we went to the Akron Airport, we could see in the distance 30 - 50 planes prepared for delivery.

People were moving from different states to Akron to work in factories dealing with war production. Every part of Akron contained small basic houses (local people called the houses shacks) to house those coming to work here. My dad was a bus driver but quit and worked at Firestone, where he worked on building the wings of C-46 transport planes. The company would have an open house where family members could tour the plant and see the rows of wings completed. My dad told us Firestone hired small people to crawl into the end of the wings to help fabricate the wingtips.

My Mom worked a few months on the night shift at General Tire, working on gas masks. Everyone worked to protect America and win the war even the kids

The young guys in the neighborhood all had army gear and would take our helmets, guns, canteens, lunch and travel over the swinging bridge to a hill overlooking two railroad tracks. We would set up camp to protect the rail line from the enemy. We dug fox holes and other "fortifications" and did out patriotic duty to guard the rail line. We could only do this during the day because our parents wanted us home by dark. A bucket list item is to revisit that hill and see if our fox holes are still there.

Akron would have occasional air raid drills in the evenings to prepare for a possible attack. A couple of us guys would hide outside, being careful the block air raid warden didn't spot us. We saw news clips of war activities between the two movies on Saturdays in Akron. Winning the war was our goal.

One activity everyone participated in was buying saving bonds. You would save $18.75 and would receive a 25 dollars saving bond. You would buy stamps worth .25 cents in school, paste them in a book, and when filled, you would receive the bond.

The war ended in Europe on V-E Day. It was a happy day, but the best celebration was V- J Day 1946, when Japan surrendered. I was 11 years old and remembered walking down the middle of Main Street in Akron, with thousands of people cheering. It was a great feeling to think "no more wars!" Now people can think about buying a new car and house appliances again and nylons for women. For those young people in their early teens, it was a time to be in America. Instead of building one merchant ship or one Corsair per day, we can now create items for our homes.

SMOKING AND CHEWING TOBACCO

My dad smoked, and I did too when no one was looking. There was smoking on Otto St. and I had to be six or seven years old. The boy across the street and I obtained a couple of cigarettes and felt we were adults just puffing away and feeling we were big guys. Our parents found out, and we both got a spanking. We tried smoking the black silk from an ear of corn using part of the newspaper to roll it into a cigarette.

On Mustill St. I borrowed a quarter from my dad and bought a pack of Pall Mall cigarettes. I walked into the house and had to go to the Lawson store for a gallon of milk. I hid the cigarettes in my room before I left. I returned, and my dad was holding the pack of cigarettes in his hand. He asked me, "where did I get the money?" "From you," was my reply. He said, "It's okay if you want to smoke, but you have to earn your own money. You are to go with Steve tomorrow to the Portage Country Club to caddy and make money for the cigarettes." I said I couldn't go tomorrow because I have a baseball game. My dad said he would call Joe, the manager, and tell him you have to make some money tomorrow an will miss the game. I couldn't miss the game, and that made me stop smoking.

I did smoke an "It's a Girl" cigar when our first daughter was born. On the way home from the hospital, I lit the cigar and took one or two puffs and gagged driving on Main St. I threw it out of the car and opened the windows because of the smell.

Chewing tobacco was tried. A new family moved in the neighborhood, and the other guys and I chummed around for a while. The kid would take his can, take a pinch, and place it in his mouth and play like everyone else. Of course, he would spit often. As you can imagine, the others and I were curious and tried a pinch. We chewed and watched each other, and I forgot you spit out the juice, I swallowed it. I gagged for a minute and thought, why would someone like hacking your tonsils out. I was done with Mail Pouch. (Mail Pouch did show later in my life.)

MY FOOTBALL PLAYING DAYS

My dad wanted me to try out for the North Commandos pre-high school football team. I didn't start at the beginning of football practice because I was playing baseball, and we were in tournaments. At my first practice, we are doing the exercising drills and time for scrimmage. I'm on defense and a middle linebacker. The coach tells me the runner is coming through the line in front of me. Get ready. The ball is snapped guys are moving, here comes the runner, I grab him. The next thing I know, I'm on my back with a coach holding a capsule of smelling salts under my nose. I look down at my shirt, and there's blond, my blood on my shirt. They walked me to the sidelines, and that's my experience as a football player - one play. The helmets didn't have any nose protection. I knew the runner who ran over me, and later in life, I would kid him how he messed up a great passer on that one play. The player was a feature running back for North High School and at a college in Ohio. His father and my dad played baseball on the same team, and our families would visit each other.

HIGH SCHOOL –1948-1952– HOWER VOCATIONAL HIGH SCHOOL

I lived in the North High School district in Akron, Ohio, and North didn't have a varsity baseball team, and I wanted to play baseball. I could have attended a Catholic High School, but we couldn't afford the tuition. We knew people who attended Hower Vocational High School, and they commented they learned skills for good-paying jobs. Hower had distinct vocational classes that allowed graduates to enter the workforce with two years of entry-level skills in a particular field. The word "college" wasn't used in my family when I entered high school. I tried auto mechanics, machine shop, drafting, and machine shop again for one semester the first two years and then picked machine shop for the last two years.

MORE SOUTH BENDS ARE USED FOR SHOP TRAINING THAN ANY OTHER MAKE OF MACHINE TOOL!
Hower Vocational School, Akron, Ohio, equipped with 32 South Bend Lathes – a total of 77 South Bend Lathes now in use in Akron schools.

Courtesy of the South Bend Lathe Company

This picture was taken in 1952, just before the bell at the end of the day. During the three periods, the guys would wear different shirts because there could be oil spills and mess up the nice shirts they have on now. I'm standing next to Leonard Marzano like I'm showing him something. No one standing by all the lathes is doing anything, no machines are running, just pretending like they are machining something. It was staged. This picture was used in The South Bend Lathe Company advertising brochure.

PIN BOY AND BASEBALL

I entered high school and worked as a pin boy at Akron Recreation Bowling Center in the evening. My mom would say, "if you get a job and make money, you don't have to wash or dry the dishes," Besides earning money, I didn't have to do half of the dishes. My sister Rita was the other half. Of course, mom would take some for "rent."

I would work (jump or take care of) two alleys five evenings, two leagues each day, plus some weekends. That would be 300 plus games each week and earn $28 to $30. Mom would take $22.00 each pay, and I would be rich with 8.00

dollars (like $80 today). I didn't mind because it helped with expenses. I learned what a mortgage was, and we ate better.

One benefit of working each night was I lifted 16-pound bowling balls and 2-pound pins for 60 games each night amounted to 6 tons per night. That workload helped my arm strength. Now, young athletes enroll in strength programs that cost thousands; mine was free.

The pin boys used Saturday morning to bowl free. My starting bowling averaged was near 100, and after two years, my average increased to 175. In 1950, in the Akron Junior Bowling League, my 246 was the high game in the city. Bowling was another way to develop my arm strength.

I was able the play baseball all four years, graduate, and continued to work at Sackmanns. In my junior year, our team advanced in the Ohio State Championship. We were one of 16 teams vie for the title. The game was played in the old Cleveland Indian's Stadium, which had a capacity of 80,000 people. We had about 300 fans. The game went 11 innings, and we lost by one run.

An example of the thrill of victory and agony of defeat in one week occurred as a 14-year old freshman. We are playing Kenmore High School's baseball team, last years' city champions. I relieved the starting pitcher in the third inning, and we were losing, and got out of the inning, didn't allow any more runs, and we won. I was the winning pitcher – the thrill of victory. The next day my name was in the headlines of the Akron Beacon Journal's sports page, but the reporter didn't know my first name, so I was Ed Sipka in the story. The feeling was, "I have arrived!" In class the next day, a classmate was at the game and told me his neighbor was the starting catcher and was mad because "some little s*** stuck him out."

The following week I was the starting pitcher and couldn't finish the inning. In one week, I went from winning the game - the <u>thrill</u>, to not even finishing the inning – the <u>agony</u>. More about baseball later.

SACKMANN STAMP AND STENCIL CO.

At the end of my junior year, I was asked if I wanted a job in a machine shop during the summer between my junior and senior years. I always worked at night, setting up pins at a bowling alley, and working during the summer in a machine shop was the thing to do. As the summer weeks came to an end, the company asked my parents if they and the school could arrange for me to work in the morning at Sackmann and attend Hower in the afternoon. This company was across the street from Hower, and I would walk the 300 feet to school each mid-day. Thus I would work at Sackmanns instead of working in the high school shop with the senior class. This procedure is now called "co-op" and is an arrangement between parents, school, and a company. I worked at Sackmanns in the morning and went to school in the afternoon.

The work at Sackmanns was machine engraving various materials and metal stamps used in the local companies like B.F.Goodrich, Firestone, General, Cooper Tire Companies, and other companies.

The machine I'm working on is a Gorton Pantograph, which was the primary machine I used for years. My right arm and hand are on the top table where the master is positioned. My left hand is moving the rotating cutter to produce the desired outline or details. My experience with this machine helped me obtained employment at Main Mold and Machine and engrave the details for the coasters made in the Cuyahoga Falls machine shop classes in 1971 and 1972. In 2016 I visited Sackmann, and they still have this machine. I sat down and moved the upper arm around as I did in 1951. The manager showed me how engraving is done now by computer numerical controlled (CNC) machines.

Photo courtesy of the Michelin Company North America

The stamp in the picture was the medallion for the B.F.Goodwich Company at that time. This stamp is two inches square and five inches long. I imagined a guy holding this stamp and hitting it more than once to transfer the image to the inside of the tire mold. Many stamps were larger than this one. When stamps were for truck tire molds, the weight of the stamp was an effort for me to handle when it had to be heat treated.

The company was noted for making metal stamps that were used to identify tires. Every tire is identified by letters unique to that company. Sackmann would make different sizes because there are different size tires. One of my jobs was to heat treat the stamps.

Now the words on the sides of tires are engraved by machines controlled by computers, no men with hammers pounding these metal stamps into the steel tire mold to identify the tire company now.

The shop had two skilled engravers, a helper and me. I did everything and learned what I still used today. One gentleman, Arthur, impressed me with his skill of using unique hand tools to shape pieces of metal. I watched his hand engrave silver plates for anniversaries and special awards; he could not make one wrong slip placing fancy letters on the silver plate. I was told not to talk to him when he was working on delicate work. - No distraction!!!!

He was born in Germany and still had an accent. On Saturdays, we were to listen to the New York Metropolitan Opera and not talk to him. Arthur would sit there working and singing with the performers; he knew the words and sounded good.

FANCY DINNER

The company would have dinner for the workers, wives, and husbands, two times a year. I didn't have a wife or girlfriend for the first dinner but was encouraged to attend; they insisted I bring my mom. When I asked my mom to go with me, she said yes before I finished the sentence. She bought a new dress and got her hair done. Me? I shined my shoes, washed my face, and combed my hair. We attended a pre-dinner party at Arthur's house, located in West Akron, where the homes were elaborate. As we drove through an open metal gate entrance with stone walls, along a driveway with a stream to our right, my mom kept commenting about everything. We entered the house; I introduced my mom to Arthur, he reached out, held her hand, clicked his heels together, and kissed her hand. I'm sure my dad never did that. The dinner was at a restaurant called the "Smorgasbord" located in Stow, Ohio, which was famous for its fancy buffet. My dad never took my mom or us to a place like that. When we arrived home, my mom was kidding my dad; she found another place he can take her for a date. She told him how polite Arthur was, and he (my dad) should be so nice! My dad's many comments about kissing my mom's hand entertained us.

I took my Mom to three of these treats, but on the forth, I took a new girlfriend. I think my mom was upset.

"OUTSOURCING"

The word "outsourcing" is common now because of all the discussion regarding how companies are sending jobs to other countries. In the 1950s, that word wasn't used, but I did experience the idea of work going overseas. We engraved 3 - 4 special metal inserts each month for a local company that produced license plate frames like we have today. These inserts were engraved, placed in a mold, and built frames for various car dealers. Months went by, and we received no orders for these inserts. Mr. Brownfield, the company manager, made comments about the lack of orders and wondered if something happened to the company or their owner. A week later, the owner rushes in, wants an insert made "like right now." Mr. Brownfield asked him why there were no orders for the last three months. Was there some illness? The guy said he found a company in a foreign country that does the work much cheaper and he sends the work there. Well, Mr. Brownfield took his short cigar (never lit) out of his mouth and told the guy to take his insert and send it overseas again because we will have to schedule his pieces sometime during the next two weeks because we are busy. We didn't engrave any more inserts. Today, sending work overseas is called "outsourcing." After the guy left Mr. Brownfield said he wanted to tell the guy to shove the insert up his (you know what), but the company's lady secretary was present, so he had to watch his language.

I worked there four years as an apprentice and received my journeyman toolmaker classification in 1956

ARMY - START OF SERVICE

After months of dating, we were talking about marriage, but there was one thing in the way – military obligation. In the 1955 time era, all males had a 6-year military obligation. In the normal process, the individuals would receive a letter indicating they were to report for induction into the Army - "Draft Notice" based on their age. In 1956 the draft notices were sent to men who were 23 years old. I was just 21, so it would be two more years before my letter would arrive, so I volunteered for the draft. I asked the draft board to move my name to the front of the next draft list, was drafted, and served for two years. If you join, you have to serve three or more years.

Being away from my family was a learning experience, living with hundreds of guys you don't know, adjusting to their ways and routines was interesting. Basic training was for me a good time because I was by myself and also part of a group. When I left Akron, I was with 18 guys from Akron, who stayed together the entire basic training. At Fort Chaffee, Arkansas, our company "D-1-1" lived in 4 buildings, each with two floors.

Being away was a plus for my four sisters because they would share my bedroom. I heard they missed me but were happy I wasn't there.

NEED TWO VOLUNTEERS

Lights out were at 9:00 PM because we were up at 5:30 am for training the next day. It was the routine that a Sargent from each barracks was to be the Officer in charge who stayed in the Company Headquarters during the night while the commanding staff went home. It was that Sargent's responsibility to get 2 or 3 guys from his building to come to clean the offices. We were in our 7th week and had one more week to go until we would be assigned to other Army posts. We also received our gas masks because the next day, we were to go through training using gas masks, and knew our guy was going to ask for volunteers to clean the office. We all went to bed and had all the lights out before 9 pm. He came in started to yell that he better have two guys in the office, or he would pick two guys. He left and spoke on the PA system that he wanted two guys now!! Someone yelled back, "We're all sleeping!!" He replied, "you guys have 2 minutes to get two guys here, or else I will call you guys out in formation and pick two guys." The 2 minutes went by, and sure enough, he yelled, "Fall Out!" We replied that we were sleeping and not dressed for a formation! He replied, "Fall out as you are!!!" The guys were feeling ornery and proceeded to get out our rifles, gas masks kits, boot not laced, and, for some, no clothes. A few were naked except for their helmet, boots and gas masks. I had on undershorts, unlaced shoes, rifle, and gas mask. Our barracks was the only one called as we hurried to the assembly area; the guys in the other barracks saw us and watched the show. There we were 60 or so guys standing there in formation some naked most with shorts standing there with rifles and gas masks. Two guys volunteered; the Sargent told them they could go back to their barrack because they were kind enough to volunteer. Another guy asked the Sargent if he volunteered would the good Sargent sent him back too? The Sargent said, "Maybe." The guy said he would volunteer, and the Sargent said the answer would be "maybe and maybe not!" He had to go and help clean up. Troops in the other barracks were taken pictures of us, many stark naked but all with their rifles. We didn't make the national news because our assembly area wasn't visible from any road.

Near the end of basic training, the guys were comfortable with their fellow recruits and played tricks on others. A guy would spray shaving cream in or on the hand of a guy sleeping, and then tickle his nose with a straw, and the guy would smack his nose and spread shaving cream on his face. I was one of those guys that had shaving cream on my face.

THE AKRON BEACON JOURNAL

With 18 guys from the Akron area, we kept up with the latest news just a few days late. I received the Sunday Beacon Journal about every Thursday. I received the Sunday Beacon Journal when we were in the field for a week, somewhere in the State of Arkansas. This site had outside toilets "about a 10-holer!" with no toilet paper. After taken the sports pages out, the entire company of 200 or so guys appreciated the Beacon that day, not because of the important news. Some complained the colored ink came off when they wiped too hard. I was able to keep the sports page for a few days, but I had to hide it from the guys. One guy mentioned I could have sold some parts of the paper. The guys gave a "thumbs up" to the Beacon that week.

WHERE TO NOW?

The last day of basic training was filled with excitement because each guy was to receive his orders for his next assignment. Was it Fort Sill for artillery? Fort Knox for Tanks? Where? I was lucky and was assigned to Fort Belvoir, Virginia, near Washington, D.C., to the 580th Redstone Missile Company. Again, I would be with guys I haven't met and with no Akron connection another learning experience. Fort Belvoir Army Base south of Washington, D.C., was my assignment for the last 21 months.

I was first assigned to an engineering company involved with road construction equipment. There were earthmovers, bulldozers, and graders. It looked like I was going to have one of my dreams fulfilled -moving dirt with a bulldozer. The classes were in the fall months, and for some reason, we were to wait for different weather.

I was then placed in the Redstone Missile Company. My duties were how to assist the operation of mobile plants that produced liquid oxygen and carbon dioxide, dry ice, for the Redstone missiles. As I see trucks on the road that are pulling tankers that indicate liquid oxygen, I think of my experience at Fort Belvoir and the time around the portable pairs of trailers that would produce liquid oxygen. The units were parked away from the roads and all the safety features to prevent explosions. I worked with carbon dioxide portable units, too, and handling blocks of dry ice to storage units that supplied local hospitals.

My four weeks in NCO school (non-commissioned officer's school) taught me to keep my mouth shut while going through the four weeks of harassment. I never thought I would experience polishing the brass ring in urinals!!! Remember cleaning the barracks all night because the Sargent found "animals" in the barracks; the animals were a couple of dead "nats" or mosquitoes.

COMING HOME TO AKRON

Because I was in the Washington DC area, I could return to Akron often on a 3-day pass. It wasn't an official pass; we would sign out to DC and go home. On this "sign-out" we were to stay within a 250-mile radius. Akron was beyond the 250-mile limit, and I could have been in trouble if I was found outside the 250-mile range.

The liquid oxygen units ran 24 hours, five days a week, and I would be on different shifts. On the midnight shift, I would be done Friday at 8 am and have Saturday, Sunday and most of Monday off. The Monday shift started at 4:00 pm. So, I could get a 3-day pass and take off Friday morning and catch a Greyhound bus Friday at noon and be home early Saturday morning. I would have all day Saturday and Sunday home and return the late Sunday (midnight) in time for my duty on Monday morning with time for my 4:00 pm shift. Because we were planning our wedding, June 28, 1958, and I would still be in the Army, it was vital for me to return to fulfill the church requirements before one gets married.

I was in formation one morning before one of these long weekends when I heard the Sargent say that plans were to be changed regarding this Saturday's day off. We would have training this Saturday but have the following Saturday off. Under my breath, I silently said, "O Shit." The Sargent stopped, looked around, and said: "Who said that???" I thought someone else said something and he heard that guy. Well, he repeated the question: "Who said that???" He then said if the guy who said that doesn't speak out, the next Saturday off will be canceled too!!!! This time, I looked around, and two hundred + pairs of eyes were looking at me. The Sargent surely couldn't hear me because I just whispered the saying. I raised my hand and told him I did it; he wanted to talk to me and asked me why I said that? I told him about the wedding and things needed to be completed, and how did he hear me when I was so far away? "Son, it sounded like you were standing next to me." He laughed and told me I could have the 3-day pass. He also told me to shove my fingers in my mouth when I want to say something under my breath. It's funny that I would use that suggestion to students in the years I taught. I learned how to express my feelings and not be heard. Shove your five fingers in your mouth to remind yourself people could hear you mutter to yourself.

GOING TO JAIL!

On the last day of 1957, December 31, I did something that could have sent me to jail, and my life today would have been different. I was never so happy to see one soldier wake up in the morning on New Year's Day morning, January 1, 1958.

Our wedding was to be typical, a church ceremony in the morning, a big reception in the evening with a sit-down dinner, band, beer, liquor, and dancing. I could buy alcohol at a reduced price at the Post Exchange (PX) at Fort Belvoir. The plan was to buy 3 or 4 bottles, 3 or 4 times, bring them home and use the liquor for the wedding. This New Year's Eve, I had three bottles in my footlocker ready to take home the weekend after New Year's Day when I had a 3-day pass. There were four guys in the barracks, including me. A new guy was in the barracks and found out I had liquor in my footlocker and asked if he could buy a bottle, and I sold him a bottle. Another guy and I just sat around and talked while this young guy started to drink the whiskey like most guys would drink pop. We told him to take it easy, and he went out and came back an hour later with an empty bottle. He was very agitated and started to turn over bunks, footlockers, and yelling. The other guy and I tried to stop him, but he was out of control. The idea of a cold shower was next; we turned on the four showers with COLD water and pushed him to the back of the shower hitting the four showers going in and out. We stopped him and did the routine again for three times. He seemed to settle down, so we took him back to his bunk, and he went to sleep. The two of us walked away but kept an eye on him, and we thought it was ok, so we relaxed. He awoke again and ran outside. After putting on our shoes, We both ran after him, but he disappeared. We looked for several minutes around the grounds, then under the barrack, and found him asleep next to a column. We carried him back and put him in his bunk, tied him in the cot, and stood there for several minutes. He struggled against the covers, yelling, throwing up, and urinating and then became quiet. I stood there a lot longer than the other guy to make sure he was asleep. The guy who helped said I should get rid of the bottle because this guy could die from drinking so much so fast. To hear the word, "DIE!" scared me. He went to sleep, and I stayed up as long as I could to watch him. I took the empty bottle and hid it in my locker and wondered if I should wipe my fingerprints off the bottle and throw it away in a different trash container down the street. My bunk was across the aisle and down a few beds. I woke up, and the first thing was to go over to the guy and talk to him. He moved started to talk realized what he was lying in, and that made him sick. The kid didn't remember anything, and he didn't feel OK for a couple of days. I was scared this young guy would die from drinking so much, so fast. I'm sure I would have been sent to jail, maybe a dishonorable discharge and other things that would have affected my life. I stopped buying liquor to save money for our wedding.

MEETING JOANNE'S FAMILY

In 1955, I met Joanne Braghieri on a blind date. My friend Steve kept asking me, and I kept saying, "no.". After many "no," replies, I said, OK!. Steve arranged the evening with three couples, so Joanne would sit next to me driving. We arrived at Joanne's house, and when she opened the door, I saw her and silently said, "she's pretty'. We played miniature golf and didn't keep score; just enjoy our talking and listening. Back at her house, I leaned over and gave her an ever so gentle kiss, backed up, and looked at her. She said, "I don't let guys kiss me on the first date!". My reply was, "There's always a first time for everything!". I drove home a happy guy, and glad I said "OK" to this blind date. (yes, I repeated this from the beginning)

Joanne was a student nurse and had to return to the nurse's dormitory on Sunday. I asked her if I could take her back and meet her parents. She accepted, and that made me happy after the kiss last night. Recall I mentioned Joanne lived with her grandparents when I was walking to St. Hedwig's, and they moved when she was six years old. I returned to Joanne's house and spent time talking to her parents and noticed a picture of a lady I've seen many times catching a bus on Cuyahoga Street. "Who's this lady?" I asked? Aunt Dolores was Joanne's reply. Who is this in another picture? That's my uncle Donald. I said I know these people. My dad, who drove the bus on the Cuyahoga Street route, commented how nice your Aunt is, and Uncle Donald is a guy in the neighborhood and had a crazy looking car. Her parents start asking me questions as to where I live and the different Italian stores on Cuyahoga Street and how they buy food at Christmas time from those stores. Joanne then asked me, "Whatever happen to a little boy she played with named -Stevie?" I looked at her and said, "Stevie"? She said he lived around the corner from her grandma's house and two sisters who couldn't talk. "You're kidding!" She said, "no." I said, "little Stevie" is Steve Wronkovich, who just fixed us up on the blind date. Joanne and her parents were ecstatic. They asked me all kinds of questions about Steve and his family. Finally, it was time to return to the dorm, and Joanne was going to find Steve if he was with his girlfriend to tell him what she just found out. Steve also didn't think this girl, Joanne, was his friend when they were 5 and 6 years old. He, too, was excited when he found out Joanne was his former playmate.

OUR WEDDING ON JUNE 28,1958

June 28, 1958, Saturday was a beautiful sunshiny day. Stan and Joanne were to become husband and wife at a 9:00 mass at St. Joseph Catholic Church in Cuyahoga Falls, Ohio.

I was in a room adjacent to the sacristy waiting and watched the ushers guiding people to their seats. The church began to fill with family and friends. Joanne's mom was escorted to the seat in the front row. The priest and I walked to the front of the altar; now, I was nervous. The music was playing, and people turned to watch each bridesmaid slowly meet their partner. As I stood there, I could not see Joanne at the end of the aisle. The music changed, people stood, and I could see Joanne and her father slowly walking down the aisle. What a sight. She was beautiful. I almost said, "hurry up." Taking her hand was the start of the journey I wanted with her. As we repeated the words, we looked at each other, and everything changed as two became one. Father McCausland then looked at us and said:" I now pronounce you, husband and wife!" Looking at each other and hearing those words was a lasting memory. The mass ended; the walk out with my wife on my arm was too quick. The first kiss out of the church was like that first one on the blind date. We drove around with our horns sounding and just looking at each other. On many dates, I would ask if I can stay with her tonight? Her reply was, "no, you have to go home tonight!" She said there were times she wanted to say yes, but we had to wait. As we drove around, Joanne looked at me and said, "you don't have to go home tonight!" My reply was, "good!"

Photo courtesy of my Uncle John
I just heard I don't have to go home tonight!

The mass ended at 10:30; we arrived at Joanne's parents' house for sandwiches and drinks. The ushers opened a bottle of whiskey, and we had a toast to my life with Joanne. I held my shot glass and touched the other glasses and downed the drink. One of the guys started to fill the glasses again. I stopped and put my glass down. I had this thought; two or more drinks of whiskey for me could make my wedding a disaster.

We drove downtown and had pictures taken and returned. Because the reception was at 6:00, it was decided the ladies would stay at Joanne's house, and the guys would drive to my house to rest. I took off my tux, played catch with some of my cousins, and did rest a little.

The reception was at the Italian club, and I think everyone had a good time, Joanne and I did. After the meal tables were removed and we danced the traditional dances. We both had grandparents and included them in the dances. We left about 10:30, drove to Joanne's parents' house, and wondered if our friends pulled tricks with our clothes. Joanne's mom told us later she made sure no one messed with our suitcase. She hid it in the closet of her bedroom. Our honeymoon location was Parma, Ohio. On Sunday, we drove to the Cleveland Airport and sent postcards as though we flew somewhere on a grand honeymoon. We took a one-day boat ride to Detroit and a two-day trip to Niagara Falls, where we took a nice tour. Our last day in Cleveland, we had to eat at the White Castle restaurant because we had to watch our money. We arrived home on Sunday with $1.95, when to church, and put the $1.95 in the offertory. We started our life together broke.

OUT OF THE SERVICE – 1958 MAIN MOLD

I was out of the service, married, and was able to return to Sackmann, and regained the routine of working there. I was not happy regarding my future. I wanted to learn more, and Sackmann was limited in providing experiences and skills. After Thanksgiving in 1958, I quit Sackmann and looked for work. Shops I went to told me it was not smart to leave at this time because the economy was terrible, with a lot of unemployment. They all wished me, "good luck." I went to Main Mold and Machine, filled out the job application, handed it to Mr. Andy Donavan; he looked it over, stated he had to check on something, and would be right back. After a few minutes, he returned and said I had a job because one of his workers was leaving for the service, and he needed a person who could run the Gorton engraving machines like those at Sackmanns.

Being hired at Main Mold and Machine controlled my life because this one moment happened to allow me to reach this day. Working at Main Mold provided me with experiences in the metal machining industry in plastic mold making procedures and machining. I was able to work on engraving and other aspects of machining.

I did work on one unique item, and that was the astronauts' space suits. It was 1961 when John Glenn was to travel in space. The B.F. Goodrich Company had the contract to build the first group of Astronauts' suits. I was asked to work on Saturdays with Mr. Donavan and an engineer from BFG to work on details of the zipper seal on the suits. I was surprised that we were working on different configurations for the zipper seal when the astronauts were going in space, I wondered if the outfits were safe. The seal is where the zipper stops. We spent several Saturdays making sketches and models from clay and then machine a sample part. I asked the engineer if I could keep some of the drawings and sample parts so I could show my family and friends. He was adamant that nothing remains at Main Mold, and explained the designs were secret, and many companies will compete for the next contract for the next phase of space exploration suits.

John Glenn was the astronaut in the next space shot, but the space shot was canceled 3 or 4 times. At Main Mold, we joked that John's zipper was stuck!!

Main Mold would do small jobs for the Cleveland NASA facility. One task required the lathe operator to sweep and clean the area around the lathe. Paper was placed on the floor and on the bed of the lathe where the chips would fall. An acetylene torch was positioned behind the rotating round bar so that the metal would be at a specific temperature for machining. There were two guys from NASA watching the machining, and we were not to talk to any of the three guys. I remember each day, all the metal chips were collected, the floor swept clean and all placed in a bag, and returned to NASA.

On numerous occasions, we machined solid blocks of graphite for the NASA Lab. There are no chips machining graphite, just fine dirty black dust. The Cleveland NASA lab worked on the heat shields on the space capsule, and graphite was the answer to protecting the astronauts and space capsule returning from space.

KENT STATE UNIVERSITY -1960

My wife insisted, and I agreed that I should obtain more education. At first, it was the local for-profit schools and then the idea of Kent State University. I didn't have confidence in my ability to succeed in college classes because I went to Hower Vocational High School, and it wasn't a college-prep high school. I talked to Mr. Donavan about Kent, and he said the company would work around my class hours for part-time work. That was the one thing that helped us decide to try Kent State University.

What did I want to be? I thought maybe a coach and an elementary teacher. In the last quarter of my first year, I was returning home, walking to my car, it began to rain very hard and took a short cut through a building I never entered - Van Dussen Hall. As I walked down the hall, I noticed a room full of machine shop equipment like I experienced at Hower. I stopped, talked to the instructor found out that this was an Industrial Arts program and building. I inquired into the Industrial Arts programs the next day, and before the end of my first year, I was an Industrial Arts major. While attending classes in Van Dussen Hall, I discovered the Vocational Education Program was located there too. Again I inquired and found my second major – Vocational Education at the end of my second year at Kent State University.

CHRISTINE - OUR FIRST DAUGHTER

Joanne was expecting our first child around January 1, 1962. I decided to take 18 hours (three 5 hour classes and a 3-hour class) of classes in the fall quarter so I could take a smaller class load the next quarter. It was Friday, November 17, 1961. Joanne, her father, sister, and I are watching the Steve Allen show (Steve Allen's show was like Jonny Carson or Jay Leno). Joanne's mom is in St Thomas hospital, scheduled to return home on Saturday. Albert, Joanne's dad goes to bed because he has to get up at 5 am to go to work at the B.F.Goodwich company. Albert leaves the house, crosses the street, and catches the 5:30 bus. Just before 6 am, Joanne wakes me up very upset because "her water broke." She tells me we have six more weeks to go for the projected birth; this is too early. During this time, families expecting were given a pocket-size book to read about what to do during the nine months. I didn't read it but was going to after my classes were over in 2 or 3 weeks. She asks what did it say about what to do when the water breaks? I grabbed the book and opened it, and the page I was on was the page that explains what to do. That was divine intervention. This baby had a garden angel who opened that book for me. We called the doctor and rushed to the hospital. It's about 8:30 when the doctor tells me we have a little girl who weighs 3pounds 9 oz. I sat down and thought about what I just heard. I'm a father! I talked to Joanne, and she was concerned due to the weight, but the baby's features were beautiful. What now?

I'm standing there thinking about what I should do. Julia is upstairs waiting to come home, Albert, at work until noon. And my dad's birthday is today. I went upstairs to tell Julia but stopped outside her room wondering what or should I tell her about the baby. A nurse asks me if she can help me. I tell her the situation, and she suggests Julia not be told at this time and wait until she is leaving the hospital. Good thinking. I drove down South Main Street and found Albert waiting for the bus. He was concerned but quickly was all smiles when he heard the good news. We both when back to the hospital to see Joanne and the baby but not Julia. We both drove back to the hospital for Albert to take Julia home. Joanne's mom was told she couldn't see her daughter and new grandchild because she was a surgical patient, and those patients can't visit the maternity ward. Julia was upset, but an older nurse would take care of this problem. Julia would be moved in a wheelchair outside as an outpatient as though she is going home. Get back in the chair as a visitor now, and see Joanne and baby. Joanne returned home, but the baby stayed at the hospital until it weighed five pounds. Both Joanne and her mom were told to stay home because of doctors' orders. Albert and I would visit every day.

I called my mom and told her we have a present for my dad. She said, "wrap it up and bring it over tonight for his birthday party." We couldn't because it was a baby girl. My dad and family came, and all were happy about the birth. My dad told Joanne that baby was the nicest present he ever received.

Three weeks later, my sister Rita gave birth to twins, and a month later, my sister Betty gave birth to a girl. My dad commented he now has four grandkids in three months

LIFE AT KENT STATE

I spent the next four years in classes in Industrial Arts (IA) and Vocational Education (Vo Ed). The difference is Vo. Ed was involved in one skill trade occupation, not all the trade areas. I remember one test in Vo Ed that lasted 5 hours on just machining issues. The Vo Ed certification would allow me to become a machine trade's instructor upon graduation and teach machine trades at Hower Vocational High School. As I worked my way to my junior and senior years, I had to adjust my school and work schedule. In the beginning, I worked about 5 – 7 hours a week; usually, those hours were on Saturday. My hours of work increased from 5 – 7 hours to 30 to 40 hours in my last year. I started Kent just married and finished Kent with a house and two daughters. My wife couldn't work when she was pregnant, and that was the reason I needed to work. Again Main Mold and Machine helped me with this schedule, and it took five years to complete the regular four-year program.

STUDENT TEACHING

Student teaching is mandatory for all teachers-to-be. The student-teacher spends the semester at a school observing and participating in the classroom related to their teaching major. A college teacher will periodically observe the student-teacher and evaluate the student teacher's performance. One of the rules that the college insists on is that the student-teacher not be given a class without supervision. I requested Sill Middle School for student teaching because this school was close enough to walk to from my home. This period for Sill was rough because of the large number of students. The school system was planning another middle school, and in the meantime, those students were attending Sill. Mr. William Watts was my supervising teacher and was a couple of years older than me. He did what he was supposed to do let me teach the classes, watching me, giving me advice when needed.

One eighth-grade class was too crowded for the shop, so Mr. Watts suggested I take half the 8-graders to a classroom and teach mechanical drawing. We would switch students every other day, and I had no problem with this request and felt qualified teaching the class. The Principal, Mr. Clinton Elmerick, would come in occasionally and observe. The representative from Kent didn't know I was doing this and would have objected to this if he found out. I was 28 years old, which is old for a student-teacher and knew the subject material. It's November, a Friday, and I was waiting by the open door for the last class of eighth-graders that day to enter my classroom. Teachers were to stand in the hallway by the doors to help the student traffic. I'm standing there when a student mentioned a teacher had a radio on and said there was a bulletin regarding President Kennedy being shot. I cautioned him to check out that statement because it could be a joke. My group came in and started to mention what the other student had said. I said if this happened, we would hear something from the office. One minute later, the principal, speaking on the public address system, said there was a bulletin that President Kennedy was shot. It's Friday, the day before the weekend, when these guys would be all over the place, but this day the students were quiet and just sitting there. This scene was different. Five to ten minutes later, Mr. Elmerick announces the President has died! These guys just looked at each other and were unusually quiet. In the third announcement, Mr. Elmerick tells us that the following Monday, there would be no school because Monday would be a day of national mourning. At that moment, one kid jumps up, starts yelling because he is happy there would be no school on Monday. All eyes are on this kid who is just thinking about a day off. I'm in front and amazed at this kid when another kid jumps up, starts yelling at this kid, and begins to approach the kid happy about a day off. I thought he doesn't realize the President was killed; this is not a happy event? The first kid sits down; the second kid hovered over the kid with his fists clenched, ready to hit him. I hurry over and calm the kid down because it looked like he was going to punch the kid who was sitting down and now afraid. When the bell rings, I keep the kid who was happy for a few minutes and told him he should go home in a different way. At the teacher's meeting after school, I mentioned what happened. They asked who the boys were; when they heard the student's names, they told me I should have taken my time getting there.

That experience happened in 1964, and now it's 1990, I'm laid off from teaching and working in a local company, I worked with a man who was in that class, and he remembered that day and the two boys and their encounter. He also said the guys wished I took more time separating the two.

BEING HIRED – 1964

I graduated in June of 1964 and was hired by Cuyahoga Falls School System before I graduated. There were two openings in Industrial Arts, and I was offered the machine shop position. I also knew there was a vocational machine shop position available at Hower Vocational High School too. Akron's pay scale was higher than Cuyahoga Falls, and I was qualified for that job because of my Vocational Certification. Joanne and I talked about what I should do. I found out that Mr. Elmerick, the Principal at Sill Middle School, recommended me, and that was the reason I received the offer. The Falls shop was well equipped, like the machine shops at Hower Vocation High School, only the room was too small for all the new equipment. The decision to take the Falls job was thought to be the best for our family.

THE FIRST YEAR OF TEACHING

SAFETY

SAFETY was a big concern because the machines we had were not toys. There was one sentence that stood out "YOU COULD BE SUED!" All classes at Kent State University regarding Industrial Arts and Vocational Education stressed safety because of the environment and activities in a shop class invite accidents and injuries. The shop teacher has to show proof he or she introduced safety in the first class and had a regular program after the first day. There were posters provided by the State that illustrated eye, personal, fellow student, and school equipment suggestions.

We did show a movie that showed a person having a piece of metal removed from his eye. Many students had a hard time watching when they could see the doctor placing an electromagnet over the person's eye and drawing the metal sliver out. You could see the eyeball bulged.

I had two experiences with eye injuries and would describe the most serious one with the class on the first day. (I would act out my time in that chair with gestures.) This eye injury scared me because I sat in the chair that held my head firmly like it was in a vise. The doctor moves forward with a pointed instrument and moves it over my eyeball. I pushed back, but the headrest held me from moving back. I heard the device hit the small piece of metal; after several swipes, the piece was removed. I asked to see what was removed. The nurse held a white cloth that had a dark speck nearly invisible. I expected a larger piece of metal. What was hard to understand was I had safety glasses and a face shield on, and still, this tiny, like a grain of salt, particle traveled past two devices, settled in my eye.

Have more on this later dealing with a blind student. The words "you can be sued" were the magic words I remembered. I wore glasses all the time, so safety glasses were not a problem, but for those who didn't wear glasses, this was a headache. No rings, bracelets, watches, or loose necklaces were allowed from my first day to the last day in 1987. At the end of every accident-free school year, I would say, "thank you, God!"

We did have one cut that required a couple of stitches when a boy cut his hand while working on a lathe. The chip was coming off the machine in a continuous curl, and the boy was allowing it to move over his palm, for some reason the chip pulled back, the boy closed his hand, and the chip cut his hand. He went to the doctor and returned because he wanted to finish the job. I asked him why he did that. His answer was, "I didn't think it would happen to me!!!" We had a liquid (we called "mother's kiss") we would place on minor cuts. That isn't allowed now (the year was 1965).

Eyes were my main concern regarding safety in my classes from high school, junior high school to adult shop classes. One thing I remembered the last minute, hour, and day, I thanked God a lot for helping me with safety procedures.

SPECIAL CLASSES

Besides my machine shop classes, I had one period, a 54-minute class of students from the special education program. The lady teacher told me these kids are respectful to the teacher, but they pick on each other and should not expect a lot from them. In the back of my mind, I imagine what marvelous things these guys would accomplish because I was their teacher. They would be up there with rocket scientists!! Stan had arrived!!!

COMBAT BOOTS

Special (a term used then but not now) education students were new to me, and I had to consider what was enough and not too much. My first encounter with a student occurred when he approached me crying. I asked him, "What's the matter?" He replied the guys are picking on him. What are they saying? They are saying, "My mother wears combat boots!" (I quickly begin to review how I should handle this from my Kent State education classes. I couldn't remember any class at Kent State that could help me with a problem that deals with combat boots.) I paused for a moment and proceeded to tell the young man, "I just got out of the Army and had to wear combat boots every day. I enjoyed the boots because they were comfortable for me and I would wear them in school if I could, but the school wants me to wear shoes like those I'm wearing now. For me, those boots were the greatest if your mom does wear combat boots; she must be pretty smart because she knows combat boots are good shoes." He looked at me, smiled, and returned to his group, and I could see him controlling the conversation with his friends. Yes! I do like combat boots

STOP SIGN

In a metal class, we went over different materials and shapes. We talked round, square, rectangle, hexagon shapes. Because the bell was going to ring, we would talk tomorrow about the "octagon." On their way home, each was to notice a stop sign and count the number of sides because a stop sign is an octagon. The bell rings, and they leave. The next day I was reminded the first question was, how many sides on an octagon? After the question, everyone raised their hands, some both hands. I called on one student, and he proudly said "7" sides. He proudly looked around and smiled like his answer was correct. Well, the hands went up again, so I called on another. I heard "9" sides!!!! These two answers were a learning experience for me. The idea these guys were going to be rocket scientists departed from my mind. I then walk to the blackboard, drew an octagon, and called the last kid up to show me "9". Well, he just pointed to the eight sides, counted "1, 2, 3, 4, 5, 6, 7, 8, and counted the first side again for a total of nine. You learn to control your facial expressions; this was one time I had to put on my "expressionless face." I wrote down numbers on each side, and we got "8". This octagon experience made me think about individual differences and how to present information to the student's ability. After the school day, I sat down and thought of that experience with the stop sign and individual difference. I learned something that day

THE BUILDING IS ON FIRE

My class was in a room where a welding class was in session at the same time. We made sure the two groups were separated. Mr. Ingram Smith had the welding class and kept his class busy, and I kept my guys busy at the other end. One of the special students walks up to me and whispers in my ear.

Can I tell you something? He said

Sure, what is it??

He whispered, "The building is on fire!!"

That was an ear full, and he showed me a barrel by the welding area and smoke coming from the barrel. As soon as I saw the smoke, Mr. Smith saw it too; we rolled the barrel out the door, away from the building, and douse the smoldering paper with water. Both classes were excited about our "fire." Both groups talked about fire safety until the period ended. After school, Mr. Smith and I went to the office and told our unit Principal, Mr. Jenkins, about the "fire." All of a sudden, the guy standing next to us, looking over some papers, came over and started yelling at the two of us about not pulling the fire alarm to allow the students to evacuate the buildings. Both of us were surprised by this criticism. We heard there are State laws and rules on procedures for fires in schools. If this happens again, we would have to answer for our actions. Mr. Smith and I thought we would get a "good job" comment. Instead, we heard we did the wrong thing. The guy yelling was an off duty fireman who works the study halls on his days off. The fireman leaves, we stare at the Principal who was looking at us and tells us we did the right thing. The Industrial Arts building is not attached to the main building, and there were no flames. What we learned was to look around before we tell the Principal about a similar fire.

BLACK AND GOLD

The students in the machine shop complained they needed more time. The nature of machining requires time to set up the equipment, and with one period, little machining happens. Many enjoyed this class. The other machining instructor and I developed a plan that would give the student more time but would make drastic changes in the school's period arrangement. Dr. Gilbert Welty was the Administrative Principal who made the idea work. My only contact with him was when we were trying to start this unique program where the student would spend two periods in a row in the same class. We called this "double periods" "BLACK AND GOLD." In a machine shop, if the period is 52 minutes long, the student doesn't have time to work on any job because of the time factor. Very little would be completed. We worked out an idea to have two groups of students spend two periods one day in the shop and spend the next day in 2 different classes. We could show how much time the student had with this program to complete work.

The two periods in a row would give a student 52 + 5 (pass time) + 52 minutes or 109 minutes or one hour and 40 minutes. Dr. Weldy studied our presentation, approved the program, and was called "Black and Gold." It stopped when we started the Vocational Machine Shop program in 1968. The students liked the program because they could spend 109+ minutes working on skills and get jobs done. A few students commented that they were tired of working for the hour and 40 minutes, but we mentioned this is the way it is in the world of work. I felt good, allowing the students to experience working two periods.

DRIVING SCHOOL BUS

In 1967 the Cuyahoga Falls School System was overcrowded with students. The graduating classes were near 1000 students. The administration wanted to have a period before the regular school day to help the large class sizes. They called this period the "zero period." They couldn't assign teachers but asked for volunteers. A teacher would start at 7 am with the zero periods and be excused one hour sooner in the afternoon. Mr. John Lilly and I volunteered with three others to start the zero periods. Those teachers were done at 2:00 pm.

There was an announcement for school bus drivers. John and I signed up, practiced, took the test and passed

SINGING ON THE BUS

The first trip for me was from St. Joseph grade school to the Bailey road area. I found out quickly the kids pick on each other and always seem to argue. One day two girls ask if they could sing a song they learned that day. I replied, "sure." The two girls started, and then the others joined in and stopped arguing until their stop. The next day they asked if they could sing, and I asked if they knew any other songs? They did and sang a couple until the bus was empty. When the weather was nice, we opened the windows, and they sang and watched the people notice the bus as we went by. A few full-time drivers didn't like the idea of singing. It worked for me.

STUDENT DOESN'T KNOW WHERE HE LIVES

When the public school doesn't have school, the Catholic school could, so the bus has to be used. One time Mr. Ed Ocher, the bus supervisor, asked if I could drive for one run from St. Joseph's school. At the garage, Ed shows me the route and tells me not to travel to this one area because the three kids from that stop didn't go to school that morning. I'm following my instruction, and a student tells me a little boy is crying in the back of the bus and saying he's lost. I carefully park the bus and walk back to ask the boy where he lives. He doesn't know. We look in his lunch box and book bag for an address and find none. Finally, a student asks him if he has a brother and sister who ride with him. He tells us they were sick, and his mother took him to school. Well, I carefully turned the bus around and went the way I was told not to travel. At the stop, the mother looked upset about the lateness; I told her we couldn't find any address and was told none of your children were in school. She understood and would mark the lunch box. Back at the garage, Ed also was wondering why I was so late. I told him he almost had to take home this lost student.

SNOWBALL

My last run was from Sill Middle School to the Roberts school area. Roberts was not built at this time but was planned. The bus was full as I drove onto Seral St. We had a light coating of snow. We are moving, and I see a guy on the right sidewalk reach down, grab some snow, make it into a ball and throw it at the bus as we passed. There was a terrifying glass breaking sound that made the students scream. I imagined a shattered window. I stopped the bus, removed the key, to see what happen, and saw four guys run into a house.

After seeing no damage, I went to the house and knocked on the door. A boy came to the door, and I asked him who threw the snowball. He replied he didn't know. I started to write down the address and asked him his name, which I wrote down, and walked away. He asked why I want his name? I said I was going to tell school officials he threw the snowball and walked to the bus. The kids on the bus cheered. I looked back and saw four guys walking toward me. A different boy said he threw the snowball but was aiming at some guys across the street, and the bus happened to pass at that moment. I took his name. Ed was waiting for me at the garage and asked why the delay. I told him the story and the boy's name. He yelled that he caught the same boy this morning, throwing a snowball. He said he is going to talk to the principal personally regarding some discipline for this guy. He also said I did the right thing in checking the bus for damage.

CAR PASSING SCHOOL BUS

One frightening experience happened when one student could have been hurt or killed. I turned the corner, had the flashing lights, check the rearview mirror, and was watching one student exit the bus. As he walked in front of the bus, I glanced in the rearview mirror and saw a car driving past the bus. For some reason, I honked the horn, and the student stopped in front of the bus for 2 or 3 seconds, enough time to allow the speeding car to pass the bus. Those seconds kept the boy from being hit. The boy walked across the street and entered his home as though nothing happened. I followed the car, saw it stop and let off a passenger. I stopped the bus and asked the boy, who was the driver of that car? The boy said he didn't know. I considered that answer false. I remember the car and the license number; the next day, I looked at the records of students who park in the school lots. I got the telephone number and called the number and explained who I was and why I was calling. I asked the lady to tell her son or the driver of that car how close he was to killing or hurting someone. The lady thanked me and said she and the father would talk to their son.

BEGINNING VOCATIONAL MACHINE SHOP

LOCAL ADVISORY COMMITTEE

With Black and Gold double periods, we were able to instill necessary skills that allowed many students to find employment in the Cuyahoga Falls Area. Falls Engineering and Machine Company (FEMCO) hired several students and helped us with their scrap materials that we couldn't afford. It was scrap material to them; however, to us, it was usable and valuable. Also, I had attended a Vocational High School and knew that the equipment Cuyahoga Falls had was the same as what Hower had, but Cuyahoga Falls room was too small. I was taking classes at Kent State in Vocational Education and begin to meet people who would answer my questions - how to get a Vocational Machine Shop program started? The faculty at Kent State University said the Cuyahoga Falls school system could become a vocational program. The first step was organizing an advisory committee of people outside the school system involved with the machining industry. No problem with that. We had the following members on the committee, Mr. Ray Cook, Owner of R.F. Cook Company; Mr. Dave Wright Owner of FEMCO (Falls Engineering and Manufacturing Company) also Mr. Ed Weber plant manager at FEMCO; Mr. Bill Montieth owners of Akromold and Mr. Bob Byrely, and Mr. Don Hatherall plant manager at Akromold. I talked to all these people, and they all thought this was a good idea for the students and companies. The school officials were cautious; they always are because this would be a big decision. The school officials met with the advisory committee in the shop one day, and the advisory individuals examined all the equipment. Mr. Montieth didn't like a vertical mill that was obsolete and very old, sitting in the corner. He could see that the piece of equipment was ancient compared to the other machines that were two years old. Mr. Montieth asks me if we use this machine and do I think a modern Bridgeport would be better?? I answered a Bridgeport would be better, but there is a money problem. Mr. Montieth asked Don Hatherill if they received their company's yearly new Bridgeport for this year. Don replied it would arrive in 5 weeks! Mr. Montieth then said to the school officials that he would ship his new Bridgeport to the school, and the school can sell the old machine and pay Akromold. Akromold can then order another vertical milling machine. I'm standing there saying "YES, YES" to myself. (I remembered the message from the Sargent about sticking your five fingers in your mouth). One school official asked Mr. Montieth about the value of this machine. He replied, "Enough to pay for his machine. If it sells for more than $1800, the school can keep the rest." Mr. Montieth was impressive in his presence, and with this offer, the school officials approved the sale. At the auction, the machine brought in over 3000 dollars. There is one thing to mention, the obtaining of the new Bridport machine, and the sale took a few weeks when it would take months if done by the Cuyahoga Falls Board of Education.

KENT STATE VOCATIONAL COMMITTEE

The next important meeting was with the committee from Kent State University Vocational Program that would approve or not approve the program. I had been attending night classes at Kent in the Vocational program, knew and had all the Kent officials coming to Cuyahoga Falls to discuss approving Vocational Education. The night before the gathering, I talked to the man that would lead the meeting, who I had for an instructor in several classes. He knew a lot about our program, equipment, and room size before the important meeting with school officials.

There was a big emphasis on Vocational Education in the State of Ohio. Governor Jim Rhodes wanted these types of programs, and there was money for schools to set up facilities. In 1963 voters in Ohio approved a $250,000,000 bond issue for programs for "Jobs and Progress."

The people from Kent State knew of this program, and Cuyahoga Falls School Officials wanted to offer vocational programs. Still, money was the issue and being approved by the Ohio State Officials. Two were approved after this and maybe other meetings: Vocation Machine Shop and Vocational Drafting. The application was submitted, and the Cuyahoga Falls Administration had to wait to see if the Cuyahoga Falls application would be accepted. The Kent State Committee did put one condition on the machine program that was the school had to plan on a larger facility. This room was too small.

The term "compact" was a new concept in vocational programs where several schools would combine their facilities to provide classes for students from other schools. The Cuyahoga Falls System moved into a compact with Stow, Hudson, Woodridge, Tallmadge, and Kent. Mr. Warren Anderson was the Cuyahoga Falls representative and told me our 6-District Compact didn't make the first list of approved compacts. Our 6-district compact was rejected but placed first on a waiting list. When that school before us, was rejected, we were accepted.

With the approval of the vocational machine class in 1967, my teaching schedule was different. There would be one related and three periods of lab (I called it shop), but I still had a single period class of Industrial Arts. All the first-year vocational machine trades students would be juniors. When the year ended, another vocational teacher was employed. I would become the senior class teacher. While still in the small annex, another vocational teacher was to teach the junior class. Mr. Bob Gruber was hired and started the junior class in 1968. Mr. Gruber also graduated from Hower Vocation High School in 1954.

GIFTS

BOTTLE OF WHISKEY

My first Christmas teaching, we had cookies and punch the last day before the Christmas break. The guys handed me a gift, wrapped up, that looked like a bottle of liquor. "I would open it up at home," was my reply. At home, sure enough, it was a bottle of Canadian Club! My wife and I exchanged looks and wondered what I should do? Could there be trouble for me in accepting the whiskey? We just started a two week Christmas break, and I wouldn't be back at school for two weeks. I decided to call Mr. Jenkins, my unit principal, tell him about the gift, and ask for suggestions. Mr. Jenkins laughed when I told him it was a bottle of liquor and said I did inquire about my next move. He would check with the administration as to their opinion but don't open it, wait for a reply. We returned from the Christmas break, asked him if he discussed the gift, and he said "no" but would get back to me. That was 1966, and I haven't heard anything yet. I still have the bottle and thought about taking it to the CFHS class of 1967 50th class reunion and opening it there. So, it looks like I will open the bottle in 2017, or later by then, these guys will be old enough to drink. I missed the 1967 reunion and hope the '67 class has another get together soon because I may not be around for the 60th reunion in 2027.

APPLES FOR THE TEACHER? NO! FOR STUDENTS

I had apple trees in my back yard that produced more apples then we could eat or sell. My Uncle, who lived next door, and I did all the things necessary to grow bug-free apples. I begin to bring in golden delicious apples and give them to the students at the end of the day. No one refused a free apple. Some commented this seemed different where the teacher gives the students apples. Once after taking a bite of the apple, a student yelled out that he could see a wormhole; another student quickly told him only to worry if he sees half a worm!! Other teachers learned I had apples and arranged to buy bags of apples. If you looked in my van, you would see 6 - 8 Acme bags of apples that the teachers would order and pick up after school.

SAINT PATRICK

It was Friday, March 17, St. Patrick's Day. I went to the main office and return to my class office. On my desk was a big cardboard box. I opened the box and saw a big white rabbit. I looked around and saw no one. So, what do I do? Its Friday and I couldn't leave it there until Monday. I planned to return the rabbit to the owner on Monday, so I took it home, which was not a good thing because my three young daughters wanted to keep the rabbit. We named it "St. Patrick" because we got it on St. Patrick's Day. Like all pets, the kids care of it for about a week and then forgot the rabbit. We had to get rid of it and talked about what we could do? I mentioned to my wife when we were by ourselves; I am thinking of "rabbit stew." Her look told me that it was not going to happen. We finally gave the rabbit to the Akron Zoo, and we think St. Patrick lived happily ever after.

THE NEW ROOM

The Vocational building was built and used in 1970 for the six other vocational classes. Mr. Gruber and I helped in selecting, placing the equipment in our room, and couldn't wait to start school. After the first day in the new classroom, I mentioned I was tired at the end of the day from walking so much, but it was exciting to have this facility. For me, this was why I didn't take the Akron teaching position. It was like being in Mr. Alex Musser's class in 1952; only I was the Mr. Musser guy now.

SUMMER JOBS 1965 – 1970

FERRIOT BROTHERS

Teachers teach for 9 ½ months and have time during the summers for other activities. I had to work during the summers because my wife was a stay at home mother with our three daughters. My first job was at the Ferriot Brothers Company in the summer of 1965. I was to engraved molds for the plastic industry, like the work done at Main Mold and Sackmanns. One day I met my high school machine shop teacher, who asked me what I was going to do during the summer? I mentioned I was going to work at Ferriot. He shook his head like he didn't think that was a good idea and said the guys in the shop would play games with me after they found out I was a machine shop teacher. I begin to worry but was going to fulfill my commitment to work there.

I started, was able to do the job, and make friends in the shop. I could sharpen end mills on angles for the machining requirements and did one for a guy, and he thanked me. Next, two and three guys asked me if I could grind a tool for them too. I did and was happy to do these guys a favor and make more friends. One day Ed, the foreman, told me I was doing a good thing BUT, there is a guy downstairs whose job is to grind tools for the guys. They wanted me to do the engraving. I asked the foreman why the guys don't ask that guy. Ed mentioned the guys don't like the guy because he is mean and nasty! I asked Ed if I should tell the guys "no"? He said to tell the guys you have to finish your job, and when you're done, you will work on their cutters. It worked, and the guys went downstairs. I made friends, and they did ask me questions and answered as many as I could. Frank, the tool room guy, who helped with shop procedures, was my best friend. Ferriot makes a lot of toys for the Mattel Toy Company, and the job was dollhouse furniture. I would pass a "try out press" and see complete sample sets of furniture checked to meet the company requirements. If correct, the mold would be placed in the production line to complete the order. Since I had three daughters, a set of dollhouse furniture could be in the next Christmas plans. I mentioned this to Frank, and he said he would find me a set. I was working my last day; here comes Frank with others carrying a full black plastic trash bag for me to take home. "What's in the bag?" I asked. Frank said the boss told him to clean out the old samples or toys and other samples the tool room keeps for reference. Frank included three sets of dollhouse furniture. When asked if I would come back next year, I told them, "I'll be back!" My old high school teacher was wrong about my experience. I saw and learned many things that helped me in teaching and meeting people who were able to hire students to work there. Several students were employed.

I returned the next year and did some engraving but filled in for guys going on vacations. These men would have an area enclosed or cubical where they would work on parts and usually had a vertical milling machine in front of their work area. Also, these bench men were guys who were old and who worked there for years. I was given a job and needed a mill, but the mill in front of my cubical was set up and couldn't use it. So, I went to the next one, proceeded to set up the machine and machine the part in a couple of hours. Two guys came to me and warned me not to take just any mill because these guys, who work here, think these machines are their property. Some of these old guys have told a lot of us what they think and can be mean. That was news to me. I asked who "belongs" to this machine and they told me the "meanest guy"! Who they pointed out. I went over to the man and told him I was sorry to use this machine, the next time I will ask him if I can use the mill. He was all smiles and told me it's OK for me to use it any time I needed a machine, all the time he was smiling and friendly. Later the two guys who warned me asked what the guy said; I told them he was not mad and that I could use the machine any time I needed it. One of these two guys said that "old Gus" is changing in his old age, and he's not that way with them.

"GUNFIGHT AT THE OK CORRAL?"

The title of this story isn't "The Gunfight at the OK Corral" but "The Gunfight at Ferriot Brothers." Ferriot produced toys for the Mattel Toy Company, guns and rifles were a major product. Mattel would send or allow Ferriot to keep samples for their display case. Mr. Ferriot, one of 2 brothers, decided to clean out the display case because it was full and needed space for new products. He removes the oversupply of toy guns and rifles, hands them to the foreman, Mr. Jack Mutchie, to give to the guys in the shop. At lunch, the guys, now kids, start a gunfight in the shop. The 8 to 10 guys are running around the machines firing their weapons at guys behind other machines. The guns and rifles had realistic sound, and the spectators stood there laughing. Mr. Ferriot, hearing the noise, comes out and walks down the aisle separating the two sides of guys. They tell him he better get out of the way because he might get shot. The gun battle ends, because they ran out of bullets, Mr. Ferriot shakes his head and tells Jack the next time they hand out toys to wait until the end of the shift.

There were days when I would work 10 to 12 hours, and if you worked more than ten, you could eat the food leftover from the noon lunch cafeteria for almost no cost.

Working at Ferriot, I saw a different aspect and learning experience of the plastic mold industry, which was the running of plastic injection machines, which produces the finished product. This part of Ferriot was a separate company but in the same building.

I also saw in 1967 a new method of drilling deep holes. The plastic injection mold must have ways to cool the base due to heat from the hot flowing plastic.

Holes must be in and around the cavities, core areas and be in a circuit. The water flows in, around, and out to cool the mold. The radial drill press was the machine that slowly did this operation. It was time-consuming. Ferriot was using a gun drilling machine that cut the time 75% or more. The drill had a unique carbide tip cutting bit that was attached to a shaft that had an opening the length of the shaft. Imagine a pie cut in 4 pieces and one quarter is missing. There was a hole through the shaft and cutting tool where the coolant was pumped to the cutting tip. The chips were flushed out the one-quarter opening to a reservoir to recycle the coolant and deposit the chips. Imagine drilling a half-inch hole 22 or more inches deep without a stop. That was a first-class time saver. I heard the saying, "saving time is money!

AKROMOLD

In my third and fourth summers, I worked for Akromold in their new EDM department. EDM stands for Electric Discharge Machining. It's 1967, the process was new and saved machine time because intricate thin, detailed shapes could be machined on graphite material and that shape produced in the metal by using electric current. In EDM, the machinist machines graphite just like the lead in a pencil, only blocks of graphite. Imagine machining blocks of graphite into unique, delicate shapes that are lowered into the metal mold, as the electrode gets close (within a .001) a spark of electricity jumps out. It vaporizes a small part of the metal. The electrode does not touch the material but is a few thousandths of an inch above the surface. This erosion or vaporizing happens a thousand times per second, and eventually, the shape will form the unique graphite shape. This experience allowed me to work with graphite and black dust from machining. If you worked in this building, you would come to work in a set of clothes, change at work, at the end of the day, shower at work, and return home in the clothes you came to work wearing. I learned you do not wear your work shoes in the house because the shoes and especially the bottoms, are graphite loaded and would see footprints on the carpet. I didn't work the EDM machines; I made the electrodes. I learned a lot and earned money doing this. All the time I worked in these companies, I met guys who helped me place students in jobs. I learned how this process could save hours, not minutes, on a job because EDM can produce thin rids or supports needed in the plastic product. In making the tiny electrodes, you would have to be careful you don't bump or drop them because some would break. Soon after, another time-saving procedure became common, and that was wire EDM. Picture a thin wire on a band saw type machine cutting through the material by vaporizing the metal. The wire diameters can be in the low thousands of an inch.

MARTZ MOLD 1970

Martz Mold and Machine was a family run business located in Cuyahoga Falls. Like most shops, the company started as a part-time, in the garage at night business with the wife helping with orders as the husband work at his regular job. Then the young boys started to work, next the move to a larger building, and Mr. Martz quitting his regular job to concentrate his effort and time on his own business. I worked there the year they moved into their present facility, which was spacious. I heard stories about their previous shop that it was so crowded they had to move the trash can out because they had no room inside the small building. Three sons worked alongside their dad, but the boys told me at the beginning that the "Main Boss was their Mom" She's the real boss! My time there was running the NC Cintamatic machine. NC stands for "Numerical Control." These machines operated by a paper tape inserted in a controller the size of a present-day refrigerator. We're talking 4 – 5 feet high, 2 feet wide and 2 feet deep. The circuitry inside the controller would produce heat that could alter the machine functions, so many control units had little air-conditional units built into the sides. The paper tape was 1 inch wide with eight rows of holes with the sprocket holes between the 5th and 3rd holes to prevent the tape from being inserted the wrong way. A regular looking typewriter or tape writer would provide a readable sheet of information (hard copy) regarding the information on the tape. At the same time, a series of holes are being punched in the 1-inch tape alongside the typewriter. The beginning of the tape had information punched to identify the order number and other details. The operator was responsible for making sure the tape number and job matched. The typed instructions listed the sequence of the operations, and the operator, after practice, could hold the tape and read the arrangement of holes if he had to check a detail. To understand what is on the modern CNC (Computer Numerical Control) machines, imagine a laptop computer connected to the machine and machining instructions downloaded with the keypad. No more refrigerator size control units. Now the machining process is called CNC, not NC. NC machines are disappearing if not already gone

Martz manufactured molds for rubber products and did a robust business. Rubber molds are less critical in many respects because the finished product can be pulled from the mold and are flexible, whereas plastic products are stable, and ejection is essential in the design of the shape. Working at Martz was very valuable because NC was the start of the revolution in machining processes, and I learned this new process that I could convey to my students. Here's a machine and process that can repeat movements with less workforce and save time too. The importance of dimension location became important because the machine moves to those points without a person turning handles. Those coordinates X, Y, and Z become part of machinist vocabulary

As I mentioned before, working in various companies allowed me to learn the newest machine processes to convey to the students. I watched Mr. Martz produce 16 cavities with his "hobbing press," which is an old process then and seldom used today. This process is where a heat-treated machined shape is forced under tremendous pressure into a block of steel. Imagine sticking your thumb into a marshmallow that is inside a round container. As you remove your finger, the imprint is there, and that is the desired shape. The machine had safety shields around the press due to the forces applied. Today that process is no longer efficient with the new technology.

Magnesium was machined there also, and I learned how extra care and safety should be present when machining this material. I appreciated the Martz Mold and Machine Company for allowing me to work and learn.

SCIENTIFIC CALULATORS

I was working at Martz in 1970 and was introduced to NC Numerical Control and my first scientific calculator. A friend, an engineer, showed me his one evening, and I went nuts at what it could do. The friend knew how to use it and showed ways to solve a trig problem. A calculator was a must, and I did obtain the cheaper of the three different Texas Instrument units, the cost was about 75 dollars. I told my wife that it could be my Christmas present. She included my birthday too. I figured this would help a student learn more and would be accepted by all. I was wrong; the message was to be proficient with the old method of adding, subtracting, dividing, and multiplication. At our advisory committee meeting, the subject of students using the calculator was discussed. The owners all stressed using the calculator in our class because this would be the place to learn. When this person is employed, he will have this skill which will be helpful to the company. We were able to buy a basic calculator for under 15 dollars. Mr. Warren Anderson, the Vocational Director, helped with the administration acceptance. The guys were told about the opposition to not working a problem to the old way of multiplying or dividing a four-place decimal number times or into a four-place decimal number to find an angle. The Delmar Company introduced a unit into the 2nd edition textbook we used and also had examples with the same calculator we were using.

The time is 1989, laid off from teaching at CFHS and obtaining a teaching job at The Akron Machining Institute in Norton, Ohio. The program is for adults and 1000 hours long. The class has the same Delmar math workbook used at CFHS. I'm teaching the shop and math the same way as I did at Cuyahoga Falls High School when I'm called into the director's office. The other instructor is there, and the subject is me using the TI calculator with the students. It's that old argument about knowing the old long way or BC math (before calculator). I stand my grounds and tell the director to contact the school's advisory committee and ask them their opinion. Soon after that meeting, both instructors used calculators.

AKRON EQUIPMENT COMPANY – "ATTENDANCE PATTERN."

Akron Equipment Company wanted to interview and maybe hire a student from our program. Jack Selgus, who did the hiring, asked if I could send a student. The young man went, had the meeting, and was considered a candidate. The student's transcript was sent and evaluated. Mr. Selgus called and said he could not hire the student because the young man's "attendance pattern" indicated he missed a lot of school, and that pattern wasn't acceptable. I was disappointed but understood. That was the first time I heard "attendance pattern" and understood why the rejection.

The Cuyahoga Falls School System had an attendance rule where a student can miss up to 12 days after which he or she will fail the class. There was an appeal process that usually gave the student another chance provided the student didn't miss any more classes. This student missed less than the limit but close to that number each year. When I would mention this to students, I would hear that he would not miss work because he is making money and not being in school. I would reply it's a fact every job gets boring for short periods and the worker will revert to his or her habits when they become tired of the work. If you miss school because you are bored, you will also miss work when you are bored. That's a fact!

In my conversation with Mr. Selgus mentioned the position was working in the programming of NC machines of tire molds. I explained what my job was at Martz and understood the concept. He asked me to come in, and after an interview, I got the job the student lost. At first, I didn't say anything to the student because he was upset. I worked all summer long and was asked to work at night, and this helped the second shift until 10 pm each weekday. I was to program an NC machine where a paper tape was produced with punched holes and threaded into a control unit to create table movement and machining operations. It was a perfect job because I was learning and getting paid at the same time. The workers in the shop were union members, and I couldn't work the machines because of union rules. There was a threat of a strike and was told I would be running machines on the floor. I programmed an eight-spindle position machine that milled, drilled, and counterbored the tops and bottoms of tire molds.

Things were going along nicely when my boss, Mike, gets a call from one angry foreman about how I screwed up a program. Mike tells me there some problems downstairs; both of us go to check the problem. The foreman is upset about how I programmed the wrong pattern of holes on a tire mold. Mike and I checked the drawings, checked the identification numbers on the tape, and found out the operator picked out the wrong tapes for the job. The operator reached above the part number and removed the tapes when he should have reached below, thus the wrong hole pattern. The job was not scrapped and was saved. When the foreman and operator realized how this happened, it wasn't my fault; I went back upstairs to the programming area. Mike stayed there and wanted the foreman to call me and apologize for his outbursts. The foreman called, and I told him it was a simple mistake, and everything is fine. I was treated differently after that experience.

Guys would ask me how to do some trig problems because they had trouble with trig. One day a worker asked me how to extract a square root because he forgot how to do it the old fashion way; he didn't have a calculator. I worked each step and made sure the guy understood, and he thanked me. I returned to the programming area and explained to the two guys what I just did downstairs. Both Mike Nonno and Hank Caiazza laughed and said they couldn't remember when they worked a square root problem longhand. I said, "You want me to show you?" They just laughed and walked away.

My wife liked me working there because each Christmas season, the company would treat management to a fancy dinner at a country club. My wife and I seldom go to these fancy clubs. For my wife, that meant a trip to the hairdresser, a new dress and shoes. For me? Wash my face, comb my hair, and shine my shoes.

I did place two students there. One worked in programming (JM), and the other worked on the floor or shop. I will write about "DR" in more detail when I write about students.

BACK TO KENT STATE UNIVERSITY

I returned to Kent State University to work part-time on my master's degree and became interested in career guidance, which helped me to understand students. One professor made an impression on me - Dr. Mark Savickas. I took three of his classes and realized if teachers had a better idea of their students, they could adapt some instruction to fit student's needs.

One of Mark's speakers talked about grants that were available for teacher education in local schools and what the application required. The speaker was also in my Army Reserve Unit, so he knew me and what I wanted to do to apply for a grant. I talked to Mark about the idea of him and me running an in-school program for the Cuyahoga Falls teachers with money from these grants. The plan was to have eight sessions on Saturday morning for no more than ten teachers with a stipend of 25 dollars per session. Mark told me he would start, and I would finish each session. I developed a written presentation to present to the Cuyahoga Falls Administration for approval, with Mark's help. I was enthusiastic about this. The school administrators spoke to me and said the school officials ruled against the idea because there was a program in the past that turned out bad. They didn't know the professor from Kent (Dr. Savickas), and the administration was afraid this program would not be good and would not approve the program. I talked to Dr. Savickas about the news, and he said he was sorry I was so disappointed. That was a learning experience for me. I learned work behind the scenes must take place to start a program.

STUDENTS 18 STORIES

(I) REX – DROPPING THE STUDENT (Name Has Been Changed)

In the first year of the vocational machine shop, I had a student who was quiet and very polite but would miss a lot of school. It seemed that Rex (not his real name) would miss Monday and Tuesday two weeks out of three weeks. I talked to Mr. Jenkins about Rex missing school, and maybe he should be dropped from the program. Mr. Jenkins took me into his office and closed the door. He proceeded to tell me Rex's parents were the reason he stays home. It seems the parents have some problems, so Rex stays home to take care of his younger brothers and sisters. Mr. Jenkins mentioned to me that his experience with Rex after talking to him, maybe the machine shop experience would be good for Rex. My opinion of this young man changed after this conversation with Mr. Jenkins. Rex continued in the program, and we were able to find employment in the machining industry. Rex worked in a specialized area of this company that required advanced skills. I often wonder what happened to this young man. He would be about 65+ years of age now.

Rex is an example of learning about the life of the students in my class. I learned to ask questions and seek advice about issues that affect a student's life. I think about Rex and wonder what could have happened if he was removed from the program. As I said, Teaching was an education.

(II) MARY – "DON'T DROP THIS STUDENT!"
(Name Has Been Changed)

The above example happen in 1965, when I was thinking about dropping a student because of absences and found out his reason, changed my mind, and that change helped the student. This example is just the opposite. It is 1988, I was a substitute teacher in the Cuyahoga Falls System, substituting for a member of the school's attendance committee, and I was to take her place at a meeting at the end of the day. This committee could recommend a student not be given credit for her or his class and require her or his to take it over next year or allow the student to continue with conditions. My wife worked as an aide for two special education classes at a middle school and had this young lady, Mary, as a student. This young girl looked like an ordinary student but had problems like where she would forget things, where her next class was, or where she placed her books or gym clothes even if those items were under her desk. Mary missed several gym classes and was to appear before the attendance committee of teachers who would recommend 1) no credit and have to repeat the course or 2) to be allowed the missed time and be approved for credit. This young lady came in, sat down, and looked very relaxed, and presented herself very well. Mary mentioned she forgets to bring her gym outfit to class and can't dress and doesn't receive credit for that day. She has more non-credit days than allowed; thus, she has to come before this committee. The girl leaves, thanks us, and closes the door. The first comment is not to grant her an extension of time, and she is to receive no credit for her physical education class. I speak up and tell the committee things my wife has said to me about this girl and that she was in a special program at the middle school, and she can't remember things. There were more questions asked about the girl, and one counselor did mention Mary did have a problem. "Academic challenged" students were to be included in regular classes. After this discussion, the young lady was allowed to receive credit. One fellow teacher mentioned to me you would never think anything about this girl by the way she looks and presents herself in front of the committee. I felt lucky I was substituting that day.

(III) LEONARD AND TEEPEEING

"Teepeeing" describes an activity where people, usually students, throw toilet paper on and over a tree, car, or house to show they like you. Before I started to grade papers at home, I called a student, Leonard, about an interview at a local company scheduled for him the next day. Leonard's Mom answered and said Leonard wasn't home and would give him that message. I started grading papers after my three daughters were in bed because it would be quiet. As I was looking at the homework, the neighbor's large German shepherd was barking, but different. I went to the back door, turn on the rear house light, saw toilet paper on the little tree we had in our back yard, and then saw two people running through the neighbor's yard next to his 6-foot high fence. I could see the German shepherd running along the fence, barking at these two "dangers" to his house. I can imagine what the dog would have done if there was no fence. I yelled, "LEONARD!" but the two guys ran to the other side of the neighbor's house and the street. I went to the front door, open it, and saw our trees in front also covered in paper. By this time, my wife and daughters came to the door to see why I was yelling. We all stood on our stoup and looked at the front yard while the three or four cars with the guys who did the teepeeing would drive pass in one direction, yelling out the window, go up the street, turn around and repeat the drive pass. After several passes, the guys drove in the driveway, got out, and were asking us what we thought about the trees. My daughters were young and ask, "Why do they throw toilet paper on the trees?" The guys then began to remove the paper and clean the yard. While the guys were cleaning up, my next-door neighbor came out with his wife and mother and watched from their driveway. As the guys drove away, I walked to the neighbor and explained what had happened. They said they didn't understand "these young people these days." As they began to return to their house, the man's light jacket opened up, and I could see a gun inside his belt. (In my comments to the students I stressed a BIG gun) That gun scared me, and the next day I told the guys about the weapon, was glad Leonard or no one didn't get shot. I told Leonard about the interview that evening, and when his Mother said I called about an interview, Leonard said I already told him. She wondered how Leonard found out.

(IV) RICK

In 1969, Rich was a student who was competent, skilled, and a pleasure to have in class. One day I asked him if he had an Aunt named "Donna." He said, "Yes." I asked him if his father was in the Korean War, again a "Yes.", was his father blind? He said yes again. I told him I went to school with his Aunt Donna and remembered when his Mother and Dad married around 1950. I asked Rick what his father did for a living. Rick said he works in his machine shop! I had to be so surprised that Rick noticed the expression on my face. "Your father has a machine shop? What type of work does he do in his shop?" Rick said he does work for AAmco Transmission and turns shafts down for the company. I asked one more question; does your father has some fingers missing? Another "yes," I told Rick I remember the experience of seeing dark spots on the floor of the junior machine shop in 1950 at Hower and thinking the spots must be layout dye an adult evening student spilled the night before. Our junior instructor told us the evening before, a student cut off three fingers running a milling machine. Mr. Kleckner also said the student was blind. The class just stood there and wondered why a blind guy would want to run a horizontal mill. That was Rick's father in 1950. We had eyes, and we were afraid of the machine.

The year is 1969, and this experience appears again with Rick's father. I questioned Rick as to how does his father maintains dimensions to a plus or minus .003 tolerance? Rick told me, "You don't want to see him work on his lathe!" I guess my facial expression indicated surprise and safety concerns again. Rick knew how I stressed safety, and he anticipated my interest. It seems that Rick's father would position his finger next to the tool cutting the material because he couldn't see the cut. I asked Rick if he would ask his father if I could visit the shop and talk to his father. The next day Rick said his dad said the following Friday after school would be fine. I arrived, but Rick's father had to be away, and I didn't meet him. I saw the shop and if was perfect for one man with all the necessary machines and equipment to earn a living "with normal eyesight." I asked Rick if he helps his dad. He said his dad gets mad at him because he forgets to replace the tools in their exact place, and when his father reaches for it and if it is not where it's supposed to be, he yells at Rick. Of course, the tool is just a couple of inches away, but his father is blind and can't see the item is just a couple of inches away. All the tools in the roll-a-way were in pockets, and he knew where each one was located. The dials on his machines were marked in brail so he could feel precise movement. What I saw was extraordinary. I would have like to make a movie about Rick's father's accomplishments and show what's possible with determination. It's 2020, and I hope to meet this amazing gentleman and Rick because I found a couple of assignments from Rick's time in the class, and it's time to return them.

(V) ONLY ONE IN THE UNIVERSE

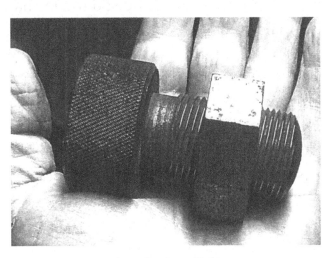

Photo by Stan Sipka

Universe means every aspect of outer-space – aliens, planets, and the unknown. Each senior was to machine a multiple lead left-hand thread and nut. Tom decided on a 1.250 diameter left-hand quad lead project. "Quad" means there would be four starts to the thread, and it was a challenge. Many containers used in every house have multiple threads on the lid. Tom machined the shaft under the 1.250 dimension and was upset and wanted to scrap the piece and start over. We continued with the 1.189 diameter. Both shaft and nut were completed, and information was stamped on the head of the shaft. Tom was upset; the 1.250 dimension was missed and commented about his grade. The grade was still high because of his achievement of making the matching thread that fit. I made a comment his dimensions and uniqueness would make this matched pair "The Only one in the Universe!" nowhere in space. The class enjoyed the comment, and others wanted to copy Tom's dimensions? I told them no one would copy Tom's work.

Tom took his pride and joy home and announced to his dad this was the only one in the universe. Dad looked at it and said something like "Big Deal!"

Tom gave me his "Only One in the Universe" and said he was not seeking a job in machining.

Other guys tried to copy the dimensions, but I threaten them with a failing grade. Different diameters would make their pair the only one in the universe too.

(VI) BOB JENKINS

Bob and I talked and mentioned I was writing about things that happen as a result of learning and wanted to know if I could use his name. He told me to go ahead and say "me and twist drills and grandpa" We're talking about the 1967-68 school year, and Bob was in the 2-period machining class. I required all the students to learn how to sharpen a twist drill, which is a common tool in everyone's' toolbox. Some students catch on quickly, and others take more time. Bob caught on quick, as I would comment how fast he was, he would say he's going to take me on in a drill sharpening contest! My answer would be that I will not get in a contest with a student because I can't stand the student crying to his mother when he loses!

Bob shares with me a story where his skill in sharpening drills allowed him to find a "buddy" - his grandpa. Bob said he wasn't close to his grandpa because both had different interests. His parents and Bob went to visit the grandparents and was told to "go downstairs and say hello to grandpa in his basement workshop." Bob goes down, said hello, looks around, and notices the equipment in grandpa's shop. He glances down and sees a pile of drills in a box, picks up one, notices it needs sharpening and asks why all these in this box look like they need sharpening? When a drill becomes dull, Grandpa buys another drill. Bob asks if he can sharpen one? "Sure, go ahead." Bob picks up a drill, proceeds to sharpen the twist drill, positioning his hands, and frequently looks at it to checks the angles while grandpa watches. Finally, he hands it to grandpa. Grandpa examines it and wants to know where Bob learned how to do that? Bob mentions he's in a machine shop class, and one thing everyone has to know is how to sharpen a drill. All of a sudden, Bob and grandpa have something in common. Grandpa has a slew of dull drills, and Bob can fix them. Bob then sharpens several more, comes back another day, and finishes the others. Bob says his grandpa seemed like a regular guy because they seemed to have a lot in common. Grandpa would ask Bob what he's doing in school, and Bob would ask questions about what grandpa was doing. Bob said, "I feel good because I have a buddy - grandpa."

Bob was in another story about him knowing Stan Sipka. I rented some device from Home Depot and was returning the tool. I drove, and my son-in-law took the item in the store. The clerk asked for a name, and the son-in-law said, "STAN SIPKA." Bob was there returning something and started to question this guy who said, "SIPKA." My son-in-law later said this guy (Bob) wasn't smiling when told me that "you are not Stan Sipka because I know Sipka!" My son-in-law said Stan would be in the store as soon as he parks the car", satisfying Bob until I arrived. We shook hands, exchanged greetings, and I thanked him for looking out for me. My son-in-law said it was a good thing I came to the store because this guy thought I was doing something wrong.

(VII) SHARPENING TWIST DRILLS

Every student should know how to sharpen a twist drill because the drill is a common tool for repair work in every home. Three things are needed to sharpen a drill 1) the same angle on each flute, 2) the same length of cutting edge, and 3) clearance behind the cutting edge. Each student learns to sharpen a twist drill. Most were successful. A few would brag how fast they could sharpen a drill. A few would challenge me to a timed contest in sharpening a twist drill. I would tell them I won't because I don't want the loser's mother telling the school officials how I embarrassed their child.

I did have a left-hand drill where the twists were opposite the standard drill. When I would have a student bragging how good and fast he is, I would tell him we would time him when for the record. We would give him this left-hand drill. We would have another student watch the time, give him the drill, and say "GO." The student would position himself with his hands placed on the tool rest and move the drill towards the grinding wheel, but soon he would stop and look at the end of it and reposition his hands. To the student, something wasn't right, and again, he would pause. The guys watching would make some comment about the time wasted with no grinding. Most of the students would stop and pick up a standard one and examine the ends of both drills and realize they were different. We didn't let the student grind this drill because I wanted to use it as an example for other guys.

Another exercise with drills was to flat bottom a drill in case there was a need to counterbore (a hole with a flat bottom) a hole, and there was no counterbore tool available. We used drill gages and squares to check and an optical comparator unit to check with magnification.

(VIII) DENNY

Denny was a student, who had the necessary entry-level skills, Cooped at Ferriot Brothers, and continued working there after graduation. Coop means a student is allowed to work at a company instead of attending the senior class time. I talk to the seniors that their job could lead to a journeyman classification, which is like a college diploma. When you are in a company that sponsors an apprenticeship program, papers have to be signed, so the State of Ohio knows you are in a program. So, you, the company, and the state must have this information. After you work full time, the hours you work counts towards the 2000 hours per year for the four years. There should be a schedule of the different machines and hours you should experience to gain the journeyman skills. Denny graduates and is working. School starts in the fall, and he is a memory. One afternoon in October, Denny walks in the shop and needs to talk to me. The guys are busy, and Denny tells me he's going to quit Ferriot because they haven't spoken to him about the apprenticeship program. I asked him if he likes working there. His reply was "yes," but nothing is being said about the apprenticeship program. I recommend he try something first. Talk to his foreman "Ed" about the apprenticeship and the needed papers to sign. Later that day, speak to Ed again in a friendly way and ask him if he had luck finding the documents? Ed, no doubt, forgot what you asked him before and will probably ignore the second time. The next day ask Ed again in a subtle way and smile and wish him a good day. Ask, Ed again, be friendly and smile. Give this a few days before you quit. Denny leaves, and I forget what I told him. A few months later, I take the senior class on tour at Ferriot's. As we walked past the machines, Denny motions for me to come over to him because he wanted to say something. The foreman tells me it's OK to talk to Denny. The first thing he says was, "That worked!" It took me a few minutes to wonder what worked. He said he kept telling Ed that his Mother wanted to see the papers and got the documents in a couple of days. Denny was happy, and so was I. I will use "mother" from now on if I have to tell another student how to get his apprenticeship papers.

(IX) IT'S MY FISH

Socializing with students is not a good idea. Students have various interests, and being a good listener, I would ask questions indicating an interest in their activity. Kevin's interest was fishing and had stories related to his skill. He kept inviting me to let him teach me "how to catch fish." The answers were "later" until I agreed to go and learn "how to catch fish." I arrived at Wingfoot Lake in Hartville mid-morning, and Kevin had the boat and fishing gear in the boat ready to go. I rowed the boat across the lake to where all the fish were waiting. Rowing to that spot, we could see the Goodyear Blimp hanger, the home of the famous Goodyear Blimp that's seen at important events. We stop, drop the anchor, and ready the fishing gear. When I looked up, I'm looking at the dock area, not the Blimp hanger; the boat turned 180 degrees.

Kevin points to the area near the seaweeds and comments, 'that's where all the fish are hiding." He will fish towards the weeds, and I will fish towards the boat dock. We are casting for 30 minutes when Kevin's line becomes active, and Kevin starts to yell his excitement with the catch. I prepare to use the fishnet to haul the fish when it's near. The fish is making life difficult for Kevin. It jumps out of the water, and Kevin sees the fish and becomes excited because of the size of the largemouth bass. The fish is in the net; Kevin holds the fish up and comments, "this is the largest bass I have ever caught and will have it mounted."

I'm looking at it as the main part of a fish dinner. I've seen mounted fish on walls but picture larger fish, not the fish Kevin is holding. We finish, and I don't remember if I caught any fish. The thrill of Kevin's success was my success. He continued to talk about keeping the bass, and the cost is not extravagant, just the trophy. That fish could have been mine, but the wind turned the boat around. I asked if he could put my name at the bottom of the plaque as a witness. I heard a "no." Kevin would be most generous with everything but not his trophy fish. I enjoyed the day.

(X) DAVE (NOT HIS REAL NAME)

Dave was a student. I will never forget and wonder what I could or should have done to help him. I met Dave when he was in the junior machine shop class. He had a beautiful smile as he talked to me and looked happy working on the machines. Mr. Gruber, the junior teacher, had a requirement that each student does an outside project regarding the machining industry. Many junior students wrote a paper like those required in many other classes. Dave and his Grandpa walk in with his project, which was a display of metal fasteners inside a case that was so large it was in two separate 2ft x 4ft hinged sections. Each section had a transparent plastic sheet, and inside were numerous fasteners fasten to the back with 3in x 5in cards neatly written describing each unique fastener. That was not an "A"; it was a triple "AAA" project. The grandpa stood by, and Dave just beamed with his smile as both teachers examined the assignment. Dave and his grandpa sent letters to different companies that produced fasteners and asked for a sample for this class project. Dave mentioned they received too many examples and didn't have room for all they received.

Dave entered the senior year and was a pleasure to have as a student. We were able to co-op Dave, and it looked like life would be kind to him. But, I receive a call from the owner who said Dave gave his tools to a worker and left the shop for no reason at all. His tools are returned, and he returns to the class, again gives his tools to another student and leaves. After a few days, Dave returns and is his old self, smiling and friendly to everyone. Both instructors are concerned and don't know what to do. Most of the time, Dave is all smiles, and those few times, there is no smile.

Dave graduates and I help him obtain a job at Akron Equipment Company, where I was working during the summer. We talk daily, and I see that beautiful smile. I'm working on a program and get a call from the foreman downstairs to come as soon as possible; it's about Dave! The foreman mentioned that Dave stopped his machine, put his tools in his toolbox, locked the box, gave the key to another worker, told him he could have the tools, walked to the time clock, punched out, and leaves. Dave was working on a vertical boring mill where the large table rotates like a record on a turntable. This machine was scheduled for maintenance because the main table bearings were wearing out and would be replaced after this last job. There was one worker who knew about the bearing problem because of the many hours of use. This guy walks over to Dave, positioned himself as if he is listening to this noise from the bearing, and asks Dave what he did to make this bearing sound so bad? This machine sounds messed up. Dave bends down listens, stops the machine, closes his toolbox, gives the key to this guy, punches out, and leaves. The guys in the shop were upset with this guy who thought he was just having a little shop fun. Dave doesn't come back, and the company makes sure he gets his tools back.

Dave travels to Texas to stay with his brother. Years later, I received several telephone calls (no cell phones), but the person doesn't leave a message or return number. Soon after, I see Dave's obituary in the Beacon Journal, and there are no calling hours. I wondered if those calls were from Dave.

When the Cuyahoga Falls Vocational Machine class stopped, I took the project of the fasteners and used it in the adult programs until 1997. So, Dave was in my thoughts for a long time because that display reminded me of that smile.

(XI) SARA (NOT HER REAL NAME)

Near the end of the school year, the seniors receive their caps and gowns for graduation. I had a senior homeroom and knew we passed out graduation caps and gowns that morning. I made arrangements with the business education teacher to have a student that could type for me in the afternoon while I had the seniors in the shop. Sara, a nice young senior girl, came and helped me in the 6th period with my year-end records and reports. The period begins, Miss Sara arrives, and I commented, "well, I guess you got your cap and gown today" before I could say anything else, she covers her eyes with her hands and cries profusely. I'm surprised, and don't know what to do and asked her, "What's the matter." She replies she won't graduate! This young lady surely has the grades and attendances to pass with honors, but yet she can't graduate? It dawn's on me to ask her, "it's because she didn't take a specific class requirement?" She replies, "Yes," she didn't take the required health class. I tell her she doesn't have to help me today and can return to the study hall. She said she's OK and comes into the room where there is the typewriter. After school, I talk to the senior class principal, mention this lady, and what I just experienced. The principal shook his head and said the school bent over backward for the girl and had another class that would satisfy this course requirement. The mother refused the alternative class for her daughter. Thus, this girl did not graduate. What a sad thing to happen to a person who deserved and needed to graduate.

A day or two later, I met the mother and the girl in the hall outside the machine shop classroom, and after talking to the mother, I felt sorry for this girl. The alternative was the way to satisfy the requirements, and this mother's objection made no sense to me. The mother "did not want her daughter in a class with girls who were pregnant." That was the mother's reason. I had wished I knew this before; I would have tried to become friends with the mother and tell her how nice her daughter was and how she has helped me. The idea was to talk to the mother about her objection and soften her objection and realize how it affected her daughter's life.

(XII) YOU CAME TO TALK TO MY DAD!

The next story was told to me when I went to visit Prospect Mold to get up-to-date information about what is being done today regarding machining compared to the 1970s and 1980s. While there, I learned another student was working there, and we talked about his time in the Cuyahoga Falls machine program. I asked him if he had leukemia in his senior year, and he said, "yes." I told him I had to learn what leukemia was all about and mentioned I was happy that everything is better now. What year was he in the class? I asked. He replied 1980 and said that it was 37 years ago. He then said he will always remember me because I came to his house one evening at 8:00 pm and wanted to talk to his father. He mentioned I told his father my grades were failing, and the father should know. The former student said after that visit, his grades improved. This young man who beat leukemia said he would never forget that visit.

(XIII) "YES SIR, NO SIR."

I saw a truck next to me at a traffic light with a company logo and name of the company on the door – Esterly Mold and Machine. I met the company owner, years ago, when Mr. Adam Esterly interviewed a student. John was sent and was hired for the position. John would always say "yes sir" or "no sir" when you would typically hear "yes or yea" or "no or naw." I enjoy hearing this because it conveyed a well mannerly individual and could sense respect and parental involvement. I receive a call from the owner asking me if John is a smart-aleck kind of guy because he always said "yes sir or no sir" instead of just "no or yes." I laugh, and tell the owner that John is different, and enjoy his pleasant comments because John is serious. The owner mentioned he never had a worker that was polite and will appreciate John's comments.

My conversation with the owner was so pleasant that the owner invited me to his house someday for a beer. I think I will take him up on that offer if it's still on.

(XIII) BLIND STUDENT

Wearing safety glasses is easy or hard. Easy if you wear glasses for everyday use, difficult if you don't wear glasses. One size fits all isn't true. I had one boy who complained about the hurt and tried to talk me into, not wearing the glasses. I then suggested that he should see what it's like to be blind for one class period. We agreed to have this student "be blind" for one period in the class. The students arrived, and I placed a towel around the student's head so he could not see. Of course, he had to sit away from the machines and sit there for 50 minutes. After 40 or so minutes, the "blind" student gets up and starts to remove the towel. Other students ask him why he's removing the cloth; he still has ten more minutes to be "blind." He replies he has to go to the restroom, which was a small restroom with a sink and toilet off the room. The students told him he is still blind, and they would help him walk to the door and help him with the door. The "blind" student commented that he didn't want to miss the toilet, and the other guy said that he would watch him and make sure he didn't wet the floor! The "blind" student got excited about guys watching him and said he would "hold it" for another 10 minutes. Again the other students reminded him that blind guys don't know if anyone is watching them or not. That's being blind! This one period example did help guys think about their eyes and not me "bugging them" about their eyes and safety glasses.

(XIV) CHEWING TOBACCO

My first year back to the high school, after being laid off, I was assigned two welding classes, two woodworking classes, and a metal class. The year is 1993, and the school systems have rules regarding tobacco products. We were to take the tobacco item, turn it over to the principal, and he or she would handle the episode. I recognize the familiar round can impression in a boy's rear pocket and toll him I have to take the can to the principal. I see "Mail Pouch" open the can and see one pinch removed. I told him the principal would contact him regarding the tobacco and walked in my office and placed the container on my desk. It's after the last class; I prepare to go to the front office; look for the can of Mail Pouch; it's not there. Someone came into my office and stole the can. I was upset and decided to tell the principal what had happened the next morning. On my way home, I bought a can of Mail Pouch and removed a pinch and gave it to the principal the following morning. The principal confronted the boy and issued whatever discipline was appropriate. The idea was to surprise the student with a container that was identical to his. Would the student say that wasn't his and explain that he or a friend stole it from my desk? The Principal said the kid had a funny look on his face and said nothing. What did I learn from this?? Chewing tobacco is EXPENSIVE!

(XV) ACADEMIC CHALLENGED STUDENT

In 1993 academic challenged students were placed in regular classes. In 1967, the term "slow learners" was common. I wrote three stories about students in those 1967 classes. Things changed in 1993. I had a student in the woods class, who was a challenge for the teacher. The wood class has several machines that can hurt the operator and others in the class. This young boy was easy to spot; the other students were great in they recognized this boy as being different and stayed out of his way. Special activities were necessary for this boy that kept him from working the machines. One day the special boy was absent, and I asked the guys about what they thought about the special boy? The guys felt sorry for the boy, and one said how he would go out of his way to help because that could have been him. Another guy said this kid seems happy in his world. I don't remember what the special boy made, but he was happy. How the other guys worked with or stayed away from the boy was an educational experience for me.

(XVI) TIME CLOCK

Having equipment that requires oil and lubricants and little space, we arranged to store our few 55-gallon containers at the school's warehouse. When we needed items, we would call Ralph, manager of the warehouse, and set up a time to pick up the supplies. On one visit, I happened to see a time clock behind some barrels, out of sight, and asked Ralph why the clock was out of sight? Those school maintenance staff didn't want to use a time clock, so someone hid it. I asked Ralph if I could have it to use in the class. He hurried and placed the clock in my car before I finished the sentence. The clock didn't work, but a local company fixed it at no charge when I told him it was to be used in a high school class to experience the world of work. We used old IBM cards as time cards and set up the routine of "punching in and punching out."

We were using the clock in the vocational machine trades senior class where the student would arrive at noon and leave at 3 pm. I didn't take attendance until midway through the afternoon. We had three guys who would, on occasion, leave the school grounds for lunch and make it back in time for class. One day Dave didn't go with the other two and was in class before noon. The time was getting close to noon, and the other two guys were not in sight. I wasn't aware of these guys and the time, but Dave was, kept looking outside and watching the clock. Everyone was in class, punched in before noon except these two guys. Dave has this plan that if he pulls the electric plug on the time clock before noon and when the two guys arrive, they could be there before noon by replacing the plug. I wasn't aware of Dave's plan. Here come these two guys, Dave tells them about the time clock, they plug in the clock, they punch in at 11:58. They are there before noon by the clock. Everyone is looking at me because I stressed that we "come and go" by the clock and that these guys are in before noon. Time goes on, and we start cleaning up 15 minutes before 3:00. As a few guys start cleaning, I ask them, "What are you doing cleaning up early??" The young men point to the clock on the wall, which is the correct time, but I point to the time clock time. I stated we "come and go" by the time clock. Keep working for another 10 minutes!! All the guys followed the time clock time and were not happy. When the school bell rang, we stayed in the room because we were still 10 minutes on the time clock. One guy had a girlfriend that came to the door and wondered why her boyfriend was still in class. I later thought I should not have kept the guys who were there on time those extra minutes. I guess you can say I'm apologizing 50 + years later. We used the time clock until the end of the machine trades program in 1987.

(XVII) WINDOW WASHER

Rain or sunshine determined whether this student would be absent or present. I had a student who would miss school when the weather was rain-free and clear skies. If there were rain or threatening weather, he would be in school. I asked him about why this is happening, and he said that he works for his father and uncles washing windows, and when the weather is good, he goes to the job site and works with his family. I required homework from the students in the machining classes because homework added to their knowledge of machines and materials. This student did well in the first grading period with a grade of "C" and a "D" the second grading period. Students know that a grade average of above .5 would be a final grade of "D." A "D" grade would be OK for him. The weather in the last half of the second grading period is warming up, and this student starts to miss school. The last six weeks of school included the months of May and June. Again he misses almost every day. The final grade is the total of the 3- 6weeks grades and the final exam grade. The young man comes in, takes the final exam, walks to a desk, is still standing, signs his name, and hands the exam back to me. I'm shocked at his actions. He replies with a grade of "F," he has a grade point average of .75, which is a "D." I tell him he should try to answer the questions. He tells me he has to go to work because he is making good money and walks out. The other students sit there puzzled. I discuss this with Mr. Jenkins, who asked me if this student worked on answering at least one question? I said, "no." Mr. Jenkins said we would give this student a grade of "incomplete" and instruct the student he has a time period to complete the exam to complete the course requirements. The summer vacations start, and I forget this student's obligation until I read in the paper the obituary of this young boy. I called Mr. Jenkins, mentioned this and told him I felt sorry, but the young man's attitude was so different than any other student I've had. As far as I know, the grade was never changed.

(XVIII) BEING GOD'S MACHINIST

It is 1967, and we were in Black and Gold arrangement when we had a student who was deeply involved with his church. He would spend time each day talking to students and me about being saved and inviting all to attend his church services. He handed out pamphlets and was very active in his desire to convert or save everyone. With all this talking and moving around, he wasn't doing the machine assignments, and his grades were not good. One day I mentioned to him that God placed him in this class to learn how to work in this kind of occupation because this work may be what God wants him to do. God may be upset that he is not doing the required assignments and not gaining the skills and knowledge to become skilled and be God's machinist in heaven. The boy looked at me, nodded his head, thought for a few seconds, and said I was right. I said he could put some pamphlets on the workbenches, and the guys can pick up what they want. The shop was small and crowded with machines, and I know the other students heard what I said.

(XIX) THE 35 MINUTE BREAK

I taught in the adult apprenticeship program for many years and had just one bad experience with young adults. I never let students sit in the last row of seats because I wanted them close so I could look at their work as we did problems. I knew that those who felt they couldn't do the math wanted to sit in the back, thinking the teacher would forget them. A new class starts and three young guys sit in the last row. I move them closer. The next week they sit in the back again, and I move them again. The class is 4 hours long, and we take 2 ten minute breaks during that time. The three guys seem to be close friends and started to act like high school students. I announce the second break, and these three guys take a 35-minute break, not 10 minutes. They drove somewhere. They came and sat and acted as if the 35-minute break is okay. The older guys are watching me to see what I'm going to do. At 9:50 pm, I tell the class it's time to go, but these three students are not excused and have to stay. They argue they only have to be there till 10 pm, and I mention the keyword is EXCUSED. The regular guys leave, and these three guys stay. I explain that they missed some features they have to know and proceed to work the board and overhead projector with the lesson just for them. Two of them get real busy, and the other guy tells me he knows what I'm presenting. He gives me an answer, and I ask him to show me his work because I think his result is wrong. I mention the response is OK, but how he arrived at the answer is more important, and besides, he didn't use a check step. The 30 extra minutes are up and toll them that the next time they pull this crap, I will contact their company. Also, each student must sit in a different seat and not be next to each other. The guys realized now this is not a high school class. They acted like apprentices for the rest of the 18 weeks.

(XX) HANDWRITING FROM THE PAST

Former students pass away happens more often as the days turn into years. I opened the Akron Beacon Journal and noticed a former student had died. My mind quickly returned to the time he was in class and remembered him as a pleasure to have as a student. On the first day of class, students are to fill out 5 x 7 cards with basic information. Two days before seeing the notice, I see the student card as I glance through items to be discarded. My one thought was to return the card to the family instead of throwing it away. I attend the wake and realize the line is very long, so I walk to a young girl who I believe is a daughter, and quietly tells her who I am. I give her the card explaining why I still have it; she looks at it and begins to cry aloud. That attracts the attention of her mother and other sisters. The young girl is so excited about this card that was written by her father and it's his handwriting. They all look at it and thank me for this memory of their dad and husband. I didn't expect that reaction, but after I realize the feeling of just seeing the handwriting can make her or someone feel better. She said, "It's my dad's writing!" and held it to her chest. On my way home, I begin to feel the power of handwriting.

DUTIES WITHIN THE SCHOOL

CHILDREN HAVING CHILDREN

The saying "children having children" describes a shocking experience I had writing admit slips for a 9th-grade students. A little girl walks up to counter and gives me her name. I notice the time and ask her the reason for being late. She tells me her baby is ill, and the daycare center will not take the baby with an illness; she had to take the baby to her grandmother's house. I froze for a good 20 seconds when I heard "my baby." Here's a girl in the 9th grade with a baby. My heart went out to this little girl – mother and wondered about her and the baby's life. I mentioned this encounter with the secretary, and she said you have to get use to that kind of excuse.

A DIFFERENT KIND OF DISCIPLINE

I had a small study hall for 9th graders in a regular classroom one semester. The students were seated apart, and I explained my rules about being quiet for all but the last 5 minutes of the period. After a couple of days, one boy acted up and was told to calm down. He continues; I give him the final notice; the next outburst will be a detention -my detention. Well, as day turns into night, he continued, and I assign him detention in my machine shop room after school. He said he should go to the regular detention room. I said, "no," I have my detention room. He shows up; I hand him a sheet of paper that has two questions that he must answer before he can leave. He argues he just has to sit there and not answer any question. I tell him to sit down and write and walk in my office a few feet away and looked busy. He quickly writes some answers, hands me the paper, and I give him another sheet with two more questions about why he is disturbing those in the study hall who want to use their time wisely. What right does he have to mess with them wanting to use their time for class assignments? He writes about each, hands me the second paper, and prepares to leave. I tell him, wait, we have to talk about his answers first. We spend 4 -5 minutes talking about what he wrote. I told him to go and mentioned, "you don't want to do this tomorrow too."

The next day, the class comes in; this student opens a book, takes out paper and pencil, and gets busy. Another guy starts to act up as I start to warn him about my detention; the kid who was with me yesterday yells, "you don't want his detention because he makes you write and keeps you until you finish!" The second kid hears this, stops his antics, and the room is a pleasure to supervise the rest of the year.

ADULT PROGRAMS IN 1967

My first experience with teaching adults was in the summer of 1967. There was a need for machinists, and the local chapter of the National Tool and Precision Die Machining Association (NTDPMA) sponsored an adult program using the school's machine shop facility. The class started a day after the regular school year ended in June and was from 7 am until 4 pm Monday thru Friday or a 40 hour week. This summer week schedule was long because when the regular high school starts in September, fewer hours for adults were scheduled. When the regular high school began in September, these students would then arrive at 3:30 pm and leave at 10:00 pm for another 6 or 7 weeks. I had a 7 to 4 day during the summer, but it was difficult when school started in the fall because I would start at 8 AM to 3:30 pm for the high school classes and 4 to 10 PM five days a week for the adults.

PLAYBOY CENTERFOLD

Because of the summer heat, the shop time was in the mornings and classroom instruction in the afternoon. We used a room in the high school that had a forced-air feature and was more comfortable. We didn't have air condition back "in the old days." We had 10-15 minute breaks during the 3 hours of related instruction. During the class breaks, the guys would leave in a hurry, go to the cafeteria where there were some vending machines. I would be the last person to exit the room. This one particular day the break was announced, I left the room and didn't notice the guys weren't in a hurry to leave. Off I go for some quiet time. I returned and saw no students outside waiting for me to enter first, when I came in I noticed the guys were sitting down all had this funny look on their faces. I was suspicious and looked around but didn't see anything. We were learning geometric principles involving circles, radii, and the blending of arcs and circles. I was using an opaque projector that allows you to use an actual photo, which would project it to the screen. I positioned myself and turned on the projector and was going to continue what we were viewing before the break. The guys laughed; I turned around and saw a picture of a naked lady, a Playboy centerfold. The time is 1967, so these pictures in 1967 were different than those of today. I stood there; these guys were watching me more than the screen and wondered what I would do? I had a pointer and proceeded to describe how the different radii blended into the shapes and emphasized there were no sharp corners as I moved the tip of the pointer around the different curved surfaces of the picture. I mentioned we don't want sharp edges on this object. He guys laughed, and I finally said, let's go to something else. I was worried that someone from the main office would hear the laughter and look in and see this picture in full view from the corridor. This projector has a conveyor belt, you crank the handle, and the copy comes off. I quickly turned the crank to get rid of this picture, and these guys taped another image on the reverse side on the belt, so here's another example of circles and arcs blending into recognizable shapes. I finished and went to our book examples. These guys were a pleasure to teach, and I know many students obtained employment from companies in the Association. As I reflect on this class, I believe these guys are near retirement age (70 – 80 years old) now.

Writing this story and the next one made me think how long ago this happen. Like that saying, "time goes by fast when you are having fun!"

FORD'S APPRENTICE PROGRAM

In Vocational Educational classes at Kent State, I met a school administrator from the Bedford School System who administered the Ford Apprenticeship program for the State of Ohio. The administrator was begging someone to finish one class of 4th-year apprenticeship because the regular teacher resigned before the end of the year. The subject was Metallurgy - The science of metals. I was given the position for the few weeks remaining. In the first class, I was nervous, but the guys told me they would not cause any trouble because they were near the end of their four-year apprenticeship. I was comfortable with the subject and was able to complete the units. After the last class, I was invited to a party at a local bar to celebrate their achievement, but I told them I had to teach the next day, thanked them for the offer and wished them good luck.

I understand what happens when a piece of steel is transformed from machineable to a hardened piece of steel. I show by using my hands the process occurring at specific temperatures. I intertwine my fingers loosely to represent the steel being heated to 1500 degrees. At a certain temperature, the atoms of carbon and iron become intertwined and form a different structure. The idea to immerse this hot piece of steel in water or oil is to freeze this new structure. My fingers of each hand now grab the other fingers as though they are one. (I show this grabbing with my hands tightly and facial features.) When I worked at Sackmann, an old steel salesman showed with his hands how steel changes from being machinable to not machineable. This class at Ford added and reinforced what I learned at Sackmanns while listening to the steel salesman regarding heat treatment.

I also taught a class in drafting, where I obtained many examples used in later geometry and trig assignments for high school and apprenticeship classes. The drawings were used for trig and geometry assignments.

TEACHING ADULTS -The above story happened in 1967-1968, and I didn't work with adults until later in my teaching career.

TEACHERS

GOLF LEAGUE – PERCY AND HINKEL

In the spring of 1968, I started a golf league for 5 or 6 weeks at Brookside golf course, where Giant Eagle is located in the Chapel Hill complex in Cuyahoga Falls, Ohio. We had two-man teams and paired a "good" golfer with "a not so good" golfer. Before the last week, I asked for money for prizes because we were going to have a series of contests in the final week. Prizes for the longest drive and closest to the pin on selected holes were sleeves of golf balls, and each golfer received a package of golf balls before we teed off. We had a putting contest where each golfer was to putt three balls and try to sink a putt or be closest to the hole. One of the last golfers was Percy Grenfell, an excellent left-handed golfer. It was Percy's turn; I positioned the three balls in the same place for Percy to putt. The only difference was I had a weighted golf ball and placed it in the third spot. Percy putts the first ball on the sloping path and goes past the hole, and he sees the slope. The second ball stops just past the hole. Percy looks up and yells, "get the prize ready cause this one is going in!!!" He putts the weighted ball, and it travels the other way, up the slope! Percy looks up with this strange look on his face. By now, the guys, who knew the last ball was "strange," bust out laughing at Percy's reaction. After we played that final round, the guys asked me about the golf balls each received before we started. They commented the golf balls did funny things. Where did I get them? I told them I got a good deal at a store that sold used golf balls because we were a low budget league. I remembered the golf ball well because each ball had a gorilla face on the ball. I still have one.

MR. CLARENCE HINKLE

Mr. Hinkle was teaching when most of us were in grade school. (I should say he was the oldest teacher playing) And couldn't hit the ball very far. Mr. Hinkle, known as "Maj," was a respected teacher and was near retirement and had a different golf bag and set of clubs. Where everyone had 10-12 clubs and a sturdy bag, Maj had an old cloth bag with three clubs, which included a putter, an iron, and an old wood club. He would say he's winning because he always had the most strokes like bowling where the high number wins. As he would get ready to hit another shot, the guys would ask him what club he is using. "Maj use your no.3 wood!" could be heard. He would pause, say he will use his driver or pitching wedge and reach in his bag and pull out his only wood or iron. He mentioned his golf balls were old and didn't need any because he never hit them far, just far enough to see where they went. We had fun for the few weeks.

I did get chewed out when a lady teacher chewed me out for not inviting females in the league. I found out this lady was an excellent golfer, and I promised her we would include ladies next year. We played the next year at Valley View Golf Course off of Cuyahoga Street. I also invited ladies, but none played.

PRO FOOTBALL PLAYER PLAYING GOLF

We had a new Industrial Arts Teacher who was a part-time pro football player with the Akron Vulcans. The Vulcans were in a new Professional Football League, like the National Football League. He was a fullback, played college ball at Bowling Green University, and was a typical looking fullback, big and strong. He was next to tee off. Golf courses have their unique markers for the men and women's tees. These markers at Valley View were 6x6x6 wooden blocks that were positioned a few inches out of the ground. On the first hole, the lady's tees are 30 or so feet on the left and right of the men's tees. The husky fullback golfer winds up, strikes the ball, it travels low over the distance to one of the ladies markers, hits the block and ricochets back through the golfers waiting to tee off. The ball bounces off some pop machines and comes to a stop well behind the teed off area. The scary part was guys were standing there talking or stretching and waiting their turn. After everyone settled down, the talk was the guy had to hit the ball from where it was lying. He approached the ball, and all the guys hid behind the pop machines. This young man never got to play with the Akron Vulcans because the team folded. The cleaning company kept the uniforms until the owner paid the bill; it was never paid.

BEING EMBARRASSED

Teachers sometimes have to leave the building for an hour or less. The rule is to find another teacher with a free period to "cover" your class. This day I was with the seniors in the related classroom, in walks this young attractive female teacher. In our school, the male students (teachers too) have their "favorite" female teachers. This lady was near the top of their list. I stopped my presentation; she walked right in front of me, not more than 6 – 8 inches from me. I'm one of those that need some space between the person and me. I slowly back up and then feel the full wall blackboard behind me. She moved to that 6-8 inch distance and asked me if I could cover her class (during my free or planning period the next day) because she had to leave for a few minutes? I replied that I could, and she answered, "Thanks, and I'll pay you back!" As she left the room, she turned and repeated that she would pay me back! When she was in front of me, I had to look at her face and not at the students. When she closed the door, there was a moment or three of silence, and then I heard some comments like

"How's she going to pay you back"?

"Mr. Sipka, your face is turning red."

"She was close to you, almost too close!"

"Mr. Sipka, you got chalk dust on the back of your pants."

"You were pinned against the chalkboard."

"We can see where the back of your head left a mark on the board!"

"I'll bet you forgot what you were talking about!"

As a joke, I started to talk about something unrelated like "Lake Erie is located North of Ohio….." boy did they kid me about that.

JOHN LILLY

Mr. John Lilly was one of two Vocational Drafting Instructors. I experience John getting himself into a heap of trouble. The Vocational addition built in 1970, included classrooms for an Adult Practical Nursing program. Many of the vocational teachers would sit in the rest area of the LPN room, during their conference period. John would enjoy the ladies by talking like he was a doctor. He would ask them to let him know when the adult ladies were giving baths, or could they assist him when he performs "surgery"? This particular day John and I walked into the main office. I was looking at the mail by the main counter; John walked away. Ray, a teacher, was in charge of the school's public address system and was in that room, checking the PA system. John saw Ray, had an idea, and walked in. John intended to kid around with the LPN's by talking to them over the PA system but only to that one room. John asked Ray how he could speak to just that one room? Ray flipped a few switches and told John it was ready. Ray leaves; John proceeds to push the button and announce, "Attention Please, Attention Please will Doctor John Lilly report to room 707 (LPN room) for surgery!" I'm standing by the counter looking at a folder when I hear this announcement; in fact, the whole school heard it because Ray must have flipped the wrong switch or switches. The three secretaries looked up as I did. Mr. Parson, the Administrative Principal, walked out of his office, stood across the counter from me, and we both looked down the hall to the entrance of the PA room. John walks out and sees all of us looking at him and says, "O shit! I will never listen to Ray again". Mr. Parson request that he and Dr. Lilly move into Mr. Parson's office to discuss this "Surgery"! Nothing came of this disturbance during the day, but it was funny to see the expression on John's face. Someone mentioned Dr. Lilly might be in for bedpan duty.

John Lilly was in the US Navy during the Second World War and served as a blimp pilot. He spent his time in the blimp patrolling along the West coast.

RON SIMON

Ron Simon was the art teacher for many years, and like most art teachers had a particular skill or specialty, they practice during the year in private. Ron did metal sculpture. He would weld the pieces of metal into shapes, and these works of art would be sold and or placed in various locations. Ron also knew we received scrap steel from local companies for the machining students to use. Occasionally we would receive drops (scrap pieces) from companies which were the middles of round pieces the company did not need. Imagine the hole of the donut as a piece of scrap. It seemed that Ron and another art teacher could smell the scrap metal because as we would unload the material, these two teachers would show up and watch us unload the steel. As the students would push the metal off the truck, these two teachers would get very excited with "ooh's" and "aah's" when they would see a piece of steel they could use. They would "ooh" and "aah" like someone who just received an ice cream cone. The students would watch these grown men droll over a piece of steel. The usual comment was these two are weird!

GOING OUT IN STYLE

On the last day of the year, there is a meeting when teachers retiring would be recognized. There would be some roasting by fellow teachers and then a nice present. Ron said his last day would be a day we would all remember. It was time at this meeting to bid farewell to Ron Simon. The comments about Ron were appropriate, and then Ron had his say. He thanked everyone and said he would miss the staff. He then stated he wanted everyone to remember this day when Ron left the room. Just then, a song was played, and from the storage room, a young lady who had the minimum amount of clothes on danced out doing a tantalizing dance up to Ron. After a few minutes, they both danced out of the room, waving to the group as they left. That was an exit like no other, and everyone was speechless for a few moments. The principal just stood there and watched. The comments were, how's anyone going to top that last day!

MILT LANG

Milt Lang was the head of the math department and would visit the shop a lot because he was fascinated by the things the guys were doing in the senior class. He would wear his safety glasses, watch the young men, and maybe ask a question when the student was not involved with working the machine. The math department had a device, or visual aid called a light refractor set used to demonstrate light rays for a mathematic principle. Milt brought this thing down and wondered if we could make one? We searched and found two pieces of scrap steel we obtain from local companies. This extra job would highlight using our tracing attachment. Math was involved, and templates made using the math. We had different students work on this job, and we completed both the top and bottom half's. Next was the polishing of the concave surfaces to a mirror finish. We emphasized surface finish because students would encounter that requirement in machining. Again Akromold helped us with the abrasive cloths and polishing rouges. The students took turns hand working the surfaces. This procedure is not easy, and many students hated this job. One senior, Randy, said he likes to polish, he got the job, was doing a great job, it was a matter of 2 more days, the surface would be a mirror, and done. For some reason, we had an assembly in the afternoon, and the class had to go. I was the last out and locked the door. We returned to our machines and jobs; all of a sudden, Randy starts yelling, "look what someone did to the highly polished disks!" We all looked and saw scratch marks in the mirror-like surface. We had a mystery on our hands. Who did this? And how did they get into the room? We were standing there trying to figure it out when Milt walks in. He comes over and apologizes for "helping with the polishing when we were at the assembly" He then realized he was doing more damage than good and stopped. He was sorry and said he would not try to help without knowing how to do the job. Randy was still not happy, but at least we found out who "helped us." Randy liked to polish, and he was hired by Akromold as soon as he graduated.

Photo by Stan Sipka
Randy is in the background

SAD DAYS - 3 TEACHERS DYING ON A WEEKEND

In the 30 plus years, we had teachers dying, but one weekend three teachers died. The one teacher who shocked me was Dick Shine. In the related classroom, there is a partition that separates two classes. I had one side, and Dick had the other. This Friday our classes both left the room, Dick and I talked about the weekend and that we needed a couple of days off. Dick said, "you're right!" and walked out. He died, refereeing a basketball game. Dick was a pleasure to work with and had a pleasant smile when he greeted me.

Mr. Shine was young, had a young family. The Cuyahoga Falls school system found places for Mrs. Shine to work to help with the family.

Mr. Alfred "Al" Marshall was a principal who was walking to his seat to watch a basketball game at the University of Pittsburgh Gymnasium. A graduated Cuyahoga Falls student was playing for the University of Georgia, and they were playing the University of Pittsburgh that night.

Next, Mr. Ennis Walker died that weekend. Ennis was a guidance counselor and was talking about retiring to Jeckel Island, GA., and be a starter on a golf course there. Years later, I was able to visit the island, and as I passed a golf course, I thought of Ennis working there.

Others died but not 2 or 3 the same time. One that was close to me was Mrs. Loreen Lipinski, a cosmetology teacher. Loreen had heart problems and received a pace-maker. Soon after, she had issues with the pace-maker; it had to be recalled – it was doing more harm than good. So, Loreen had another pacemaker implanted and was able to keep the bad one. She wanted people to see a pacemaker, and my class was able to handle it, and they commented it was "heavy." Learning that a pacemaker is heavy was not an item found in our math textbook.

ANOTHER SAD DAY

Five young men were coming home after watching the Cleveland Cavaliers play at the Richfield Colosseum. The normal route #303 was under construction, so a parallel road was used. The car with five young men failed to turn where this road ended, went straight through a yard and over an embankment into a ravine. Two young men died, two were severely injured, and the driver was unhurt. I didn't know anything regarding this tragedy when I arrived at school the next morning. I walked to the office and noticed no one in the halls –empty. I stopped at the intersection of 4 hallways and saw no one. That was unusual. Just then, Mr. Raybuck came out of the cafeteria, walks up the steps, and told me to walk the halls in the old building to see if there were any students in the classrooms.

I asked, "what's the matter?"

He replied, "you didn't hear?"

"No," I said

He then told me that two students died the night before, and we would like all students to be in the cafeteria so they can be told what had happened. I walked the first floor and found no one in any rooms. As I walked to the office, I looked in the cafeteria and saw girls crying and small groups hugging each other. In the office, I learned the two boys who died were sons of two of our teachers. The fathers have the same lunch period I have and even sat at the same table. I don't remember what happened during the day. I was in my class and tried to pretend it was a typical day. The students were somber, even those that came from the other schools in the compact. Occurrences like this happen at other schools, not ours. This time it was here.

I went to the wake, which was in the sacristy of a local church where both young men were in front near the altar. People of all ages filled the large room. I got in the long line slowly moved up, as I looked at the fathers and mothers I couldn't go any further. I like the majority had a handkerchief or tissue wiping away the tears. I remember looking at the faces of the two fathers and two mothers and marveled at how they conducted themselves. At home, my wife and I talked about how parents can survive after the loss of a child.

The two young men who were injured lost the use of their legs. The driver of the car was unhurt.

STEALING SOAP FROM THE SUPERINTENDENT

The academic year goes from early September to late August. The fiscal year goes from January 1st to Dec 31st. Because the end of the fiscal year is Dec. 31, financial problems develop for needed supplies like soap, paper, and office supplies. These items are to wait until the New Year's funds are available. The custodians always had standard supplies for the shop teachers like soap and paper towels. The students need to wash their hands because of working with materials and machines they encountered. Early in October, the custodian said the soap order would wait until after the first of the year, and we are in October, ten weeks to go. So, I planned to buy soap at the local store. I received a message to talk to the superintendent's secretary about my teaching certificate, went there, and did what was needed to satisfy the request. On my way back, I had to use the restroom on the second floor. I looked at the sink and saw a full bar of soap. Just one male using this restroom with a whole bar of soap. I went downstairs to visit the assistant superintendent's men's room, and he too had a full bar of Lava soap. My mind begins working as I walked back to the shop. Our shop had 30 to 40 students needing soap, and the superintendent was the only one with a full bar. So, I took the one bar we had left, went to the band saw, turned it on and cut the bar in half. I went back to the administration building, gave some reason why I had to talk to the secretary, on the way back, went into both restrooms, took the full bar replaced the full bar with half a bar. I did this about 2 or 3 times or until the New Year was near.

One day in early December, the woodshop teacher came into our office and was complaining to Mr. Gruber and me about not having any soap. To stop the woodshop teacher complaining, I opened up the cabinet and gave him a bar of soap. He saw my 4 bars and wanted to know how I was getting all that soap, and even Mr. Gruber didn't know. I told him and Mr. Gruber, "I have friends in high places" This happened around 1968, and nothing was ever said and never told anyone until I retired.

When a teacher retires, there is a small presentation by the faculty on the last day of the school year. The kids are gone, and there is usually a final meeting. Here those that retire are recognized. I decided to tell this story. The teachers laughed and asked me if I felt better after keeping this secret for all these years? I said, "I feel I can enjoy my retirement now!" The year was 1997. That's not the end of the story.

We are in the year 2008, and I'm in an elementary school in Tallmadge to pick up my granddaughter. I notice the name of the school principal is "Wilson." I see the young man who looks like Dr. Harold Wilson and asks him if his father was Dr. Wilson? He replied, "Yes!" I ask him if he has a few minutes to hear a story about his father, and he said, "sure." He laughed at this stealing soap story, and I asked about his father, and how's Dr. Wilson? He replied his Dad is fine and enjoying life.

A couple of weeks later, I saw Dr. Wilson himself in the local food store, introduced myself, and asked him if his son told him about the soap? He said he hadn't seen him recently. I then told Dr. Wilson the soap story, he said he never remembered seeing half a bar of soap, but because it was for the students, it was OK.

DONUTS

The end of the year for the shop is different than the regular classes like English or World History because there is no equipment to be cleaned or inventory or supplies to be ordered. Another thing the seniors do not attend school the last few days because there are many special occasions and ceremonies in graduating. In the last few days, the juniors are the only students in the shop, so they have the privilege of cleaning the shop the final day. The senior machine teacher, not having any students, is assigned some duty within the school, but must still do the shop inventory and order supplies for next year. One year I felt good and went out and bought two dozen donuts and some drinks to treat the juniors for cleaning the shop. The money was well spent. I continued this tradition for a couple of years as long as the senior teachers had a day free of teaching. Well, it's time for me to pick up the donuts and drinks and return to treat the juniors. This year for some reason, I drove past the High School on 4th Street doing 30 mph and notice a police car behind some bushes with his radar gun. No problem because I'm going slow. I'm thinking about the donuts and the students when I notice the police car behind me with his lights flashing. Surely he made a mistake because I wasn't speeding! Well, I end up with a ticket for going 31 mph in a school zone and have a date to appear in traffic court to pay a fine. I'm upset because I saw the car and wasn't going that fast. I pull in the school parking lot upset because now I'm out $50 or more just because I wanted to buy donuts. I carry the donuts and drinks in the room, throw them down and yell, "You guys better enjoy these donuts because they are costly donuts," go into my office and slam the door shut. The guys upfront look at me and have this puzzled look on their faces. Mr. Gruber is in the back of the shop, comes into the office and asks me, "what's wrong?" I tell him about the ticket, he looks at me and walks out to talk to the guys. He probably had a smile on his face, but I wasn't looking at him. After I settle down, I believe I wanted to eat one of my soon-to-be-expensive donuts. I received a lot of kidding about that ticket. I remember the next year I was not going to drive on 4th St. past the school.

KENT STATE SHOOTING

I remember Monday, May 4, 1971, the day four students were killed at Kent State University by Ohio National Guard troops. We were returning to the school after a tour of the Akromold Company. As Mr. Anderson and I drove back to the school, we heard on the radio there was a shooting at Kent State University, and there were fatalities. "I hope the National Guard Troops were the fatalities." I thought to myself. Why the Guard? If the students were the victims, there would be destruction everywhere, not just at Kent State. Sure enough, students were killed. On the way back, the seniors were saying they would go to Kent and see for themselves. I mentioned I was sure the roads would be blocked off, and no one from the outside would be allowed in to cause more trouble. Besides, why ask for problems. The following day the guys who tried to see the area were stopped outside Kent and told to leave or be arrested. For me, that seemed to be the start of a different way of life for everyone.

COASTERS 1971 – 1972

THE FIRST COASTER - 1971

I met many people in local companies that helped with materials and ideas. Don Hatherill, the plant manager at Akromold, introduced me to the salesman from the Detroit Mold and Engineering Company (DME). The conversation centered on using a real mold base to teach students the skills needed to produce a plastic product from the mold base. As a result of our meeting, we received an industrial quality mold base. It was a base that weighted more than we could carry assembled. The next question, "what can we design and machine?" It was 1971, and the students had a lot of ideas. The idea of a coaster representing the class was selected. The people from Akromold helped us with a basic design, and the Cuyahoga Falls Vocational Drafting class drew the drawings. Another bit of good luck, my wife had a girlfriend whose husband owned a company that ran plastic molds and also was a graduate of Cuyahoga Falls High School in 1954. Mr. Dave Davenport's Plas-ti-MaticCompany helped us by running the two-cavity mold. The students worked on the parts, and I did the engraving. We wanted something unique, like having their names at the bottom of the coaster. The student wrote their names in the cursive form, which I called their "payroll signature." I then enlarged the names to about three times the size and transferred them in reverse, like looking at the names in a mirror. I had to engrave them in a random pattern around the center design in 2 cores. Here's where my experience with engraving paid off. Akromold allowed me to come in at night and use their engraving machine. Designing the master and engraving the enlarged signatures in reverse was what I learned years earlier. There are two pictures to show the bottom and back, and a picture showing how the names were engraved in the master. The third picture also shows our appreciation for all the help with this great project. Mr. Dave Davenport allowed us to come to his plant several miles away on a Saturday morning. Another thing was the mold base was too heavy and had to be disassembled, placed in my van, reassembled there, run, and disassembled to bring back. I didn't know who or how many students would show up because this was a Saturday a day off and was early in the morning and 10 miles away. We had more than half of the class and watched Mr. Davenport set up the mold base using a small hydraulic lift, check out the shots, and finally get a good coaster. The first run of coasters was distorted, and the students were concerned, but Mr. Davenport said he would hook up the water lines to the mold base, and shots would be good. The water is forced around the cavities and cores to reduce the heat produced by the hot molten plastic. The water lines were drilled in the shop by the students. He has some red plastic to use, and the coasters looked super. It was an experience to see the students take turns reaching in and removing the two-cavity shots and placing them in stacks ready for another run. I would guess we made 200 coasters and they were free. I believe Mr. Davenport enjoyed this experience as much as the students. Each student received 8 to 10 coasters. I still have ten or so left and get them out when I see one of the students from the class of 1971. The coaster was 3 inches in diameter. The names of each student are raised .015. I would have liked to go deeper, but it was difficult and required more time. I couldn't leave the cavities set up at Akromold Company because the engraving machine had to be made available for the day shift. It did take several hours to make the master and engrave the names in 2 cores.

The first picture is the bottom of the coaster (front), and the second picture is thanking the companies for their help for this unique project (back). The picture of the name master is next, followed by The insert showing the two letters included from the D.M.E.Company.

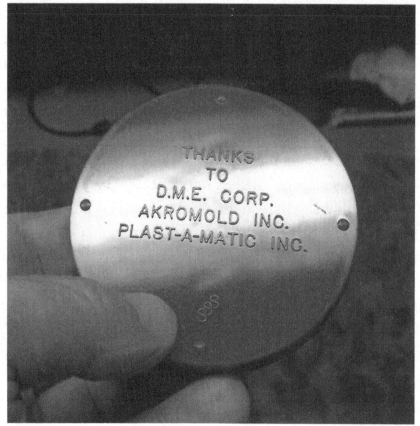

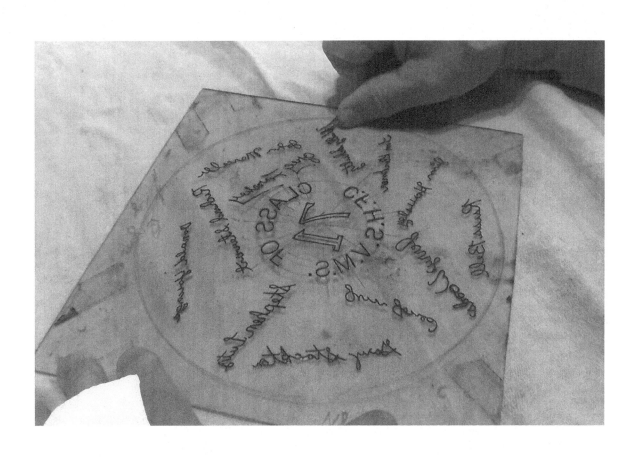

D-M-E Letters

We received a free mold base
from D-M-E and I mentioned
I would let them know how we
Used the base. It was not
small. We didn't have any way
To lift the whole base so we
had to take the plates apart
and assemble them with care
due to weight. WEtook pictures
after we ran the mold to make it
Look like we were machining
From the beginning. Akromold
helped with a couple design
changes for the tiger coasters.
The students taking the plastic
coasters from the injection press
mentioned it's "cool". That was
worth the effort.

January 15, 1973

Cuyahoga Falls High School
2300 Fourth Street
Cuyahoga Falls, Ohio 44221

    Attention: Mr. Stanley S. Sipka
            Instructor S.V.M.S.

    Reference: Letter of June 8, 1971

Dear Sir:

We are interested in obtaining the 35 m.m. slides and the cassette
narration that was made during the machining of the two cavity
injection mold of coasters. We would like to use these tools in
a traning program that we have instituted.

Please send us details as to cost and when we would be able to
obtain them.

            Sincerely yours,

            D-M-E Division of
            VSI CORPORATION

            Frank M. Wilke, Manager
            Special and Assembly Plants

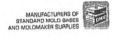

March 13, 1973

Mr. Stan Sipka
508 Southeast Avenue
Tallmadge, Ohio 44278

Dear Mr. Sipka:

    Received your packaged presentation and was most pleased
with your handling of a difficult assignment.

    With your permission, I would like to have the presentation
duplicated, and would need an additional three weeks to complete
this task.

            Sincerely yours,

            D-M-E Division of
            VSI CORPORATION

            Frank M. Wilke, Manager
            Special & Assembly Plants

      I sent a slide-tape presentation, but we took the picture after we ran the mold. We made it sound like we took pictures as we were working on the project. This year, I contacted the Company and asked if, by chance, the slide-tape presentation was still around so I could include some pictures of the students working on various facets of the project. They replied the slide-tape was discarded years ago, and the gentlemen whose names are on the letters have retired. One person, I talked to mention that it was in 1972 a very long time ago. No one there could even remember those who were involved in the correspondence. Let's see? That was 1972 or 46 years ago. Yes! I guess that was a long time ago. The red coaster was for me a pleasant surprise when we saw the final product. The photo below shows how the names are engraved in reverse deep enough to allow a pointed stylus to follow. Two cores were engraved.

TIGER COASTER - 1972

The pictures above show the tiger coaster and the four coasters in sandwich bags with the JA sticker. I kid people that air inside the package in the picture is air from 1972.

The bottom picture is the core that produced the tiger and words. Two cores were made. The depth of the words and tiger were much deeper than the names in the red coasters.

The 1972 school year begins, and another class of seniors started getting ready for the world of work. The conversation begins the first week about what they are going to make with the two-cavity mold the last senior class used for personalized coasters. In the brainstorming sessions, the idea of another coaster keeps coming up. This year we are starting in September at the beginning of the year and not halfway through the senior year. Somehow the words "Junior Achievement" (JA) came up and what that group does. I made some telephone calls and found out the purpose of JA. Students from different schools meet and form a company with officers to run this company similar to a real business. Adults are advisors of JA and help organize the group to develop a product to sell. I was able to convince the JA officials that we could have a "company" within our class and was told this is not commonly done, but they would approve this arrangement.

The class had meetings to elect officers and set responsibilities for the different facets of the company within the school. We took the name "ROLL-A-COASTER" because we were going to produce coasters with the Cuyahoga Falls Tiger logo inside the coaster. We sold 100 shares of stock at one dollar each and started to work the mold. Again I engraved the design developed by someone in the commercial art program. The vocational drafting class drew the drawings, the art class made posters to place in local businesses, and we had an article in the local newspaper.

This article appeared in the FALL CITY PRESS

Dec 22, 1971

Photo courtesy of the Cuyahoga City Press

We had everything ready by the end of January and again made arrangements with the company that ran the mold last year. The difference was last year we didn't have to pay for the coasters to be made and the cost of materials. The students had to think about the price and even a profit. We were going to need roles of black plastic to hot stamp the face, which required contact with a company and determine how many rolls we needed and white and special red paint to decorate the tiger's teeth and tongue. The class again went to the Plas-ti-Matic Company on a Saturday morning to run the injection molding machine because if we operated it, we would save money and also be part of the learning process. The class showed up, and the mold was mounted in the press. Students took turns reaching in and removing the two-cavity shots and placing them in boxes. I don't remember how many we ran, but the plan was to package four in a bag and sell them for one dollar, and each seller would earn 50 cents. The class spent many hours, hand painting the white teeth, and the red tongue with toothpicks after the coaster was hot stamped. A student had ten bags to sell. We did have some posters in local stores and the newspaper. The first number of coasters was sold and had another run of coasters. This time we didn't sell all of the coasters, and we had to liquidate those remaining coasters. I purchased the rest of them, and I still have some from 1972. We also paid for the plastic materials used in making the coasters. Another requirement of the JA program was to close our financial records, and after the ROLL-A-COASTER treasure closed the books, we were able to return money to those who bought the $1 shares. Each shareholder received their dollar plus a profit of one dollar or 100% return on their one dollar investment. A few said if they knew this would be 100% return, they would have bought all the 100 shares we were allowed to sell. I enjoyed the class and how they worked as a company with individuals taken on responsibilities.

MARK

Mark was the President of the JA company and did a great job working with all the guys. I think he learned that there is stress working with others and enjoyed the good all the class did for those seven months. I have another story about Mark and his working at Prospect Mold as a co-op student.

I was teaching adults in the NTDPMA apprenticeship program in the evenings and had a student who worked at Prospect. Mark had been working there for several weeks, and I asked this evening student, "how's Mark doing at Prospect?"

He asked," Is he a new worker?"

I said, "Yes."

The adult student said, "this new guy is "nuts," he stands on the machines and is loud and doesn't know anything.

I'm speechless and don't say anything because I can't picture Mark doing this. The next day I pulled Mark aside and ask him about what was said last night. Mark laughed and said, "that's not me, but another new guy who is "nuts." I asked what you are working on at your company?

Mark replied, "I'm roughing out pockets for molds."

The following week I talked to the evening student and mentioned that my student is Mark, not the one who is "nuts." The evening student said Mark is good and liked by the foreman and company.

What is happening with those remaining coasters? I've contact classes that are having class reunions, and many buy enough coasters to give to each a souvenir of their High School

SPECIAL BLACK AND GOLD COASTER

When the Tiger coasters were made, there was black plastic material in the machine so, Mr. Davenport runs several with the black until the system was purged. We obtained a roll of gold foil and hot-stamped real gold on the face. I wonder how to hand out a real gold and black coaster? One thought is to hand out the remaining coasters to the 50th class reunion of the class of 1972 in 2022.

SOAP BOX DERBY COASTER

I used the mold base to make coasters for the Soap Box Derby in 1972. The work was done after school and got approval, and no students were used to make the two cavities and cores. I purchased a Gorton engraving machine like the one I used at Sackmann, Main Mold, and Akromold. A few coasters were made, and the local officials approved the idea of each contestant receiving four in a bag. The final approval was obtained when I visited John DeLorean, the Chevrolet official, at the Company's temporary office. My wife and I did the hot stamping and painting at home. I took pride in the fine lines on the details of the face and wheels and car. There were 250 or so racers and all when home with a souvenir. I was planning on making coasters next year, but Mr. DeLorean felt Chevrolet should not sponsor this event, and it was stopped. The next year the Akron Chamber of Commerce was the sponsored the Derby. I reworked the two cavities with the Akron Chamber logo and made coasters the next year. In 1973 there was a big scandal regarding a device placed in the front of a car to help the car gain momentum. After that, the number of racers dwindled to less than 100, and it looked like the Derby would stop. I stopped making coasters and sold the machine soon after that.

SENIOR LOUNGE

The machine shop class of 1972 made the tiger coasters, and that was a great achievement, but the school's student council of 1972 also achieved another thing every student wanted - to get a SENIOR LOUNGE. The idea of a particular place just for seniors was there every year, and each time that request was made, the students wanted the school administration to develop the lounge. There was a set of objections that the administration would bring to the students, and the students were not able to satisfy those requests. Several faculty members, study hall monitors, and I came in contact with the student council and senior Jon Myers, council president. At a meeting, the idea was again presented, but this time the student council members were told they should anticipate the objections and show how these common objections can be solved. There were questions like: where should this lounge be located?; should it be just for seniors?; who would be the monitor?; what about noise?; should there be a special card for seniors?; can the students play cards?; would there be music?; and other questions. Council members laid out a floor plan of a room at the end of the hall by the band room for the lounge. They listed the furniture needed that was already in the school and what other items could be donated. The local funeral home offered to print unique cards for those seniors that wanted the come to the lounge during their study hall period. There was a plan for daily clean up beyond the regular evening clean up routine by the custodians. All these plans and details were written and presented to the faculty council. Jon Myers was the young man that believed in this and worked hard to overcome all the objections used in the past. The day the presentation was to be presented to the faculty, Jon wasn't in school, so a freshman council member made the presentation. Thinking that the idea would be approved and recommend it start in September, the presenter suggested this can be started this school year and open at the end of the spring or Easter week break. Members of the council will work during the week break and set up the lounge, so when school resumes that Monday, this special place can be used by seniors. The main reason to start this year, any problems can be seen so next year's room will be better for students. I think several administrators and faculty members were surprised by the quick responses to the faculty's reply "..of next year". I was one who helped with planning objections and working to remove those objections. The senior lounge was used for several years but has been eliminated.

I found several notes and written documents used when the students were developing their presentations to the faculty council. Mrs. Celli Hockberg, a study hall monitor, was a big fan of a senior lounge and did a lot of work to show data regarding how many students can be in the room and a schedule of the study halls and monitors and periods. There is the one-sheet presentation developed and presented by members of the student council at the faculty meeting that approved the request. There was a lot of effort and thought to answer those objections of the faculty. The hand-printed document was what each faculty member received at that big meeting. I included these two sheets to show how to plan when presenting a request for what is wanted. I know Leann Corby, Mrs. Hockberg, and I was three of several teachers who worked with the student council on this request. I know Mrs. Hockberg was happy to be a part of this senior lounge and was the monitor for several years.

OPEN STUDY HALL FOR SENIORS IN ROOM 623

Submitted by:
Student Council and Faculty Study Hall
and Independent Study Committees

We the members of the Faculty Study Hall and Independent Study Committee recommends the implimentation of a trial program for six weeks duration the second semester of this school year. The reasons for the recommendations are:

1. The program is the result of both monitors, students, and faculty planning.

2. The program is a trial program which will allow for elimination or continuation after the time period.

3. The program is just for seniors who have study halls.

4. The students who occupy room 623 have been relocated for the periods 1,2,3, 5, and 6. a survey was taken this semester as to the number of seniors in study halls each of the above periods. It was assumed that the number of seniors in study hall the first semester would be representative of this semester.

5. A study hall monitor has volunteered to supervise the student "lounge".

6. Rules of attendance, supervision, and activities have been suggested.

7. Rules for operations by students have been suggested.

8. The idea of such a lounge has been presented several times the past few years but always just the idea was presented. This time the effort was to answer all the objections with reasonable solutions.

9. It will be an educational experience for the seniors, class of 1972, because they will determine the duration of the program for this year and for senior classes to follow.

10. A program of senior class public relations will be conducted prior to the beginning of the program to acquaint the seniors of their opportunities and responsibilities.

11. The faculty committee function will stop when the program has ended.

12. Several members of Student Council have volunteered to help as runners and supervisors in the lounge.

13. Several monitors have volunteered to help in any way possible.

14. The noise level has not been determined but this factor will be controlled by the monitors and students.

15. The faculty members of the committee are impressed with the seriousness of student council, to help determine educational atmosphere at the high school.

by an unknown member of Student Council of 1972

HE CAN READ CHINESE

When we ordered supplies, they can come from anywhere, any country, and usually have instructions in different languages. We received an order that required someone to check if what we ordered was sent. I'm sitting at a table by the door when the students come in from lunch, some walk-in front, most look over my shoulder. One student comments the packaging instructions come in different languages. There were four columns, each in a different language. I point to the left language, which is Chinese and place my finger at the characters and keeping my head toward the Chinese instruction, but my eyes swing to the right and read the English instructions, all the time, moving my finger over the Chinese characters. The guys behind me can't see my eyes looking to the right and saying the English words. The guys behind can see both sets of instructions, and they think I know how to read Chinese. The three guys in front can see my eyes looking at the American words and laughing like crazy. I ask the guys behind if they want me to read the German version next.

PICK UP A THREAD – REPAIR A THREAD

The student learns to chase a thread in the junior program, and in the senior year, we did different operations to expand the student's skills in working with threads. The shop term" chase" means the student machines the thread on the lathe rather than using a die. (A die is a device that is turned over the shaft and completes the thread in one pass). Many students may never chase a thread on the job, but who knows what area of work a young man may obtain. When the student has to cut an internal thread to match the external thread that requires a learning process, the student would not forget. The multiple left- hand thread, both internal and external, keeps the boy involved. When done, the nut moved on the threads, and there is a sense of accomplishment. It was like, "YEA, and I did that!!"

We also required another common job task that would typically go to one of the older experienced guys in the shop, and that is to repair a damaged thread. Something drops and damages the threaded shaft, and it's either buy another or fix the damaged area. But, at your job site, there could be no one there, and the repair is needed, so you can fill a prominent position and help the company.

We had several extra threaded pieces around, and we would use a hammer and strike the threads and cause damage to the thread. A nut would not work on that shaft. The setup procedures regarding threads were to repair a damaged thread. The student had to take their time to make the few passes to repair the threads, and I would say everyone who did that operation was successful and felt skilled. When a student became involved in doing these operations, they concentrated on what they were doing and did not fool around. Many would say when told to start cleaning up, "Boy, time sure did fly today!"

The idea of repairing a thread happened to me when I worked at Main Mold and Machine while attending Kent State University. I was working on the engraving machine and had to raise the table. I turn the wheel, and the table drops down instead of moving up. The foreman and owner check the problem -we needed a new shaft. There are two choices 1) Buy a new shaft or 2) make a shaft. The time the machine would be down made, the foreman and owner decided to make a new shaft. I watched an older worker proceed to complete a new shaft in one day. That man's skills saved a lot of time; if a student could help their company like this, he would be valuable.

CLOSING FEMCO

I have mentioned FEMCO several times and how this company helped the school system by employing students and helping with materials that were scrap to them but useable for us. Another company in Akron, who competed with FEMCO, stated they were going to merge with FEMCO and become a "super company." "Merging" is typical, and after a few months, the purchased company (FEMCO) would be closed, and the workers laid off. Yes, FEMCO closed within a year. I received a message to call Mr. Ed Weber, the plant manager at FEMCO (Ed graduated from Cuyahoga Falls years ago, when asked what year? he would say "BC"); there would be some scrap for us if we wanted the materials. We made arrangements, and I drove the school truck to the factory. As I was entering the driveway, a security guard was requesting identification. Ed yelled at the guy that I was OK, and I was from the high school here to pick up some scrap. I backed in, took my gloves, and begin to help load the steel onto the truck. Ed took me aside, and we walked down the shop to his office for coffee, and he said the guys know what to give the school. I kept looking back, and many guys were putting items in the truck.

After a few minutes, I returned to the truck, shook hands with the workers, many of whom I knew. Ed told me that I should drive to the gate and just keep going to the street. As I moved forward, the guard allowed me to return to school, and everything I had was just scrap materials. The guard motioned me through, and my first move was to turn left onto Second Street and then a short way down the street, turn right. Traffic was coming, so I had to speed up as I made the turn. All of a sudden, things started to roll on the floor under my feet. I had to turn right quickly, and more items moved around on the floor. At a stop sign, I looked down and could see many different size end mills; many never used and spotted two micrometers. I returned, and as the seniors unloaded the truck, we found four-jaw chucks and vices that we could use. Mr. Gruber, who watched my class as I went to pick up this "scrap," commented I could have been arrested for taking this stuff; it would have been at least grand theft for 2 to 3 years. As I left the dock, the guys at FEMCO were all smiles now, I knew why. We used the four-jaw chucks and the cutters.

A couple of years later, I met Mr. Weber and mentioned I was going to write about his part in this episode and the tools, supplies, and wondered if he could get in trouble. He said he's too old to go to jail and didn't know what those workers were going to do that day. I travel Second Street a lot, and when I pass that building and see the gate, I can imagine all the end mills rolling around on the floor.

STARTING BLOCKS

There was just one time when outsiders used the shop, and that was when parents came and used the machines to make starting blocks for the Tallmadge YMCA swim team. My daughters were involved with the YMCA's swim team, and I helped with the home meets. Someone in the past made wood starting blocks, and after years of use and many repairs, the Y official told the swim parents the what we used was dangerous, and we should plan on buying new blocks. We checked prices, and for five blocks, the cost was too much for the team to purchase. The idea of making starting blocks was presented to the parent's organization. One of the parents was an architect and designed a block that would fit the contour of the pool's different end. We were able to get prices for the special marine aluminum that could be placed in chemically treated water. Arrangements were made with the Cuyahoga Valley Vocational School in Brecksville that had a vocational welding program to do the welding for the cost of the gas and materials. Several men got together and planned the operation using the machines and equipment in the shop. I received permission from school officials to do this, and we ordered the aluminum. The material was delivered, and we set up a day and had men and women there to do this production run to make five starting blocks. Several men who knew how to run milling machines, drill presses, and power saws did the precision cutting, and the others did the deburring (removing sharp edges) of machined surfaces. We made wood fixtures to ensure each side of each block was the same, and these fixtures were then used for welding.

The evening worked well because everyone contributed, and no one had to stay all night to finish parts. The next day a parent with a truck came and transported the pieces to the vocational school for welding. The instructor there called me and said what we did was right, and the students would start the next day. After the first one was done, they asked me to come to the school and check the finished block. I looked the block over and thought how beautiful these blocks were and good for the YMCA Swim team. The word was "OK" to finish the others. The parents picked up the blocks, brought them into the pool, and positioned them on the deck by each lane. They were perfect! Because the top was sloped and slippery, we glued a rubberized material on the top. The parents were able to raise the money to pay for the special aluminum for the blocks. Those blocks were used until the YMCA closed and then given to the Tallmadge summer pool. I acted as the boss and was happy to see all the people working so hard. They all were proud of those blocks.

CLOSING THE MACHINE TRADES PROGRAM

Progress is a good thing except when it happens in foreign countries and not in America. America was number one but was relaxing, and the other countries developed their machining industry, and with low wages, foreign companies began to destroy our system. My opinion was America was caught sleeping and woke up with problems completing with the nations near equal to us in manufacturing skills. One company owner told me a company who was his mainstay begin to send his orders overseas. The gentleman said the cost of the finished mold produced in that country was what it costs him just to buy the mold base. The American workers' wages were too high to compete with Japan, China, or wherever. The period was the late 1970s. Losing these orders and jobs was a wake-up call for those in business to quit or dig in and fight to save this country. The machine shops that made Northeastern Ohio one of the biggest employers had to deal with the challenge. The 1980s was a downhill ride to the bottom, and we couldn't see the bottom. We, in our machine program, sensed this concern with the employers. But there was another trend that was occurring too.

The Cuyahoga Falls machine program was the only one for several years and had no problem with students from the six school systems in our Compact. Kent Roosevelt school district started another program, and our program enrollment began to drop. With local companies reducing their workforce and another program needed students, something had to happen. One program was to be eliminated – the Cuyahoga Falls' program.

Student enrollment was down in Cuyahoga Falls Schools, and the plan was to eliminate 26 teachers, and I was one of the 26. I was qualified for another vocational program, applied, but was not selected. The new basketball coach was hired for that position

The school year ended, and The Machine Trades was no more. I helped with the arranged auction of equipment because I felt I was responsible for the program, and I will be there for the end. I felt sorry for the students not having this program

The Junior Auto Mechanics was to use the room. After a few years, that program stopped, and the room became the physical training room for athletics.

WORSE THAN BEING LAID OFF

ANGELA

Photo by Stan Sipka

Our angel in the clouds, ANGELA

When school began in September, I knew this would be my last year teaching the Machine Trades class. My oldest daughter was expecting our first grandchild. Christine was having problems and was admitted to the hospital to help her carry the baby. Christine gave birth on September 27, Sunday, in the early afternoon. My wife and I were thrilled the baby was small in weight but beautiful. Because she weighed 3 lbs 4 ozs, the baby was transported to Akron Children's Hospital special maternity section. The baby weighed the same as her mother 26 years before. My wife, I, and the father went home to tell everyone the good news, and we three returned to see the baby at Children's Hospital in the evening. We came into the neo-natal room and were met by a doctor who told us the baby had taken a turn for the worse. She is in serious condition! We went from the highest point of emotion with the birth to the lowest point in those few minutes. My first thought was maybe it wasn't our grandchild, and ours was okay. No! As we walked to the isolette, we could see many tubes and wires in and on the baby. I thought she looked like she did when we saw her for the first time a few hours ago. The doctors explained to the 3 of us what was happening, but I didn't hear anything. The doctor asked us if we wanted to hold the baby, and I had to walk away and started to cry. I walked away and noticed many little cribs with babies in each of them, and many looked different, and they were alive. I kept calling her an angel, and they thought the name "Angela" was correct. Our Angel appeared perfect and soon would be dead. Several nurses in the room talked to me and gave me hugs. I asked one nurse if they have support groups for parents. "Yes," was her reply, "and there are support groups for grandparents too." When I returned, Angela was not in the isolette. Christine wasn't able to be there because she was at City Hospital.

The services were to be only graveside service, but the father's parents wanted a funeral with full service. Angela's father refused the service, and I said I would take care of the details. We all have been to a funeral home to pay our respect to the family of the deceased, and we see a room with people, flowers, chairs, and conversation among those present. There's a casket, the person presented, allowing the viewers to remember the person as if the person is sleeping. Now picture a room with just a small coffin maybe 2 foot long against the wall with nothing around the casket – bare walls, no flowers, chairs - nothing. There are a few chairs along the sidewall, but nothing but the tiny coffin with Angela wrapped in a special blanket with only her angelic face visible. Family members come in, and the sound of crying was everywhere. I'll always remember my Father-in-law, Albert Braghieri, sobbing so hard people were concerned about him. Christine was in the hospital recuperating, and the Father was at work. He said he said his goodbyes at the hospital. I did what a grieving Grandfather would do - the worst day of my life.

My experience was different that day and moment because I had a baseball friend who died and was in the room on the other side of the partition. The wall separated the two caskets. I went to pay my respect to my friend. They thanked me for taking the time to come and pay my respects to their loved one. I didn't tell them my reason for being there.

My wife and I visit Holy Cross Cemetery because we have older family members there and always stop at the special section where the children are buried. We talk. I tell her the latest information, say a prayer, not for Angela but for her to intercede for family and me. I need help from Angela. A few rows from Angela's grave is one stone for two other grandchildren that died much later. These grandchildren are boys, Steven Micheal and Mathew Ryan. I would bring a baseball each time I visit and leave the ball on the grave. The last time I dug a hole and buried it, so it will not be in the way of the guys who maintain the grounds.

So the school year 1987-1988 was eventful. I had no job, and I lost a beautiful granddaughter. You should know that I cried as I typed this story.

R.I.F. (REDUCTION IN FORCE)

The three letters "R I F" stand for "reduction in force" or a fancy way to say "Laid Off." In Educational terms laid off means, you are on a recall list. The school year started in September of 1987 like other years but ended differently, and I would not be working in the Cuyahoga Falls School System. The day came when I was to meet the Principal, where the Superintendent gave me the official notice of my termination. I would sign a paper, leave, and hear words of encouragement from this guy. I walked out of this office, turned right; as I turned still looking at the paper, I tripped over the bottom drawer of a filing cabinet that was out blocking the aisle. I fell a few feet away and landed on my hands and knees. The secretary was upset and sorry that she left the drawer out. She said she opened the drawer, took out a file, and was going to close it, but I came out. Everyone came running and asked me if I was "OK?" I got up, rubbed my shin, and yelled, "HELL NO!" and left. I was no longer employed. What a feeling! I was 52 years old with 24 years of teaching and wondered if I would reach the 30-year mark.\

C.F.E.A.

The Cuyahoga Falls Education Association negotiated the rule that laid-off teachers are to be allowed to return when there is a vacancy. I hoped I would be recalled and finish my years in the Cuyahoga Falls School System. In 1988 at the end of the 87-88 school year, 26 teachers were laid off, but my certification was different than the 25 teachers. In retrospect, the 25 teachers did find employment in education many back with the Cuyahoga Falls School system. I joined the NEA (National Education Association), OEA (Ohio Educational Association), and CFEA (Cuyahoga Falls Educational Association) every year because I felt it was the thing to do. When the school year ended, the OEA and CFEA had meetings with the RIFed teachers indicated the Association would start legal action against the Cuyahoga Falls School System to be rehired. The main issue was a reduction of students in the school system. The meetings also showed us how to apply for unemployment benefits and other items, like health insurance.

The court proceeding went through the local court the Appeal Courts and finally the Ohio State Supreme Court. In 1990 The State Supreme ruled in favor of the Cuyahoga Falls School System and not for the 25 teachers who didn't have the certification. In the final ruling, I was not included; I was a footnote. I asked the OEA lawyer what did that mean. She said we have to repeat the process. The 25 teachers were out of the job, but I was still involved.

LIFE AS A SUBSTITUTE TEACHER

It can be hard on a person and their family to go from a full-time teacher to being laid off with an unknown source of income. Add to the hardship is the feeling of what the future will be like, not teaching. I could return to industry, but I had 24 years of teaching toward retirement that was the goal. So, my wife and I had long talks about what I should do to obtain the six +years needed for my 30 years. We mentioned I should try subbing because there would be one day credit toward the yearly total of 180 days of credit for another year. My wife worked in the Cuyahoga Falls Schools as a study hall monitor, and my three daughters were young adults. The first year I worked as a substitute for 140 days towards the 180 days one year total. The pay was $45 per day, and I had to be prepared to leave in the mornings to any of the middle schools or high school. A teaching assignment was not guaranteed every day. There were a couple of long-term assignments (2 or 3 days) but mostly here one day and the next day somewhere else.

I was aware that a sub's day in the classroom could be hectic, and I had to be different in the basic rules of substituting. The guys would sometimes sit in different seats to be near a girl or friend, and if I thought they wanted to socialize or mess around, I would stand near them, usually behind them. I would move around, spend time in front, on the sides, and in the back. There were seating charts, and listing those absent was always the first duty after I would read the instructions and expect all would use the time wisely. I announced I don't know any students and don't want to. My job is to provide time to work on assignments.

The last 5 minutes can be for socializing. It was hard not to be busy just sit or standing and move around, but that's life as a sub. I could help some, but in some classes, I would ask if someone could answer the person's question because I'm not familiar with the material.

In a tenth-grade basic math class, two girls were sitting in front and asked if they could help each other with some of their math problems? I figured it would be a learning experience for the girls. The assignment was 40 simple math problems. They open their books to the answer section in the back. One girl would do the even numbers, and the other would do the odd numbers. I watched as each girl wrote down 40 numbers, write the answer on her even or odd numbers, do the same on another sheet, hand one to the other girl, take her paper, copy her numbers down and finish the assignment. They were done with the homework and proceeded to close their books and begin to chit-chat. I told them that was not the way to learn, but their reply was Mr. XXXX thinks that's OK. I asked if they had to write the problem down too with the answer, and their comment indicated that it was a big waste of time. I did not let them talk because I told them their talking would disturb those working. They were not happy!

I could not continue to sub because we had bills to pay, and there was no assurance when or how many days I would work. Nothing was guaranteed; we decided I would return to a full-time machining job and teach evening classes. The evening classes would give me one day credit for the evening apprenticeship classes. I was able to work three nights a week for 32 weeks and earned 96 days toward the 180 needed for one year. I also started evening classes at Cuyahoga Falls and received one day for each session. One eight- week class session had just one student, but I received one more day teaching credit. It was called "Geo-Trig" and was the same math I presented in high school and adult day classes. I ended up earning about 120 days (out of 180 needed for a full year) while I worked full time, which was equal to 2/3 of a year. This 2/3 of a year helped me toward the magic number of 30 years.

DO YOU KNOW ME?

When you are working as a substitute teacher, you better be aware that some students will make your life miserable. You don't do it for the pay because it's not worth the time. Every day you sub, you get credit for one day toward the required

180 days for achieving one year of credit toward the goal of 30 years. You sign up and then wait for the telephone call in the morning for the assignment. You can be in an advanced placement class or class of students who hate school and believe having a sub means "play games" period. Usually, a sub stands there, waits for the bell, takes attendance, announces the assignment, and sits down. I guess I was different because I would use the seating chart, make the assignment, and then walk around the class. I would carry a folder and sometimes a chair and sit in the chair or stand there. The students who worked on the assignment didn't notice where I was because they were busy working. I would announce they had a 52-minute class (the time was different for different schools), and they could have 5 minutes at the end of the period to socialize. My favorite saying was that I don't know any of you, and I don't want to know who you are. If you cause trouble, I'll have to find out your name and report it to the principal.

One day near the end of the school year, my wife and I were shopping, and this young boy walks up to and asks, "do you know me?" I said, "no," He replied, "good" and walked away. My wife asked me what that was all about. I explained my statement, "I don't want to know who you are" and said a few students remember that. I did not have any real negative experience subbing. It was hard because I wondered if this is how I was going to get my 30 years of teaching.

RECALL BACK TO TEACHING

In 1991, there was an opening in Industrial Arts at Bolich Middle School, because I was on the recall list I was offered that teaching position. Instead of Bolich, I returned to The High School because the teacher at CFHS transferred to the Bolich Middle School. I had the High School assignment. It was the welding program. It was ironic the return was to the same room I started in 1965 but for the machining position. Two years later, another opening occurred at Bolich, and I wanted that position. Mr. Arden Summers, the Bolich Middle School shop teacher, became a principal in another school system, thus the vacancy.

I was teaching at Bolich when I received a telephone call from the OEA lawyer who said: "I won!!!" I replied, "What did I win?" She told me the Ohio Supreme Court ruled 7 – 0 in my favor and told me there would be another series of meetings to obtain facts about my lost earnings and time credits that I accrued the past five years for back pay and time. I worked during the time I was not teaching in the Cuyahoga Falls school system and had to spend a lot of time determining hours, days of substituting, and wages earned in the metal machine industry to determine lost wages and time. By this time, I was ready to retire and allowed to retire with the stipulation that when and if the courts determine any additional time coming to me, my retirement information will be refigured. After one year, there was a settlement and a readjustment to my benefits. Finally, I was all done in 1997. What did I learn from this? I learn that an Association like the National Education Association or/and OEA or/ and CFEA stand up for teachers. There was a position I qualified for when I was RIFed, but I was not allowed that position. I know a lot of people don't like Unions or Associations unions and claim America's problems are because of Union demands. My comment is this "union or Association" saved me.

BOLICH MIDDLE SCHOOL

In my first class, the first day was a sixth-grade class. We had square work tables and positioned chairs near the four corners. The bell rang; I just started to introduce myself when a little 6th-grade girl throws up in front of me on my shoes and the floor. What an introduction to Bolich Middle School. The little girl was embarrassed, but the class went on after a few minutes of cleaning up.

The 6th and 7th-grade students scared me, and I didn't plan any time allowing the sixth graders to work on the machines. I know the machines we had in our shop require skill and strength to operate the machines. The students did not use the table saw, jointer and planer. With the 7th grade student, there was a small project that was used by the other instructor, and the drill press was the only machine used. As a student was using the machine, I was right there watching every move. I was concerned about safety. One thing I had to worry about was the girls' hair if they were using the drill press. Their head would be 2 to 3 inches away from the revolving spindle.

Both classes were given assignments related to visualization skills. Isometric sketches were introduced using a special graph paper; most enjoyed developing a shape in 3-dimensions. On a couple of handouts, I would tell the students not to do the last one or two shapes because they are too difficult. That was a dirty trick because most did those first.

For the 6-graders, we would have "show and tell" how common items developed into what we have today. It can be titled "Show what we had to live with a long time ago!" The first topic was music. I had an eight-track player and cartridges, old records both 45's and 33 ½ to single real old records (from the 1930s and 1940s) and a record player to play that "old" music. The kids put down the eight-track outfit. Remember this is 1990 or 30 some years ago. The kids listened to the music and talked about the sound difference, both singing and instruments. We then talked about what changes to the music industry would they experience.

ARE YOU OLD?

Another topic discussed was the telephone. I printed out a series of questions; each student was interviewing an "old person" to find the answers, not their mom or dad, but a grandparent or a neighbor who looked like a grandparent. Some of the questions were: When did your family use or get a telephone? What year? How many families were on your line? Do you remember the name of the first part of your telephone number? Where you ever told to get off the phone by the other party because you were talking too much? How often did you talk to your friends? You can see these questions are for older people. The class begins; a young girl raised her hand and asked if she could ask me a question? I replied sure. She asked a neighbor who she thought was old. The neighbor answered the question, but she said she had a question too! The neighbor wanted to know if the teacher (me) was old. I told the young girl "yes" I was old like the neighbor. You can imagine the talk about the fact that more than one family would use the same line, and talking on the phone was limited to real emergencies. Many of the students said they called their friends as soon as they get home and talk about what happened at school. How did or what did the kids back then do when they got home and couldn't call or talk to their friend? I said the answer to that question should come from that older person they interviewed.

CHECK THE ANSWERS IF THEY ARE MARKED WRONG

I am a firm believer a student should check returned assignments with incorrect answers. WHY? That individual should examine why the answer was wrong and what was done wrong. Learn from a mistake. I was a student at Kent State in the Education Program. There is a requirement that each student entering their third year takes two exams before they are allowed to continue in the teaching college. One is a written paper that, if not approved, requires the person to take two remedial classes and then retake the test. It's the last day of class in the spring, and the approved list is posted, and my name is not on the list. There are general topics to write about, and I worked the topic "Married, working and college" I inquire how I can find out what was wrong with my paper to learn from my mistakes and was told to go to the English department. There I asked and was referred to a Professor who was in charge of testing. I asked nicely what did I do wrong that I have to improve on the next time. The professor obtained and read the paper, and said he thought it was good and deserved an "S" for satisfactory and not a "U" for unsatisfactory. My checking saved me time and money because I wanted to know what I did wrong. We both went out to present this change to the Department Head for approval. We met the Department head in the hall and asked him to read my paper. The Department head said, "if it's good enough for you, it's good enough for me and wrote a big "S." I didn't have to take those extra non-credit classes. I learned to check my mistakes to learn from them.

The 6th and 7th graders had assignments, and when returned, the student would shove the paper in the folder and start to talk to a friend. I kept telling them to check their answers because they will learn from a mistake. Why is your answer wrong? One day I decided to mark a correct answer wrong and return the papers. Before I did this, I wrote on the blackboard that the correct answer to question #6 was "this" and that if you had that answer, I marked it wrong. I then pulled the movie screen down so they could not see what I wrote about #6 question. I handed back the papers and asked, "how many had all the questions correct? No one raised their hand. Next, I asked how many got one wrong? Three or four raised their hands. I then reminded them to check their answers and waited to start the next presentation. All of a sudden, a little girl raised her hand asked me," Can I ask you a question?" "Sure," She said I would like to know why my answer to question 6 is wrong. I then walked to the screen and raised the screen to show what I had written on the board about question #6. I also said this young lady was the only one to check her answers that were marked wrong, and her answer is correct. I will collect her paper and give her a grade of 105, not 100, but 105 for following directions. Well, all heck broke loose then. There were 5 or 6 people who had the correct answer but didn't check their wrong answers. One student mentioned that that was the dumbest thing he ever heard! I replied a dumb thing is to not learn from your mistakes.

SAME PROBLEM DIFFERENT ANSWERS

With seniors and adults, I would hand out math assignments and occasionally mark one problem with two different numbers. If there were 15 people, I would have 2 or 3 "special" papers. All the other problems were the same. I wanted the people to develop the problem into an answer. Do one thing at a time and write the problem in vertical steps so that you can describe and show how you obtained the answer. This way, if two people got different answers, they could review each other's steps and find the error. It was encouraging to see two or three people looking over papers and backtracking from the answer to the original problem. I had to comment when the people would find out I made "special" problems to prove a point.

One example with adults in detailing work was this young man would write the problem, then the answer while everyone else would show their steps. I returned the assignments; that student had a couple of wrong answers. He told me that his answer was correct and proceeded to take the next student's paper and describe what he did and that his answer is correct. I looked at his paper, which showed nothing and asks him to show me how come the two papers have different answers? Where did the problem start towards the wrong answer? He back up paused for a few seconds and said, "ok, you proved your point." From then on, this student did the detailing routine.

ISOMETRIC AND 3 VIEW SKETCHES

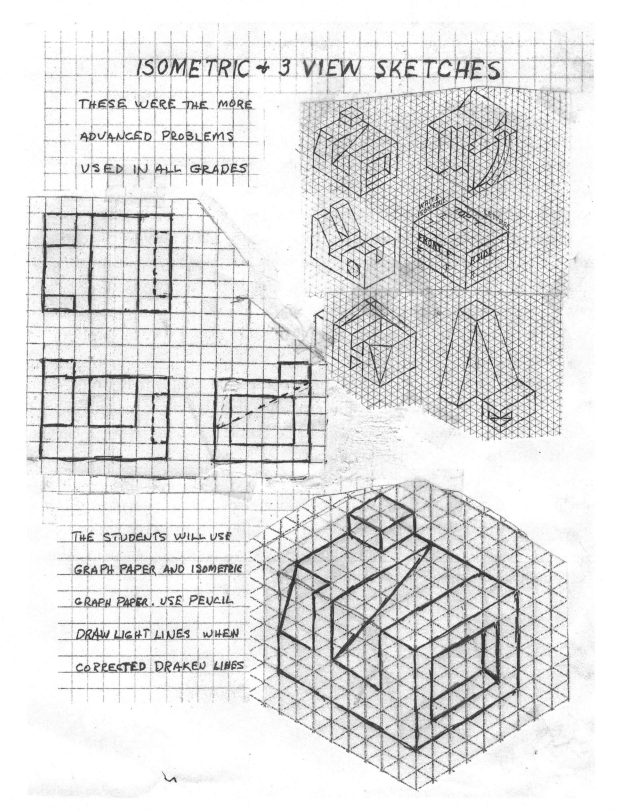

by Stan Sipka

These six examples were the ones Used and told the 6th and 7th Graders to do the easy ones. The last four are too difficult. Use a pencil and draw the lines light until the sketch is corrected, then darken the lines. Four drawings per sheet. Draw lines across and down for four sections, remember to draw the lines very light, have it checked, then darken the lines. Students enjoyed the three drawings and isometric. I had a special isometric paper to use under the paper and just trace over the line. With the three-view drawing, we use wood blocks with the sides marked – top, front, right side, bottom, back, and left side. A few assignments required to located marked letters on a 3-view drawing to a box requiring the three views. One assignment was the student makes his block from our small scrap wood and then make a three-view drawing. There some weird piece

I WILL HELP YOU SWEEP!

At Bolich Middle School, the last grade was eighth-graders. Eight graders come in all sizes, even when their ages are the same. I had a couple of projects the 8th graders could do that they could put in their home. The final project was a clock they designed. The only machine the class could use was the drill press, which produces chips. We did use some plastic but mostly wood. We had a chart showing who would clean each day. Many students would do a good job, and there was no need to sweep again. I would stand there, pointing out areas that are not clean. When the students would not do a good job, I would tell them I would help them sweep. I would sweep the areas quickly, even go over the areas they had cleaned. They were to hold the dustpan while I was sweeping quickly, hoping some would catch the hint and help sweep. The sweepers knew the bell was about to ring and told to wait because "I was helping them." The two guys on occasion would watch and were not happy because I was finding a lot more chips; they had to wait until I was done. These guys would run out of the room a couple of seconds after the bell. As they washed their hands, I would tell them they did an excellent job. The next day we had new sweepers, and if I picked up a broom and said I would help, the guys who experienced me helping them a couple of days before would yell out "you don't want him to help you sweep because he will keep you until after the bell." Usually, the guys would listen to their classmates and sweep without my help. I would stand there with the broom, ready to help; the sweepers would notice me and do the job.

GIRLS SWEEPERS

There were times when two girls would sweep. Most of the time, the girls did an excellent and quick job sweeping, but one time two girls would hold the broom with one hand and talk about their after school plans. The floor was a mess, and I told them I would show them how to sweep. I hurried and obtained a typical pile of wood chips. I asked the girls if they were watching and see the pile I got. They said, "yes," I said "good" and swept all the chips in my pile back to where the chips were before, and told the girls to give me a pile like mine! They looked at me, and one said that was the dumbest thing they'd ever seen! I replied the dumbest thing was to expect me to sweep for them. I had a broom in my hand and kept pointing out spots where there were some chips. If looks could kill, I would have been a dead man. As they were leaving, I told them they did an excellent job the second time.

WHEN YOU SWEEP BE HUMBLE, NOT PROUD

I would tell the students from middle school to be humble when you sweep; 1) you look down, 2) one hand low on the broom, 3) the other higher, 4) quick movements, and 5) the bristles bent to move the chips. A proud sweeper looks up, has both hands on top of the broom, and no pressure on the bristles. The proud sweeper will sweep the area a second time. Why have to work twice when one good, impressive sweep is enough. Remember, a clean shop is a happy shop.

IS A FOOT LONG HOT DOG - A FOOT LONG?

I used the school cafeteria for my lunch daily and wait in line with the students. I wouldn't be the first in line, and I would wait till the rush was over. This day the menu was "foot-long hot dogs with fries," milk, and fruit. I'm in line, and one of my 8th graders is ahead surrounded by girls and talking, in a loud voice, that those hot dogs better be a foot long if they aren't he going to want a reduced price or a price reduction. He's entertaining the young ladies but not the three ladies serving lunch. I looked at the ladies serving lunch, and I can see how they look at each other and (rolling their eyes) show signs they are getting tired of this 8th grader. He talks about the size and becomes more bothersome, the ladies aren't happy but don't say anything. I'm feeling sorry for the ladies, so I tell the guy we are going to check the length of the hot dog IN THE SHOP right now! He can't go to the cafeteria with the girls but go with me to the shop (next door) and measure the hot dog with a ruler. We turn right to the shop; the young girls go left to the cafeteria. We sit down and measure the hot dog, and it's less than 12 inches, and then I chew this guy out because these ladies who work in the cafeteria have nothing to do with the size of the hot dogs. It could have been 12 long before they cooked the dog, and it shrunk an inch or so, which is better a 12-inch cold-not grilled hot dog or an 11inch grilled hot dog? I told him these workers should get an apology from him because they don't deserve his loud comments like they didn't care. These ladies work hard every day to fix your lunch. The bell was going to ring, so we went back to return the trays. I mentioned I enjoyed having lunch with him, and maybe we can do this tomorrow. The ladies asked me what I did with the kid and thanked me. I kidded the ladies they should list that the foot-long hot dogs are "cold and not cooked," and the cooked hot dogs are 10 inches long. They just laughed

WORKING WITH ADULTS

I mentioned earlier my first experience working with adults was in 1967 and didn't do any more until the mid1970's with the apprenticeship program developed by the NTDPMA (National Tool and Die Precision Manufacturing Association). The local chapter started their evening program because they were unhappy with the Akron City School Apprenticeship program. John Severs was the administrator, and I was the only evening instructor. John was on loan from a local company and had teaching experience. This evening program developed into a day-night school with adult training plus apprenticeship programs. I was laid off in 1987 and became a full-time instructor there using the same math workbook, jobs, and techniques only to adults. I stopped teaching full time when the Cuyahoga Falls School system had a position for me.

MYRNA AND THE "CHEAT SHEET"

I developed a cheat sheet to save time and help solve trig problems quicker because the basic formulas would be handy. The small sheet 3 by 5 inches must fit inside the cover or lid of the calculator and used as a reference sheet. The rule was the sheet could not be seen when the plastic cover was on the calculator. It was to be out of sight. Myrna, an older student, asked me if her arrangement was OK because you could not see any paper on her calculator. She had an older version of the Texas Instrument (TI) calculator that had a hinged cover, with a pocket inside of the cover. She proceeded to open the cover and open her sheet, which was a full sheet of paper, folded like a road map. It was a full sheet of paper with notes and formulas on both sides. She then folded it back and closed the lid, and sure enough, you could not see any cheat sheet. She asked, "Is this OK?" All the guys went nuts because they had just one 2 ½ by five-inch sheet in the cover. I said it was OK, and a couple of guys wanted to know if she wanted to sell her "old" calculator.

MYRNA AND "R AND R"

This lady was a single parent of two children, a boy in high school and a girl in middle school. Myrna told the kids she needed their help at home because she had to work on her homework. I also believed that it's better to have the student rework incorrect problems than to fail and be dropped from the program. I started a program called "R and R," which stands for" Rework and Return." If a person has five correct out of 10, that's 50% and not good. So, I want the person to rework the incorrect problems in detail, not just change the answer. By working the problem, step by step, into the answer, a person can see where they went wrong. Myrna would get an R and R for almost every math assignment, would take the paper home and rework the problems. She would use some shop time to review some features of the math and finish the task at home. All correct reworks would get a grade of 70 or just passing. Myrna did tell me all her working homework around the kitchen table helped in another way because her kids started to do homework around the table too. The kid's teachers in school commented that the kid's grades improved. I was happy we got Myrna an interview and a job at a local company near her home in Ravenna. I met a gentleman, Mr. Neil Mann, at a meeting at the AMI facility and mentioned we have a lady from the Ravenna area, and she would be applying for a job. I said she is a good worker. She was hired in 1990, which was 28+ years ago. I hope to find her and talk about old times and tell her I'm going to give her a couple of trig problems to do using her cheat sheet.

I found out more about Myrna one evening during an apprentice class at the NTDA facility. The new student also worked at Allen Aircraft with Myrna. The guy commented that she is the perfect worker regarding breaks, lunch, start, and finish times. She was always there before the morning starting time; works till the beginning of the morning 15-minute break; is back at the end of the break; works till the start of lunch; was back at the end of lunch and works till the end of the shift. She cleans up after the end of the day on her time. The guy said the foremen keeps commenting to the other workers what she does, and they should follow her example. She replies to the people who ask her about her work habits; she wants to keep her job and was following the company rules. I asked him if this habit was making the people upset? He replied her work ethic makes others think about what is fair to the company. He said It was a good thing!!

THAT DEPENDS

One of my most interesting experiences was I had a mixed class of men and women. In all my years of teaching, I seldom had females in classes, maybe one or two, but never 7 to 9 women. It was 8:00 am. ready to start class when this young mother holding her two-year-old daughter, states she has to return home because the daycare center would not take the child this morning; the child was sick with a running nose and coughing. I was ready to say OK when the other ladies said all the ladies could help take care of the child while in class, and if the child cried, they would take the child out. I wasn't sure but said OK. The class started. I would notice this lady on the right, holding the quiet baby looking at me. The next time I turned, another lady on the left was holding the baby, and even guys took turns holding the baby too. (I guess I could say that was the youngest student I ever had in class) Finally, noon came this mother said she had to leave because the baby dirtied his diaper and she didn't have an extra one. I said wait a minute when to my car, reached in the pocket behind the front seat, pulled out a diaper, and gave it to the mother. Everyone looked at me, and I could see this questioned look on their faces. I mention I have young grandkids, and the extra diapers were like having a spare tire in your car. I also told them I've changed diapers too but not as nice as the mother. I was to "cover all the important places."

HELPING STUDENTS WITH EMPLOYMENT

March and April were months that we made contact with companies that hired students and set up interviews. Akromold would ask to interview two or three students because they knew what we did to prepare them with entry-level skills and were likely to hire one or two each year. Mr. Hatherill would give them a test regarding shop procedures and math problems. I didn't know the questions, and I expected the student to be able to answer the questions. One year a new company asked about interviewing a couple of students. I told the company owner to give the guys some math problems as a test. The two guys went after school, and I got a call from the owner telling me the two guys did the math, both got every math problem correct. I replied his problems were too easy. He commented the guys in his shop couldn't do those problems. I told him both young men would help his company, and wouldn't tell him which one to hire.

When the first young man was to begin working in the coop, I would mention a few things the new worker could expect. Some regular guys will try initiating the new rookie. One thing I remember was the old workers would ask the new guy to get a "thread stretcher" from a guy at the far end of the shop. When the kid asks that guy, he will say he gave it to another guy over there and point to an old guy somewhere else. Usually, a supervisor will inform the rookie what a thread stretcher is and note the kid's expression. There are other unique items to look for, like a can of "vapor." I told the guys to go along with the search because if you work there long enough, you will be asked by a new worker for a thread stretcher. Those first few days can be eventful.

AKROMOLD INC.

The established shop usually have the same beginnings. A man works in a factory, buys a machine, works in his basement or garage, becomes busy and has too many jobs to complete, gets his wife and kids to help, and because of so much work, decides to quit the full-time job and open a small shop. The man hires another worker, then another, buys a small building, obtains more equipment, and expands. Akromold Inc. started from a small one, then three-man shop to multiple extensive facilities in Cuyahoga Falls. Akromold began that way; only three guys started the company. Those three guys were Mr. Bob Montieth, Mr. Bud Bryler, and Mr. John Gazdit. I was lucky I knew the plant foreman from Hower

Vocational High School. Don Hatherill was a senior when I was a freshman, and we played on the High School Varsity baseball team. Our relationship helped students in every class because the class could tour Akromold, and Don was our guide. When a student was sent there for an interview, Don would give him a test and wanted guys who would come in with entry-level skills and improve from the first day employed. Akromold also helped us with steel that was scrap steel to them and would cut what we needed from their large blocks. The steel was pre-hardened and the kind used in making cavities and cores for the large molds they made. Imagine a mold that would make the entire dash panel of an automobile. Akromold usually hired one or two students a year for the time we had a program. I always said all this help was because of baseball at Hower.

Don and I did have some fun with a cocky student. Don said he was going to have Mr. Bryly interview the student. Mr. Bryly looked mean and had a gruff voice. It was a set-up, the kid met Don and then Mr. Bryly. Mr. Bryly was firm and talked like he would to any employee. The student told the class the next day "that this one guy" scared me at first, but after a while, he was different and helpful in a rough way. I told Don the kid's comments, and he passed the remarks to Mr. Bryly, who said he would have to work on being meaner. Mr. Bryly didn't want to be known as being nice!

We did help Akromold because Akromold helped us with steel and places for employment. I believed the company was good to its workers and treated them fairly. One year I went to visit and walked in the worker's entrance by the time clock and waited for Mr. Hatherill and noticed the time card rack. I counted about 100 workers, and 33 workers were our former students. I just recently visited Prospect Mold (Prospect purchased Akromold several years ago) and was met by eight former students. I asked them how many years they have been working here or in machining? I received 31 years to 34 years. I also commented you guys are getting old and probably are grandpas. They laughed and said, yes, they are old and know I am ancient by now, something like "old as dirt!"

R.F. COOK COMPANY

R.F. Cook was another company that hired many students. John Little, the plant foreman and I were in the same apprenticeship program, and this friendship helped students received an interview and employment. It was essential to place students that would provide an excellent example because the company would use our program to continue to hire our students. The companies wanted the guys to receive the basics, and the company would provide additional skills. Most of the companies had an Ohio State approved apprenticeship program, which leads to a journeyman's classification.

Mr. R.F. Cook was on our first advisory committee and stayed on the committee for several years. The Committee would meet at least once a year with school officials to evaluate and give suggestions about the program. I had a couple of guys who worked at R.C. Cook, who would visit and talk to the students about the company. One young man worked in the finish grinding room, a unique area, and in our conversation, he commented about the company having three sets of precision gage blocks on a shelf that are marked "Don't use." The young man said when these gage blocks show wear, they are taken out of use and just sit there. At our yearly advisory committee meeting, as we finished, I ask Mr. Cook about those blocks they can't use, but we could for basic instruction. I asked him how much would he want for them? He asked the fellow who came with him about the blocks, and this gentleman said there are three sets they can't use because they have "wore down." Mr. Cook said he would check when he gets back and let us know. A couple of days later, the company said we could pick up a set. Gage blocks come in different sets of blocks; some have a few basic blocks, and some have 50 to 60 blocks. Mr. Cook gave us the full set and said they are free.

That was in 1967 or 1968, and we kept the entire set until the program closed in 1987. Those blocks may have been "undersize" for R.F. Cook, but important for every student from that day until the end. Thanks, R.F.Cook!

One day we lost a small gage block, and the student said he was using it on a lathe, and when he cleaned the machine and floor, it must have been dumped in the trash barrel. Well, over went the barrel, the guys sorted through the chips, and we found the block.

COOP-PROGRAM

We initiated a Coop-program where a student could spend the three shop periods at a job site as an employee. The opportunities were in the last two months of the senior year. I had to visit the company to verify the experience at the facility would be equal or more than what the student would gain at the school shop. We had companies that would want to interview every year, so there was no first visit required. The goal was to find a place of employment after graduation and not for a few months. There was a lot of satisfaction seeing these guys attending the fourth period of related and then leaving for work. Those in the class were motivated to coop too.

There was one bad experience in selecting a company. I visited the new company and was shown around and told the young man's tasks. The boy starts and graduates and continues working. After a few months, I meet the young man and tells me he had to quit. After a few questions, I find out the former student is placed on a surface grinder and required to grind the jobs to ten-thousandths of an inch. That's not a task for a young man who doesn't have the experience. There was another comment that the owner seems to have been drinking. The young student said he would start painting for a neighbor.

The related class was used for "Show-and-Tell" for those working in our co-op program. The young man will spend a few minutes in front of the class, showing and telling what the individual does and what the company manufactures. One student asks if he can be excused from the S and T. The guy was shy and talked so soft one had to be in his face to hear what he said. I suggested he bring in the items to show and write down what his duties were. I would stand in front and handle the samples he brought in, and he can talk to the class while he is in the back of the room. The class will be looking at me. He agreed. The talk started, and I handled and walking around with the samples to different classmates. They began to ask questions, and I tried to point out the answers but wasn't correct, so the boy comes to the front and talks like a PRO. He didn't realize he was in the front of the class, but he knew the answers and forgot his fear. We all commented about this fear, and knowledge of the subject will overcome the fear.

When a student starts working, he doesn't attend the three periods in the shop but travels to the job site. If they didn't complete their jobs in our shop, they can take them and finish them later.

RETIREMENT KEEPING BUSY

I mentioned the first day of retirement, where I ended in the hospital. After that, I became a taxi driver for my grandkids with their daycare pre-school. It was the Tallmadge Tree House Pre-School located in the First Congregational Church. I transported Monica, Joey, Julia, and Melissa for their years of early education. I looked forward to the day each would enter the Tallmadge Public Schools – no more driving. Being there the three days a week for several years, I became friends with the young mothers and grandmothers doing the same thing. One day my wife and I were shopping at our local Acme store, we passed two of these young mothers. As they passed, they said, "Hi Mr. Sipka!" and I replied, "Hi." My wife looked at me and asked in a serious tone, "who are they?" I said they are my lady friends from the Tree House Pre School. Her comment was when she retires; she is going to take the kids to Pre School.

I had to fix lunch for the grandkids and would have egg salad sandwiches one day of the week. Melissa liked egg salad sandwiches and would help, peel and mash the eggs, get the bread ready, get the mayonnaise, and help mix the eggs and mayo. Now for the taste test, I would get a fork, put some egg salad on the fork, and have her taste the mix. No! More mayo, Yes! Spread it on the bread. I would cut the sandwich in four parts but cut diagonally (four triangles) instead of four squares. I told Melissa cutting this way makes the four pieces taste better.

One day I had to take her to Julia Braghieri's house, her great-grandma, and Julia too was going to make egg salad sandwiches. Julia boils the eggs, cools them, and starts to peel them. Melissa says, "That's my job!" Now to mix the eggs and mayo, Melissa looks in the refrigerator to bring out the mayo. Julia combined the two and started to spread the salad on the bread. Melissa tells Julia she has to taste it first to see if it's ok. Great-grandma gives her a taste, and she said: "it's OK." The spread goes on the bread; the second piece of bread covers the bottom, and Julia starts to cut the sandwich into four squares. Again, Melissa stops Great-Grandma and tells her to cut diagonally. Julia asks Melissa where she's getting all these ideas about this sandwich. Melissa says Grandpa says all this makes the egg sandwich taste better. Julia comments on how Melissa is bossy when it comes to egg salad sandwiches.

Melissa also would brag about my chicken soap and tell people, "it's the best." Julia asked what I do to make a can of Campbell chicken soup so great. I told her, with a straight face, you open the can from the bottom. I kept a serious look as I mention what I do to make my Campbell's chicken noodle soup great. After a few seconds, I laugh, get a nasty look from my mother-in-law, and a comment to get out of here along with a hand wave.

TAKING PICTURES AND OTHER PROJECTS

My first reflex camera was obtained from a tool salesman who had a hobby of going to big auto racing events like the Indianapolis 500 race and took pictures before and during the race. He said he did sell some pictures enough to cover his expenses. He would buy a new camera every two years. I bought one that year and was lucky with this photo of my daughter and others as they started a swim event in 1983 at the Ohio State Girls District Swimming Championship.

Photo by Stan Sipka

My daughter Carol is the third swimmer from the bottom with a gold-colored hat. I entered this picture in the Canon Photo contest and won a camera. The grand prize was a trip for two to the 1984 Olympics in Los Angeles, California, with tickets to your favorite event.

When our church has pancake breakfasts after the two Masses on Sundays, I'm asked to take pictures. I crop the picture, make one or two, and give them their pictures. A lady took the picture, looked at it, and said: "This picture is so nice of me that I am going to use it for my obituary." I was surprised at that statement; my facial expression showed that surprise. Yes! That's important for someone to consider. I tell people you are not a "photographer" until someone tells you they will use the picture you took for their obituary.

THE RAPIDS OF CUYAHOGA FALLS OHIO

The "Rapids of Cuyahoga Falls" was viewed the first time when I had to wait on a part for my car at the auto store. I said I would take a few minutes to walk across the street and look at the river. I walked on the bridge and saw this scene and was determined to take this view because it was beautiful. I went home, got the camera, and returned and took many pictures. Because of the beauty of the scene, enlargements of different sizes were made and given to family and friends.

Photo by Stan Sipka

ROSE PEDAL JOURNEY

The Rapids of Cuyahoga Falls is in this picture, too, alongside a poem that I wrote for a person whose husband died. People have expressed interest and have asked for one to post and reflect on the message. This picture is in vertical form, and the other is in the horizontal form with paper with a light sampling of rose petals. When my Mother-in-law, Julia Braghieri, died, we made a booklet with Julia and her Husband Albert on the cover as a together picture with a short description of the two of them. Inside was this picture in the horizontal format. We received a lot of comments, and many asked for copies to show others the picture and poem.

A ROSE PETAL'S JOURNEY

IMAGINE YOU ARE WATCHING A ROSE PEDAL TRAVELING DOWN THE STREAM AND COMING OVER THE WATERFALLS ALONG THE WAYS IT ENCOUNTERS SMOOTH AND ROUGH PASSAGES OBSTACLES ARE IN THE WAY BUT IT KEEPS GOING AND FINALLY REACHES THE SMOOTH PART OF THE REST OF THE JOURNEY. GOD'S PLAN FOR OUR LIFE'S JOURNEY IS THE SAME

"The Cuyahoga River Rapids"
This dynamic portion of the Cuyahoga River is located in Cuyahoga Falls, Oh. This forceful rapids can be viewed From a bridge in High Bridge Glens Park.

insert by Stan Sipka

BEFORE AND AFTER PICTURES

Before and after pictures are enjoyed because there is a serious and funny picture. I have taken many team pictures of my grandkids' sports teams, and the before and after are a favorite. At our churches' pancake breakfast grandma and grandpa, their grandkids want the after picture too. My biggest surprise was a picture-perfect grandma hamming it up in the "let it all hang out "picture. She was a happy woman when she saw the pictures a week later.

Our local store has beautiful flowers in the spring, and I took pictures of individual flowers. My wife is in a hospital for an operation and spends several days there. I bring in 25 + photos and tape them to a locker in her room. The workers comment about the beautiful pictures and wonder why is a picture of our little dog among the flowers. My wife tells them the dog's name is "Daisy." We tell the staff they can take a picture if they wish and more than half were taken. We received a lot of thanks.

We all have been somewhere and want to have a picture of all of us to show others, but one has to take the picture and not be in the picture. I have a habit of volunteering to take the picture so that person can be in the picture too. I was rejected once by a lady who thought I was going to steal her camera. Her husband yelled at her that I wasn't going to steal her camera and get in the picture. This favor has been returned many times.

SHUT-THE-BOX GAME

I played the shut-the-box game at a toy store, and It was fun and having a couple of old plastic VHS film containers; the idea was to make a couple. I have the woodworking machines and time and made the 3 or 4. Our family had a Christmas party, and everyone was to bring a craft item for exchange. These plastic boxes aren't used anymore, so the problem was where to get the boxes. I mentioned this need to my neighbor, and he laughed and said, wait a minute, went up to the loft in his garage and handed me 15 empty boxes. The 15 were made, and I gave my neighbor one for his gift. At the party, most were given out, and I received many nice compliments. I wanted to make more because they were easy to make and cheap, just scrap wood, a coat hanger, and felt. I went to Goodwill, Salivation Army, and junk stores and no old VHS containers. I'm stopped at a

Photo by Stan Sipka

traffic light and noticed an old gas station that advertised XXX rated movies. My thought was VHS boxes (yes, just the empty boxes). I stopped and asked if they had any old containers; the guy handed me ten or so EMPTY boxes. I hurried out of the building holding these ten and placed them in my car. I noticed people in cars, waiting for the light to turn green looking at me and wanted to yell, "THEY

ARE ALL EMPTY!" I can imagine people hearing me would say, "sure, empty!" I mentioned this embarrassing experience to my neighbors, and they commented that's why the police came to interview us about Stan's character.

JESUS, MARY, AND JOSEPH THE HOLY FAMILY

Joanne and I received two wood pieces that represented the Holy Family, Jesus, Mary, and Joseph from a friend years ago and liked it so much that we kept the pair out all year, not just at the Christmas season. With our family gatherings at Christmas, the idea was to make sets to give away. I received permission to copy the idea and made 50 or so sets again all out of scrap wood. I would plan to make 20 at a time and would be busy in the garage, keeping track of matched sets. I wanted the grain pattern to match. It's time to stop, so I have to place the 20 individual pieces in a box. I place 20 Mary and Joseph

Photo by Stan Sipka

pieces in line and start looking for Baby Jesus parts. I find 19. I look everywhere and no Baby Jesus. I walk in the house and tell Joanne, "Well, I lost Jesus!" She smiles and reassures me I will find Jesus tomorrow, or Jesus will find you. The next day I'm again working on the 20 sets and look on the floor behind a piece of wood, and I find Baby Jesus. I open the door to the kitchen and yell, "JOANNE, I FOUND JESUS!" She asked me, "do you feel better now?" "yes," was my reply.

The surface of the wood is plain, not a fancy finish. I try for a light brown color wood to match what I think what would be the color of their clothes then.

50ᵀᴴ WEDDING ANNIVERSARY

My wife and I approached our 50th wedding anniversary and wanted to celebrate the occasion differently. People usually go to dinner and then an open house gathering at their house. For our anniversary, I wanted something different, so I talked my wife into a hall reception with a meal, music, and an evening like our wedding reception, 50 years ago in 1958, except now our daughters and grandkids would be there. At the Saturday mass at our church, the priest had us repeat our wedding vowels, and two grandchildren were our

Photo by Family Member

Photo by Family Member

Photo by Family Member

witnesses. (I cried). We went to the hall and greeted the family and guests. We didn't have any liquor or beer because the priest said we would need a professional bartender and a police officer in the hall. A dish jockey provided the music who had access to all kinds of music with his computer instead of a 5 – 6 piece band like we had at our wedding. I asked the DJ if he had any Spike Jones' music. He had no idea who Spike Jones was but did locate some songs using his computer. So we had the traditional dance where the bride and groom dance to a romantic song and people watch. Now Spike Jones was a band that played a song as you would expect, but after a minute, the band members would use bells, whistles, gongs, and strange noisemakers to accent the song. The band was part of the 1940s and 1950s period. My wife and I are dancing close and looking at each other like we did 50 years ago when suddenly the music changes to "CRASH, BANG, BELLS, WHISTLES, and LORD KNOWS WHAT SOUNDS" for a good minute, then back to the slow, relaxing music. Very few people knew what Spike Jones did, and when they heard this, they all stopped and looked at us. We started to dance fast, like the typical movements of the day. I noticed the grandkids and their expressions. All the expense of the celebrations was worth watching them enjoy "OUR MUSIC." Even the DJ loved the song.

We also gave each family a gift to remember the occasion, which was a little mantel clock with a sticker on the back. I made over 100 of these clocks. (note I mention 100 an 89 clocks, 11 were not completed).

Photo by Stan Sipka

Photo by Stan Sipka

I have made a couple hundred more to give away as presents. Several times the grandkids in elementary school would give their teacher a clock for Christmas. I was told that one elementary teacher asked the principal to place one of the grandchildren in her class because she wanted a clock. Still have a few ready to hand out for special occasions

THE 60TH WEDDING ANNIVERSARY

The 60th wedding anniversary was not like the 50th. It was a family dinner, open house, and early to bed event. As for a party, DJ, catered meal, and a hall, we just showed the video of the 50th anniversary at our house. One thing there will be fewer older people around. No clocks were given this time, only a new battery for the clock given ten years ago. When asked why no clocks? I told them I would make new ones for the 70th wedding anniversary.

OUR FIRST WEDDING ANNIVERSARY

A couple's first wedding anniversary is an important event. Ours was different. Upon leaving the service, I had to join the local Army Reserve Unit as part of my six-year obligation. Our date, June 28, 1959, happened to be in the two-week reserve training schedule. A wedding anniversary is not an excuse for an exemption. One nice thing was a good friend, Joe Falkenstein, was also with me at Camp Atterbury somewhere in Indiana. He cheered me up as much as he could. His wife Phillys was home, cheering up Joanne.

OUR SECOND WEDDING ANNIVERSARY

Knowing that the reserve training would be the same for our second anniversary, I signed up for summer school at Kent State. It worked. I didn't miss our second anniversary but was assigned two weeks at Fort Belvoir in August. I was playing baseball locally and doing well, so I brought my baseball equipment just in case. After a couple of days, I talked with a fellow who was the company's team catcher and captain. We played catch and went through my routine. The guy wanted to see if I could play in the team's next game. I received an identification card (ID) that listed me as "regular army," not some other classification. The guy checked with the league official about me just coming into the company and if I could pitch. Since I was "RA," I was scheduled to throw. This team had not won any games and was playing a team tied for first place. Our ninth player showed up still in his khakis. We are into the seventh inning and winning by two runs. As we finish the inning, the other team manager talks to the umpire, he motions me to meet at home plate, and show my ID because they thought I was a "ringer." My ID listed me as RA, and the umpire was satisfied. We lost by one run, and the other team was happy. After the game, the other team's coach and two other men asked me to try out for the Fort Belvoir All-Star Team. The catcher who knew my situation was there and when I told them I was to return home because of my two-week army reserve training was up. They all laughed and asked if I could extend for a month or two to play. I wanted to be with my wife, so I declined.

HOSPITALS

KIDNEY STONES

I wrote earlier about my experience in the hospital while in the army in 1958, and my next "visit" to a hospital was in 1973 when I had trouble with kidney stones. I was admitted to the hospital early Tuesday morning. The following Friday, my family, including me, was to go to the Michigan YMCA Championship at Western Michigan University. I had three daughters swimming, and I always watched them swim. Kidney stones were new to me, and as I was in the hospital to remove the stones, my idea was they were big "rocks." I could just suffer through the stones passing, or some medical device or procedure would remove the "rocks." There is so much pain I was given drugs, if continued, could lead to drug addiction. The doctors said the stone or stones were in the duct and had to pass by themselves. I commented to visitors the stones must be the size of baseballs the way they feel, and how could they pass? With the drugs that made me feel no pain, I hatched a plan where I could ask for a release from the hospital and drive to Michigan and watch the girls swim and return on Monday and finish the treatment. I felt no pain. Well, that plan wasn't going to happen, and I was sure it would be just as I planned. My wife and another mother drove our van with the four girl swimmers to Michigan. They left early in the morning, and I knew the route they would take. I'm lying there upset because I couldn't go and following their progress on a map when I was hit with one immense pain! I never had that intense pain before. The nurses and doctors said the stone (I knew now the stone(s) was the size of a baseball) was moving through, and that's a good sign. The pain was intense and then no pain, and this cycle throughout the day. Between pains, I could picture being in the van going to Michigan with this series of shooting pains. My wife was right about not going. I would have been in a hospital somewhere in north-western Ohio or Michigan, and the kids would not have made it to the meet. The nurses were kind to me and talked to me about my progress. I told them I can picture the stone as big as a baseball; they said "no" it was like a deck of cards. They congratulated me on passing the stone and told me I just experienced the pain a woman goes through when she delivers a baby. My hat goes off to all mothers.

WHAT ARE HEMORRHOIDS?

The second hospital visit was in 1983 when I had hemorrhoids removed. I had an idea about hemorrhoids from my army days. One thing I was told to do was stay off my feet as much as possible. Our shop was large, so I prepared to walk less and was given a unique air-filled pillow to sit on that would help. It looked like a donut. The guys come in, I explain what I have to do regarding walking, but I will be around. One student asks me what the problem was. I said I had hemorrhoids removed. Another student asks, "what are hemorrhoids?" I was ready to give him the description in medical terms when a student yells? "THEY ARE THINGS THAT STICK OUT OF YOUR _____AND HURT LIKE HELL!". The guys bust our laughing and me too. After a minute of laughter, the kid who asked the question said he didn't know. Another student said, "Mr. Sipka show him your operation!" That request made the guys move to their machines in a hurry. I said I would find a picture in some medical book to show him hemorrhoids.

HEART ATTACK

My wakeup call arrived in 2002; I had a stiff neck, just a simple thing that would be ok in a few days. My wife thought differently and set up a doctor visit that day. I'm sitting in the room talking to the doctor; my wife is behind me shaking her head "no" when I tell the doctor it's ok and I'll be better tomorrow. He mentioned he wants me to go to the hospital and check it out just to be sure, and I agree. Within 24 hours, I had a stent implanted in the area called the "widowmaker." Hey! It just a stiff neck, Right? On the operating table, I remember watching the probe traveling in the veins coming to a spot that looked different. When the probe hit that spot, I felt that "stiff neck" pain. I could see the probe striking the blockage and nothing happening. I (kiddingly) told the doctor he should put a small twist drill on the end and drill out the blockage. The probe broke through, and then came the stent. Rehab was next and learning how to keep from the next heart attack. What a learning experience. I learned that there was no pain as the probe was moving through the vein.

SECOND HEART ATTACK

My second heart attack occurred in 2008 while we were in Fort Myers, Florida, playing baseball. This time I could not throw a ball in a practice session. We were staying 30 miles away at Lehigh Acres. We called the paramedics, and it was a heart attack. The fireman asked me, "what hospital do you want? I replied, "the best one!" So it was South West General in Fort Myers. Knowing we were 30+ miles away, I asked if a helicopter would be better; he replied no, and we will be there quickly. As we were traveling with the sirens and lights flashing, I mentioned it didn't seem like we were moving very fast. He replied, we are going as fast as we can, and don't worry. The time was near midnight, my wife wanted to be with me and had to drive to the hospital. She had no idea how to get to the hospital, but one of the paramedics took the time to detail a map to get to the hospital. She gets there, and the door is locked and can't get anyone's attention. Just then, a well-dressed man walks up and opens the door, and both enter the hospital. After several hours my wife is brought to my room, and who does she meet? The well-dressed man who let her in was the doctor who put three stents in my heart.

I knew many players from our area that were there, several visited, and some kidded me I should be good enough to pitch on Friday. "No! Not this Friday," was my response.

There were two visitors I will never forget. Mike Williams and his wife Cheryl came to visit on their way home to Gerard, Ohio. Mike had advanced cancer but wanted to go and play. His wife was a nurse, and as Mike and I talked,

Cheryl walked around, looking at the devices flashing numbers and zig-zag lines. She came over and said, "Stan, your vital signs look good!" That was a dose of good medicine. I told him when we were on the same team, and he was at the shortstop position, I felt like I could win the game. Mike passed away soon after we arrived home. I went to the wake and cried; I lost a friend.

BUCKET LIST

THE BEVEL STAIN GLASS WINDOW

Photo by Stan Sipka

After I watched the movie with Jack Nickleson and Morgan Freeman, I started a bucket list. My list is far out but doesn't include jumping out of an airplane. A recent accomplishment is finishing a bevel stain glass window 23 inches by 48 inches sitting in our front window. It was designed to be in a front door, but I wanted to see the window every time I look out the front window. I was retired and was interested in stain glass windows, and took lessons in 2005 at a store in Cuyahoga Falls, and made the simple pieces and was happy. My best works, until then, were two identical pieces that were placed in my Daughter's floral shop next to a fireplace. When she sold the shop, I took the two pieces and put them in our home. While taking lessons, the owner obtained some kits of full windows at a reduced price, and I purchased two packages. The sets were placed in the basement and collected dust over the ten years. In 2015 we talked about all the things we had, and the word "downsizing" came to mind. What about those two glass kits? I could sell or try making them.

In October of 2015, I decided to create one. I had the work area, time, and started the project and planned on finishing it by Christmas. Christmas came, and it was not done, not done on my birthday January 23, but was finished Feb 26. My Mother-in-law thought it was "beautiful." I have been asked how long it took to make. I would say I would work 4-6 hours for days then take time off for a couple of days. I had to be careful; I didn't drop any piece because I couldn't find replacement parts. A lady at the store that deals with this kind of glass told me to work on a carpet and try to move the glass over the table as you move pieces around. The lack of soldering skills disappointed me, and I would re-solder many joints. The beauty of this made me keep going, and finally, the soldering improved.

I made the second window and placed it in my daughter's front window because the panel is 56 inches high, and her front window is that size. It is beautiful too.

THE STARTING PITCHER IN 8 DIFFERENT AGE GROUPS

I play in the Roy Hobbs Baseball League. The league started in Akron, Ohio, in 1985 and has expanded to the whole country. The league has eight different age groups, so young guys can't play on teams with older men. In 2013 the league started the 75 and over division in Fort Myers, Florida, and I was on one of the two 75 teams. In Akron, there are five different age divisions and three in Florida. The three are 65+and over, 70+ and over, and the new 75+ division. One day I had the idea of being the starting pitcher in each age group that would be a first for me and all the old guys. The Hobbs' officials thought I was crazy but agreed. The first age division I arranged to throw was the Greater Akron AA 18 and over in Akron. These guys were talented college and high school players.

The night before the game, I told my wife I was afraid because these guys are good. At the game I went to the other team's dugout and said what I was hoping to do and please take it easy on me, it could be one pitch, one batter, and one inning. I went to the mound

Photo by Family Member

and started my warm-up throws, all the infielders and catcher walked to the mound and wished me good luck. The catcher, Justin Spicer, was my grandson. The accompanying picture was taken as Justin handed me the ball and said: "GRANDPA THROW STRIKES."

That comment made me relax because I had the guys' support. The first batter ground to short. The second batter popped a fly to the third baseman. The third hit a fly to center field. I was thrilled to imagine a 78-year-old guy pitching to these 20-year-old good players and out of the inning. I walked to the dugout and thanked the manager for letting me do that and expected to be finished. I asked him who was to take over for the rest of the game. The guys commented I had to pitch the second inning because I was working on a no-hitter. He asked me if I wanted to go out and I said sure. The next batter was the clean-up hitter who looked like a clean-up hitter – big and strong. I got two strikes on him with two pitches. I thought I better be careful, threw a bad pitch and he got a single. The manager took me out. What an exciting experience.

After the game, I looked for the clean-up batter and mentioned I was surprised to get two strikes on him and wanted to throw something unhittable but made a mistake. He mentioned he was afraid I would strike him out and said his friends would have never stopped kidding him how a 78-year-old guy could strike him out. He said he was worried. I played in the Greater Akron AA in the 1960s, and here I was playing in 2013 - Fifty years apart.

I did play in all the eight age divisions and wondered if anyone else would do the same thing. I'm 85 now and kid the Roy Hobbs Organization to start an 80 and over division. I believe there would be enough guys for two teams.

During the time in Fort Myers working on my bucket list, I watched ladies playing hardball too. There were six teams in the open division. I asked if I could be the starting pitcher in one of the girl's game and got a LOUD NO! One of my teammates on the 75 team had two daughters who played on the best team, and I talked to many of the girls. I mentioned what I did with the eight different age groups and how I was disappointed I couldn't pitch to one batter in the girl's game. The captain of the girl's team said she would play catch with me. I discovered she was the catcher; we went to the warm-up area, and I threw from the mound for 10 to 15 minutes. Her return throws were more than I expected. This young lady and most of this team were to represent the United States in a tournament somewhere. Besides being skilled ballplayers, they were pretty.

I told my family I want "GRANDPA THROW STRIKES' on my tombstone. NOTE I had to order a stone for my wife and me and had the design include "GRANDPA THROW STRIKES."

FIELD OF DREAMS

The 1989 movie Field of Dreams, was enjoyed because it was a simple experience I could relate to – playing catch with my dad. Six weeks into 2018, I saw on Facebook someone wanting to play catch with a different person every day for a year. That was crazy enough to write to Bob Dyer, a reporter for the Akron Beacon Journal, and ask him how I would get in touch with this guy. Soon I received an email from Mr. Dyer telling me the guy, Ethan Bryan, lived in Springfield, Missouri. I thought maybe he lived in the northeastern part of Ohio. Bob mentioned he, too, thought that was a good idea and said they figured the right place to play catch one day was at the Field of Dreams in the movie. I mentioned driving 500 miles to throw a few baseballs and drive back was not a good idea. My wife and I hatched Plan "B." We could visit my wife's cousin in Mishawaka, Indiana, on the way there for a day or two, drive to Dyersville, Iowa, play catch for a day, and visit an army friend in the Quad City Illinois area for a day. The two visits made this crazy idea make sense.

Photo by Stan Sipka

Photo by visitor
We are looking for "Shoeless Joe Jackson"

On July 24, the four of us, Ethan Bryan, Bob Dyer, my wife and I arrived at the Field of Dreams mid-morning. The corn was tall, very few people, and beautiful weather; the three men took turns pitching and catching; we were like a bunch of kids. I kicked the dirt, wanted to go into the left-field corn, and look for Shoeless Joe Jackson. Shoeless was an old player in the movie. When two of us were playing catch, the third guy would stand in the batter's box, ready to jump out of the way. I told the batter, "just don't wink at me!" In the movie, the batter winked at the pitcher, and the next pitch was aimed at his head. It was three hours of being kids again.

While I was pitching, I was asked if "do you throw smoke?" My reply was, "no! it's like a slow-moving fog!"

Photo by Joanne Sipka
Bob Dyer taking pictures, Ethan Bryan catching and me pitching

Photo by Joanne Sipka
Ethan Byran, Bob Dyer and me holding signed baseballs

Photo by Joanne Sipka
Don Hull and me

After three hours of playing, my wife and the "three kids" were sitting in the shade writing about this moment; Bob Dyer ran out to the field because he saw an old man slowly walking the bases, hunched over, with a cane rounding second on his way to third and home. Don Hunt, age 84, was with a group of senior citizens from Reedsburg, Wisconsin. Don came over, and We talked. He said he was a catcher years ago. I gave him an old baseball, and Don wanted me to give it to some younger people on the field. I told him to hold the ball as he is relaxing at home and remember how he used to throw out those guys trying to steal second base. He smiled, nodded, and went back to Reedsburg, Wisconsin, with his fellow senior citizens

My wife and I drove to Moline Il. and spent two days visiting my Army buddy. Lloyd Whitsell was a farmer who had to retire due to health and is less active on his farm. For years our families exchanged visits, and each experienced different daily routines – city and farm. One routine Lloyd and I talked about, was sleeping, their farm was away from any busy roads so that it would be quiet at night from cars and large trucks driving past the house. Lloyd commented about the noise from the traffic past our house. Our house is 125 feet from a road, which is a main route to the interstate. I was told it's quiet on the farm away from those busy roads, but the sound of his large pig herd eating all times of the day and night kept me up. As I would doze off one or more pigs would venture to the large food containers, lift the metal lid, with their nose, reach in and eat. When they finished and backed away, the metal lid would slam down and hit the bottom of the metal container. There was no rhythm to the lids hitting the edge. The next day, I mentioned I had an idea to eliminate that noise. Put some foam rubber on the underside of the lid; thus, there would be no sound when the lid falls. Lloyd answered, "they did that, and the pigs ate the foam rubber." Well, I thought it was a good idea.

I always enjoyed looking out over the farm and comparing my city life to this scene. It seemed slow-moving.

We returned home and survived the drive around Chicago and reflected on what a nice eventful trip it was. The first part was to visit her cousin Dolores Verbicky. A few weeks after our visit, Dolores passed away. We felt good to see her and me kidding her about me being her favorite cousin-in-law.

Sunday morning, I get the Sunday paper, open the bundle and see the front page – I'm on the front page! Naturally, I yelled and showed Joanne the top haft of the page showing me throwing from the mound on the Field of Dreams. The article also covered all of page 6 with pictures of Ethan, Bob Dyer, and me.

After the excitement subsided, I thought how this started: a simple request to a reporter. Mr. Dyer mentioned he, too, was surprised the story was on the front page. (The Ohio Editors Association awarded this story 1st place in the general category for 2018).

Part two to this experience. Ethan knows the actor, Dwier Brown, who played Kevin Costner's father in the movie. After reading the story, He wanted to play catch with me at the IX Center in Cleveland at a Sport's memorabilia Show. Bob Dyer set this visit up, and Dwier and I played catch in the corner of the Center for 5 minutes. As we walked back to the booth, Dwier said I surprised him with my throws and accuracy. That was fun at age 83.

Part three of this story is Bob Dyer placed the story on the internet with three 15 second videoes. I was in 2, and Don Hull was in the other. I thought Don Hull doesn't know he's on the internet and wondered how to tell him. He lives in Reedsburg WI with thousands of citizens. I called the Reedsburg's Chamber of Commerce and mentioned what I was trying to accomplish. When I said, "Don Hull," the lady yelled, "we know Don Hull, he's a member of the

Chamber!" How's that for luck. Copies of the Akron Beacon Journal and internet information was sent to Don and Reedsburg to enjoy Don's 15 seconds of fame.

Part four, Don and I, both being the same age, began to exchange letters and items we have to share. We talk on the cell phones, and this past week I somehow was able to speak with him, and we could see each other. Don said he enjoys talking and hopes we can continue this connection. I told Don about this story in the book, and he placed an order for a book.

BOWLING

I retired in 1997 and tried to keep busy and became a taxi driver for my grandkids. I told them I was going to put a meter in the car and figure how much they would owe me for my trips. Tips would not be counted.

I begin to bowl with a Tallmadge senior citizen group "Primetimers" and a Stow senior group. After a few weeks of bowling, I rolled a 654 series; the alley manager asked where do I bowl? I told him I'm not on a team just bowling with this group once a week. He said, you just bowled 654 with three 200 games and don't bowl in a league? I replied, "yes." He wanted to set me up with the senior's travel league, which is the best league for old guys that can bowl. I said, not now. Bowling in the Stow league, I did roll a 279 game with 11 strikes and a spare. That was one pin away from a 300 game. All the time before my 279, Joanne had bowled a higher game of 267 to my 246. It was something she would remind me when it came to bowled years before bragging about bowling. It didn't bother me; she had a higher game than me.

HILTON HEAD ISLAND

For the last 25 years, Hilton Head Island South Carolina has become our location for vacations because of the Ocean. The distance is 750 miles and a one day drive on the interstates. In our first few years, we stayed in units away from the Ocean and had to travel to the public beaches. Once we had an oceanfront unit, we were hooked on a beachfront location. As we grew older, Joanne and I enjoyed knowing what we had and enjoyed the week stay. We obtained two weeks in a row in the middle of June. Father's Day is always involved with one of the weeks. We go the first week because of the fourth-floor oceanfront view.

There were a couple of years we stayed both weeks. The ladies know the stores to visit while I enjoy just watching the waves and people. I do take three gloves (one is a left-hand glove) and 4 or 5 baseballs with me and walk the beach asking older guys if they want to play catch. Most look surprised, but if they seem to agree, I ask them if the lady there is their wife, and I want to ask her if it's ok for her husband to play catch. Most laugh and comment they will not rub his sore muscles later, or ask where his life insurance policy is? I was embarrassed once when I asked a guy, with teenage sons, if he could play some catch. He said later. He came over, and we played, and he squatted down like a catcher and caught my throws with strong return throws. After I asked him where he played ball? His son said he played with the Minnesota Twins Professional team. I told him I felt foolish asking him if he can play catch.

JOHN AND ME AT THE OCEAN

Another feel-good experience was giving a baseball to John Krabbe of Hamilton, Ohio, who was special. I asked his father first if it was okay. The young man held the ball and had a smile on his face. I told John not to throw the ball in the house.

Photo by Joanne Sipka
John and Me at the Ocean

That happened five years ago, and each time we see them, I ask the father about the young man, and also ask about the ball. The father says the ball is on his dresser on a little stand. It's a good feeling to do that. Just think an old dirty ball can make someone feel good. The young man calls me "Mr. Baseball."

WE ALMOST KILLED EACH OTHER

In the first few years of vacations at Hilton Head, Joanne was determined to collect all the shells and sand dollars in the Ocean. She bought books on how to make things out of shells and sand dollars. We learned you wait for low tide and walk out as far as possible and feel with your feet for the sharp point for conk shells and dollars. She couldn't dive down to dig the shell out, so that was my job. She would say she is standing on one, and I was to dive and follow her leg and retrieve the item. One day I couldn't stay down long enough to get the shell. She had this idea to place her hand on my head as I went under head first and help me stay down. She tells me she has her foot on a shell under her left leg; down, I go with her help; I get the shell, but can't get back because she is holding my head down. I finally pop back up, gasping for air. The first thing I hear is, "Did you get the shell?" I'm a little excited about the concern for shells and not breathing. I asked if she wanted to kill me? Again she asks if I got the shell. The next time she does that, I will pinch her on her butt.

One common activity there is bike riding along the Ocean. The beaches are ideal for riding, wide and hard-surfaced. This day I talk her into biking down the Island; we have water and towels and suntan lotion to enjoy the trip. The trip down is effortless and enjoyed, and we stopped occasionally and looked at the mansions. Time to return. We start to pedal back and discover we are going into a strong wind. That's why it was easy going down the beach. We are struggling, and Joanne comments, "you're trying to kill me!". I, too, am thinking we went too far, but I keep telling her those tall buildings far up the beach is where our place is located. I was told you check the direction of the wind and travel into the wind and use the wind to help you return. Joanne would tell people how I tried to kill her with that bike ride.

We eat out once or twice while there. We seem to be the ones who pay the bill so, The Crab Shack" is one place for sure. I get the seafood platter, and Joanne gets the swimp dinner. The one item I think enjoyed is eating their "hushpuppies." When our group of 4 to 6 people is there, I don't get my share of the puppies. I complained to the waitress, and she gave me a take-home box full of hush puppies for the next day. I was happy. The next day afternoon, I went to get a couple of hush puppies, and they are all gone. I did raise my voice and told them the next time I will hide them in my bedroom.

ORANGE MOON ON THE OCEAN

moon

Normally people are asked to keep from walking the beach and using flashlights because the turtles lay their eggs at night. On most nights, we do not look at the ocean, but on our last visit, we experience a full moon and a beautiful sight. This was the first time we saw a full moon like this, and Joanne and I enjoyed sitting on the balcony. A day before, the moon was white, and the pictures were just as nice.

WE BOTH LOVED THE BEACH

jo and i

You can see we enjoy just sitting looking at the ocean and occasionally taking a little nap. The naps happen after we obtained high back chairs. I have a special set of wheels that can carry all the items and make the trip easy. The first 75 feet is soft sand that is difficult to walk on but once past that sand, and it is easy to find a spot. At low tide, there are 250 feet of beach, and even at high tide, there is a hard surface. My job is to return to the unit and bring lunch and what else we forgot. On the last day there, we talk about how nice the stay was, and we give each a long kiss usually standing in the ocean and while embraced talk about next year.

In this picture, I marked our villa that is oceanfront that allowed us to take the two pictures because of the full moon and a clear sky at night. The other picture that is included is the day time picture with the angel in the clouds. That is with the story about Angela, our first granddaughter.

MY DAD AND ME AND BASEBALL

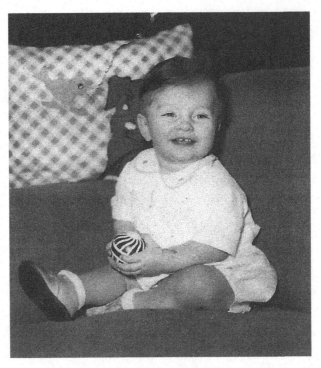

Photo by Daughter

My dad was an excellent ballplayer, but I never watched him play. He was 33 years old when I was born. We played catch almost every day, and he told me he hurt his arm when he was late to a game and didn't warm up and went to 3rd base. The first ball was hit to him; he threw to first, and something snapped in his shoulder, and that was it for his bullet-like throws to first. Several friends told me he was an excellent hitter, fielder and could run. Someone in the family has a small gold ball; he was awarded for the highest batting average in the league of .424. I was the first child and male; a ball was soon in my crib and first-year portrait

My older cousin said she remembers seeing me in a diaper sitting on the floor, rolling a ball back and forth to my dad. I guess I had to be two years old. We played catch daily and had to get a better catcher's glove because my throws were stronger. We did have a tradition to play catch on New Years' Day. Some years there were just a few tosses and back in the house. I guess this habit of playing catch was noticed because I met a person from our street years later and described where we lived, and his reply was, "you and your dad were always playing catch."

Photo by my Sister Rita
In from of our house on Mustill Street with sister Arlene watching

MY BASEBALL BEGINING

My early years of sports were exceptional. It started when my dad enrolled me for bowling instructions at the Firestone clubhouse. There I met a boy whose father coached a ten and under GABF (Greater Akron Baseball Federation) baseball team in the Firestone Park area. I went out and played in the ten and under league, and "Joe-All-Stars" won the city Championship in 1946. Each player had a jersey with a different sponsor. My jersey had "ROOP ELECTIC." The next year we were Cline's Drain Service Company with uniforms just like the Cleveland Indians. The uniforms were intimidating. In the 12 and 14 and under leagues, we won the championship both years in each age group, four years, four league championships in 2 age groups. We also won the Ohio State Championship in 1950. We were awesome! I would say no 14 and under team could beat us. I won 40 games and no losses in the last three years. I knew what the "Thrill of Victory" meant. My baseball experience between the age of 11 and 15 was exceptional.

Photo by my Father
Joe's Allstars names: back row left to right Ron Hill, Dick Valentine, Larry Carbaugh, me, Gary Snyder, Bob Raynow, Ira Duffield, Bob Wynes, Mr. Joe Marnics-Manager, front row left to right; Norman Menendez, Mike Marnics, Tom Jackson, Don Oldham, Tim Bittinger, Dave Larrymore, Bill Cunningham, Don Warren, Dale Riley.

RETURN TO BASEBALL FORTY YEARS LATER

ROY HOBBS BASEBALL LEAGUES

After my heart attack in 2002, I was in rehab and met a friend who had his hand in a splint, and I asked him about the injury. He mentioned it happen while playing baseball, which surprised me because he was my age – 67 years old. He explained the Roy Hobbs league as an organization started local but has expanded to all the states; it made me think baseball again. Their leagues are set up in different age groups.

I found out where the old guys were practicing and told my wife I was going to the practice of the "young guys" (she thought my grandson's practice). In the rehab classes, I was aware of heart rate and bought a heart rate monitor that is strapped to my chest over the heart and transferred the heart rate number to a special wristwatch. I arrive, introduce myself, and ask if I can throw some batting practice. I kept looking at the numbers and how quickly it returns to a low rate. It's time to leave and mentioned to the guy helping me that I have to go. He comments he noticed me looking at my "watch." I told him, "no! It's a heart rate monitor" and walked to the car. I guess all the guys went nuts with a guy throwing and checking his heart rate. At the year-end gathering, this story was told and enjoyed by all.

I returned home but wasn't sure when or how to tell my wife where I went to practice. The old guys were younger than me, but not Justin's age group. I got up enough nerve to tell her, and she was Ok with that. That was in 2002. From 1962 to 2002, looks like 40 years, I didn't play baseball. Now, it was fun again!

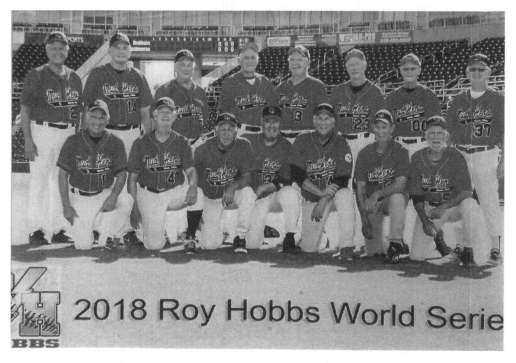

Photo courtesy of Wagner Photography
Front row P. Perantinides, J. Parrish, P. Kellerling, R. Rupp, J. Wasko, J. Nickelson, N. Reash
Back row D. Manuseles, J. Jacobson, S. Sipka, D. Drown, D. Booth, A. Green, E. Clark, B. Leech

The other picture is a team I played on in 2017 Kent Mud Hens. The difference is 70 years. The 1947 team played on a small field with a house close by and no restroom facility. There was a wooded area across the street. Foul balls hit to the left landed on Archwood Street. There were no lines to indicate the first and third base foul areas. This field was in Firestone Park, and I lived in North Akron. Some times I would have to catch two busses to get there. Most of the time, I peddled my bike there and back.

Now the 2017 team and picture. We are playing in the Boston Red Sock's Spring Training facilities. There are spacious dugouts with restrooms. The fans had comfortable seats, and they, too, had restroom facilities. There was a place to buy food and drinks. I, as a pitcher, became overjoyed standing on the mound and digging a little trench in front of the rubber. To stand there and look around 360 degrees was worth the trip to Fort Myers, Florida, in November. One thing pitchers had to think about was throwing a wild pitch because the distance behind the catcher is normal for the professionals but too far for old guys. A couple of times, there would be an announcer and would indicate the batter and those pitching. All this for a bunch of old guys trying to be young again. It wasn't the thrill of victory but the thrill of participating.

The teams there are made up of guys from different parts of America. The Kent Mud Hens home is Kent Ohio, and there were 8 – 10 guys from the Kent area; the others are from everywhere. It's amazing the number of tournaments for old guys during the year. I would hear guys talking about where they have played before this week and their plans for the next tournament. The league official sets up the week's schedule, so there are divisions within age groups, and each group with have a champion. I have played in the championship game, and the teams line up before the game on the foul line and listen to the National Anthem. At the end of the game, the winning team and runner up receives medals. Every team can select a "most valuable" player, and the league will provide a nice award. One year, I received that award. It's a fantasy.

LADIES

Photo by Stan Sipka

Joanne looked forwarded to going there because there were other wives to socialize with and make friends. We kidded the 6 – 8 ladies about them following us around the country like we were famous ballplayers. We did tell them they should sit in different sections, so when they cheered, it would sound like we had a big crowd following us. One comment was, "well, do something we can cheer about!"

THE EAGLES NEST IN FLORIDA

This eagle's nest near Fort Myers, Florida, was the talk of Joanne's and her friends. An Insurance Company had on their property a nest of eagles that would hatch one of more eagles each year. There were cameras on almost seven days and 24 hours. Joanne would watch and inform me when important things happen, like the appearance of one egg and a day or two later, the second egg. I knew when the eggshells were cracking; the first sight of an eaglet, and even their names or numbers. There were times I was called to watch important occurrences like the eaglet out of the shell or eating or moving around. I saw the mother and father bring food to feed the always hungry babies. Joanne said we had

eagles

to see these eagles in person. The site was a couple of miles away from our motel, and I, too, enjoyed sitting and becoming excited when one eagle flew away and returned with something in its mouth. It was nice because a nearby church provided places to park and benches to sit and relax, watching something to happen. The many visitors would comment on where they are from and how they spend time daily watching the eagles. The nest is in the tree that is behind us. You can see the large nest. We spent an hour or more watching and talking with other visitors. All had a camera, some with telephoto lenses that could take the eagle's faces and beautiful colors. Joanne found the site by typing Ft Myers's eagle cam.

MUNSON

My favorite picture is me pitching at Thurman Munson Stadium in Canton, Ohio, about 2015. I can relive the five to six seconds of motion, throwing the ball to the catcher. At the beginning of the game or start of an inning, I would look at all the players. Position my right foot on the rubber with my weight on my left foot, look for the catcher's signal, maybe rearrange my fingers, start the arm movement, move forward, push off the rubber, rotate the body, and lunge toward the plate, forcefully moving my arm and twisting the body to send the ball toward the plate. Five or six seconds of movement performed many times an inning, hoping the movements stays the same with each throw. The first thing a pitcher must do after the throw is to expect the ball to be hit at your face. I can't count the number of throws I have completed. Yes! Some didn't get to the catcher or my teammates. It's the thrill of participating. The success I had was because of the players on my team. Every position was important to win a game. I knew the guys would be upset if they made an error, but they wanted to win too. The loss of a game was possible, and it should be expected at times. Watching a Cleveland Indians' pitcher, I could feel what he was doing and say I can do that too. Not as fast but getting the ball over the plate. I was asked if I throw smoke. My reply was, "no, it's more like a slow-moving fog!"

IS THERE BASEBALL IN HEAVEN?

Photo by Joanne Sipka

This picture reminds me of the story of the two old baseball buddies sitting on a bench, reminiscing their early years. The subject came up if there's baseball in heaven. There were all kinds of comments, and it was a topic that brought out an agreement. The first one who dies is to return and let the other one know if there is baseball in heaven. Soon after, one man dies, and the other is left to sit on the bench and think about his friend. Suddenly the friend appears and tells the guy he has good news and bad news. The guy wants the good news first. "There is baseball in heaven!" was the comment. The friend on the bench smiles. What is the bad news? "You are scheduled to pitch on Wednesday!"

There I am standing on the mound on this field in Florida and imagining the field in heaven. I can not imagine advertising on the outfield wall. Next, who will be my teammates? I know my Dad will be the third baseman and bat third. He was an excellent hitter. My Uncle Johnny would be the catcher, and the others are unknown. I would see many old teammates and want them to play. I see Joe, Billy, who both died young. There is Bobby, Warren, Norman, Micky, and Donny to list a few. I am sure there is a lot of competition for players.

Donny would also pitch because he most likely is a star there. The first game I played after my 40 year lay off Donny was pitching. I was positioned at third base; the first batter hit a hard ground ball to me, and I picked it up and threw it to first. The throw was low, but our first baseman scooped it up for the out. I looked up at the sky and thanked my dad for helping me. The manager let me pitch the last inning, and we were ahead by seven runs. Donny was moved to first base. I got the first two batters out but ran into trouble and was replaced by Donny with a two-run lead. Donny got the third out, and we won. I told Donny he was the winning pitcher, and he got a safe too.

Another thought was the umpires in heaven. Guys talk that all the umpires go to the other place. I can imagine George and George, Herman there working the games. Herman was a colorful umpire, and one episode stands out with Herman. My team is playing at George Sisler's field (it was named different back then). An opposing batter hit a ball to right-center field, and it rolls past the outfield into the weeds past the edge of the field. The runner is running while the center and right fielders are looking in the weeds for the ball. The center fielder picks up the ball and throws it to the relay man, who throws it to the catcher. The ball arrives just before the runner and the catcher tags the runner out. Wait, the ball rolls out of the catcher's glove, so he is safe. Herman looks at the ball and sees it is not the game ball but a weather-beaten ball that been lost in the weeds. Herman comments if the ball had stayed in the glove, he would not notice the condition of the ball. After a few minutes, the game ball was found. The outfielders were kidded that they acted like that was the game ball.

HOWER VOCATIONAL HIGH SCHOOL

In high school at Hower Vocational High School, I made the team but was down the list of pitchers being a 14-year-old freshman, and I didn't expect anything else. We are playing Kenmore High School, reining city champs, and we can't get out of the third inning. I enter the game with guys on base and one out and losing. I get out of the inning; we score runs and won the game. I was the winning pitcher. That was the first time I had to throw 60 feet 6 inches. The distance in the 14 and under league was 56 feet. The 60 feet 6inches made me feel like I was pitching from second base. We beat the city champions. The next day the headlines in the Akron Beacon Journal had us beating Kenmore, but the reporter didn't know my first name, so I was Ed Sipka. One of my classmates told me he lives next to the star of the Kenmore team and was mad that some little (s---) beat them, and he didn't get any hits. Of course, I felt Sipka had arrived, and the other teams in the city better watch out. The next game I pitched, I couldn't get out of the first inning, but we won because their pitcher had the same problem. In one week, I experienced the thrill of victory and the agony of defeat.

In my junior year, we won the district championship and played in the old Cleveland Indians Stadium, which seats 80,000, and our crowd of 300 was lost that day. When our fans cheered, there was an echo. We lost in 11 innings.

At the end of my senior year on the team, I was disappointed because I missed the awards assembly. Assemblies are usually in the afternoon, but this one was changed to the morning. I was working in the morning and missed hearing what was said about me. My classmates said I was mentioned last, and the coach had good things to say about me.

After graduation in 1952, I played in the Greater Akron Baseball AA League until 1956 when I entered the service. I played in the Army in1957 and 1958 and was invited to try out for the Fort Belvoir Post All-Star team, but I was leaving the service to return home. I played in Akron until 1962.

I stopped playing because I was attending Kent State University, married and working as much as I could.

I'm 85 years old and a retired teacher. I was an old fashion SHOP TEACHER the taught vocational machine shop for 33 years. The reason I was a machine shop teacher is also related to baseball. When I was to enter high school, my local high school, North High, didn't have a baseball team, and I had to play. We couldn't afford St Vincent High School (Labron James's school), so I attended Hower. At Hower, I liked working with machines, playing high school ball, learning, got a job from my education, received my journeyman's "Tool Maker" card, and continued to enter Kent State University. So, baseball is responsible for who and what I am today. I would do the same because I am happy and thankful for what I have.

WAS THERE LIFE WITHOUT BASEBALL?

There was life without baseball for 40 years. I last played in 1962. I tried out for the Kent State Baseball team and had to stop because of family responsibilities. We had our first daughter, Christine, November 18, 1961, and living with my wife's parents. Main Mold and Machine helped us by allowing me to work hours and maintain my hours at Kent. I didn't read the local sports results and kept busy with KSU. In 1963 we built a house in Tallmadge, Ohio, and Cathy was born September 19. I was student teaching at Sill Middle School and experienced John F. Kennedy's assassination and watched on Sunday, Lee Harvey Osway being shot by Ruby on TV. My hours working at Main Mold increased to near a full 40 hours per week. With two daughters, the experience I had with my dad playing with a ball while in diapers didn't happen. The Cleveland Indians and Browns kept me aware of the sports scene but not the local baseball results.

We kept busy by joining the Tallmadge Jaycees, an organization for young people where the whole family met families like ours. The wives have activities that helped Joanne enjoy others and connect with other mothers. In September 1965, Carol, our third daughter, was born, and I graduated from Kent State and was hired by the Cuyahoga Falls School System. There was also a teaching position at Hower Vocational High School that has some appeal, but we thought the Falls position was better. When I signed the contract, the position was to be an Industrial Arts teacher, not Vocational.

With three daughters, just starting teaching, I had to work during the summer months to help with expenses. With no sons to play catch with and no softball programs in high school, there was no reason to think BALL. In 1969 Title 9 change sports for females in schools. Softball, basketball, and track open the door for girls to complete like the males

The first year Tallmadge High School had a girl's basketball team; the girls had to wear the boy's wrestler's warm-up jackets. The Jaycees donated money for warm-ups, and nothing happened. When we were told that money was to pay for the girls' uniforms, the guys went to a board of education meeting and expressed their displeasure, soon after new warm-up jackets were obtained.

OBTAINING SWIMMING SKILLS

The daughter's daily routine was typical as they enjoyed the various activities in and out of school. Our family and others would enjoy summers at Munroe Falls Swim Park. Our groups had a special place we would place our blankets so the adults and children would enjoy the day. We all had to be alert regarding swimming safety.

My wife and I lacked knowledge and skills in swimming safety, so we enrolled them in swim classes at the Tallmadge YMCA. Christine was eight years old, and we enrolled her in their swim programs. As she advanced in the skill groups, one instructor told us, we should think about her joining the local AAU summer swim team. We were unaware of the swim team competition. She joined the Cuyahoga Falls YMCA team that swam in a league, did well, and wanted to join the summer team. Because Chris was having a lot of fun, the other two daughters wanted to take lessons too. Cathy, age 8, was able to swim in one meet with Chris's relay because they needed another ten and under girl. Chris and Cathy were on the Falls Y team, and Carol was taking lessons and doing well. The Y has a series of classes that a swimmer takes, and after the series, the swimmer is a "shark." They then can take lessons to be a lifeguard. Chris and Cathy asked and were allowed to test out for the last program and passed. Because they were too young, they couldn't take the lifeguard class.

Carol, age 7, did win or place many of the few seven and under events. The metals and ribbons were posted on a corkboard. Soon, we had to buy another board. The girls improved their speed and skills with the four strokes – freestyle, backstroke, breaststroke, and butterfly as they advanced to the different age groups. Soon all were swimming AAU, and our family traveled to different cities and states. We took a trip to California to visit my sister, and they joined the local team – STOP - Swim Team of Placentia for one week and one meet. That was a fun meet because the STOP team beat the Mission Viejo Nadadores team by 10 points, and Cathy and Carol scored 10 points in individual events and helped the relay events. That was the Mission's team's first loss in a long time. Our girls wore black suits, and the STOP team had red. That meet was remembered a few years later when Cathy was visiting Ohio State University regarding attending OSU and may be awarded a swimming scholarship. Cathy was introduced to the coaching staff, and one lady coach mentioned she helped the Mission Viejo team. Cathy said she and her sisters swam against the Mission team a few years ago. That lady coach yelled, "YOU AND YOUR SISTERS WERE WEARING BLACK SUITS!" "Yes," was Cathy's reply. The lady coach said they wondered where you girls lived.

TALLMADGE VARSITY GIRLS SWIM TEAM

In 1979 The Ohio High School Athletic Association allowed girls swimming to be a High School Varsity team sport. The first year the girls swam in the spring sports season. The boys swam in the winter season. In 1980 Chris, a senior, and Cathy, a 10th grader (Tallmadge High School was a three year school), were able to represent Tallmadge HS. Cathy advanced to the State Championship and didn't place.

All this time, the Tallmadge Y was developing a talented girl's swim team, and eight were now in high school as 10th graders. We had a group of girls that could surprise other high schools, but Tallmadge didn't have a Varsity Girls swim team. School administrators said there was no money to have a girl's swim team. Ohio State Athletic Association had a rule that said a high school could be considered a varsity team for purposes of team points for the district meets if that school had two sanction meets with two other high school varsity swim teams. Knowing that rule, several parents developed a proposal, presented it to the school administration for approval. We did ask for three meets in case one had to be canceled. They approved the plan but said the school would not provide any money for suits. The ten girls had a car wash on Tallmadge Circle at Bob's Big Boy Restaurant and made enough to help buy the same black suits. Tallmadge HS had a faculty advisor who helped with the team from the school, and I had the team at the meet.

Photo by Stan Sipka
The picture was taken at C.T. Branin Natatorium In Canton, Ohio Front row from
left to right: Mr. Thompson, Adviser, Kari Mayfield, Carol McDanials, Denice
Dukeman, Kay Firestone, Kris Wright. Back row left to right Carol Sipka, Chris
Polefrone, Kim Holly, Patti Polefrone, Darla Carpender, Cathy Sipka

The first meet was against St. Thomas Acquirius at Malone College. The St. Thomas girls were told this was our first swim meet, and they expected to win every event – a blowout. We took five individual events and the 400-yard free relay. St Thomas swimmers and parents commented about our team's skills.

We lost to Firestone High School, and in the Cuyahoga Falls High School's meet, I listed our two girls in lanes and told the two the wrong ones. We would have scored points, but we were disqualified, and the Falls team took the points. That point difference would have given Tallmadge the win. I felt bad.

Next were two meets for the team – one was the district championship and for those who qualify, the State Championship. The Tallmadge girls' team finished 5th in the district and 8th in the Ohio State Championship. Cathy and Carol placed in each of their two events, and the 400 free relay scored points. Carol was third in the 500-yard freestyle as a 10th grader. The parents returned to tell our Board of Education the results. When we mentioned we placed 8th in the State, a board member asked us how many teams were there. We said 56. I believe the person thought we would say nine.

Carol second from left level receiving her third-place award
for the 500-yard event. Her time was 5:12.70

The following year we again swam the three meets and beat Barberton. The girls threw Mrs. Jenkins and me in the pool. Mrs. Shirley Polefrone got wind of this and left before the girls knew we had won the meet. There was one difference with the team; we had a girl diver. The girls talked a senior girl into trying out for the diving event. She was in gymnastics for years but never dove, but her gymnastic coach was a diving coach too. He liked the idea, and the two of them practice several evenings at the Cuyahoga Falls Natatorium. He said she learned the 5-6 necessary dives and dove in the three meets. She entered the district competition and performed her five dives. The diving coach tells me, "we have a problem!" I can't imagine what the problem can be. He tells me she made the 2nd round of diving and needed to dive again. The question was, should she back out or try the next round of 3 – 5 dives. The coach and girl did some quick training, and she did the new dives. She didn't make the final round because she didn't know those advanced dives. That young lady was well-liked by all, and she enjoyed the experience.

In 1982, the girls placed 10th in the district and 15th in the Ohio State Championships. Cathy received a scholarship to Youngstown State University.

In 1983 Tallmadge could not field a team because many of the swimmers graduated last year. Carol swam as an individual in the district and twice in the State meet. Carol also received a partial swimming scholarship to YSU. Another Tallmadge swimmer, Kathy Jenkins, earned a swimming Scholarship and attended Wright State University

That was the end of the first girls' Varsity Swim Team at Tallmadge, but swimming for both boys and girls did return in 20??.

THE FAMILY AND ACTIVITIES

Carol who lives in Tallmadge, Ohio, has four children, Joey and Melissa swam for Tallmadge High School, and Monica and Julia swam at Kent Roosevelt High School. The reason the kids swam at different high schools? Carol is a teacher at Kent Roosevelt, and Monica and Julia can attend the same school. Joey and Melissa stayed at Tallmadge High School.

Julia swam in the breaststroke event at the Ohio Districts and scored points for Kent Roosevelt's Swim Team. On the track team, she did the high jump and ran the short distances events as well as hurdles, plus was on the volleyball team and golf team.

Melissa swam and played tennis for Tallmadge High School and is a freshman at Kent State University.

Joey played football and scored a touchdown on a trick play near the goal line. He decided to swim instead of playing football and swam all the strokes and distances except the 500-yard freestyle event. He knew his mother's times when she swam for Tallmadge; Joey worked his way into shape to beat his mother's time in nearly every event. There was one event and time Joey did not break, and it was 5:12 minutes in the 500-yard freestyle. That was Carol's time when she placed 3rd in the Ohio State Championship in 1983. Joey kept saying, "your time is going down, MOM!" and swam the 500 yards in the last school meet. Joey went out like he was swimming the 100-yard freestyle and was up to Carol's 100-yard time. He was still even with Carol's time at the 200 and 300-yard times. The last eight laps (200 yards), took a toll on Joey and finished nowhere near his mother's time. As he exited the pool and said, his mom can keep her time. All Carol's kids have something to do with water, either coaching or lifeguards.

Cathy's boys were involved in baseball, basketball, football, track, wrestling, and swimming. Nicholas threw the shot put and discus and wrestled. Cathy's boys also are involved with water in some form. Cathy was inducted into the YSU Sports Hall of Fame and, at present, is the pool manager of the Akron General Medical Center in Green, Ohio.

Christine became a guard, coach, and a swimming official, and Katie tried many sports and had success with those sports.

Baseball appeared when Cathy's three boys – Justin, Corey and Nicklaus, and Carol's – Joey started playing sports. The relationship wasn't like what I experienced with my dad but was a gradual return to baseball and sports. I was more involved with Joey and little league. His success was in swimming and being involved with swimming and coaching swimming.

Cathy's three were all involved in sports at Kent Roosevelt. Justin ran cross-country, which helped with his speed running on the basketball court and baseball field. He lettered in all three but excelled in baseball. His skill position was catcher but often pitched. His senior year, he was awarded the Roughrider Award for the team's most valuable player. At present, he is working for the Cal Ripkin Baseball Facility in Baltimore, Maryland. He attended Tiffin University but finished at Akron University.

Corey played varsity baseball, swimming, and football teams for three years and had success in football playing both ways – middle linebacker and tight end. His interception and a 79 yard run back for a touchdown made the local sports news. It happens that Friday night was grandma Joanne's birthday, and Corey told grandma the touchdown was his birthday present to her. She said that was the nicest present she ever received. He was awarded the Roughrider Award outstanding player of the year. He is involved with water as a coach and position with the Akron General Medical Recreation Center

Nicklaus was on the swim and track teams and threw the disk and shot put. I watched him on numerous meets and was amazed at this event. He won an award in the school athletic conference for the shot put event. Joanne and I were amazed at him wrestling, and she would not go to see him at a meet. She was afraid he would get hurt. Football was his game, and he played on the line, both on offense and defense, and did well. The team didn't have a good record, but Nick played hard every down. Nick also was presented with the Roughrider Award. He is a sophomore and on the Kent State University football team.

PART 3 – YOU HAVE HOMEWORK

Your homework is the third part of my title. Included are numerous copies of assignments presented to high school, adults, and middle school students. The homework was my attempt to combine related information to working on shop equipment. Many students thought it was just time in the shop not looking in a book, but as they achieved success with the classroom assignments, they accepted what was asked of them.

Safety was my number one concern because our machines were not toys, but a small version of those in industry. In the beginning, the student was to walk-around the assigned machine and see if something is not correct that couldn't be seen from the operating position. The first safety assignment was written safety instruction, word for word, from the book. On the right side of the sheet were numbers and lines down the sheet to write the correct word, for example,

The student is to be (-1-) with any cut and obtain (-2-) to cover 1)-_____
the injury. The (-3-) also should be notified to (-4-) the covering 2)_____
3)_____

1, concerned, 2, bandages, 3, instructor, 4, inspect. The student was to read that section of the book and fill in the missing word. There were complaints the lines were too close together. I also switched a couple of sentences that made the student read the troubled area more than once. When a student would mention the mix-up, I acted surprised and commented, "I'm sorry! I did all the typing and probably was tired about that time".

There are samples of what was assigned in the math (basic, algebra, geometry, and trig), blueprint reading, and procedure sheets for jobs. Some were typed, and others were hand-drawn. I used all capital letters and required the guys to think capital too.

When you see the sheets the students were given, you can try to work on the problems. I would say, "don't work certain problems because they could be difficult," and people would try just because of my comment. I learned with middle school students telling them specific drawing problems were too complicated and don't do those; those were the ones they worked because they wanted the "hard" problems. A sixth-grade student asked me if I was using psychology on her with my telling them some problems were too challenging. I asked her which ones she worked on? – the hard problems.

THINGS I DO IN SHOP MATH

The workbook "Mathematics for Machine Technology" from the Delmar Company was used from 1969 until 1987 for the Cuyahoga Falls classes. The same book was used in the adult programs at Akron Machining Institute until 2002. The students kept the math book because the cost was included in their shop fee.

One important feature of this book was it used the basic Texas Instrument TI-30 scientific calculator in the examples. These were inexpensive and easy to obtain. There were times a student would use a different brand but realized they had to adapt to the instruction provided for the TI-30s.

R & R

Cuyahoga Falls High School required three 6-weeks and a semester grade to determine semester grade and two-semester grades for the final year grade. Assignment grades were not always passing, and that upset the student and me. When several answers were wrong, I didn't mark a failing grade; I would write R&R, which means "rework and return." An R&R required me to take time with the student to review the concept not understood. Talking to the student, I would look at the student's face to see or hear a word or sound, indicating more understanding of the concept. Sometimes I would kneel to get a better view of the face and eyes. My job was to find a magic word(s), phrase, a sentence that points to some aspect of the problem that would elicit a look or comment indicating an added understanding of the problem. This one on one could have been one on two or more. When the problems are corrected, the paper is returned, and a passing grade "70" is issued. The student can't just mark the correct answer but has to rework the steps needed to obtain the right result. When learning takes place, confidence appears. This attitude happens as I was teaching. I learned this.

REDUCE THE NUMBER OF FORMULAS TO KNOW

Handbooks are necessary for our trade because it is not possible to know what the next question might be. Formulas are one of those items needed to find dimensions or angles. The following is an example of how to reduce the need to know several formulas and know three instead of 20. Again use one letter (I use "A" for my unknown) and not "B" and "C."

BELOW are 4 pages of formulas found in the small pocket handbooks. For me, these handbooks were what I had and others working in the trade used to solve trig problems. It's obvious things are different today. These pocket handbooks are in drawers collecting dust because the calculator has eliminated the need for books such as these. I apologize for the small print but I wanted to show what was common before the mid 1970's. One of the covers (and pages inside) is dark from use in the shop by the machines. ~~The cheat sheet was an idea to help learn formulas.~~

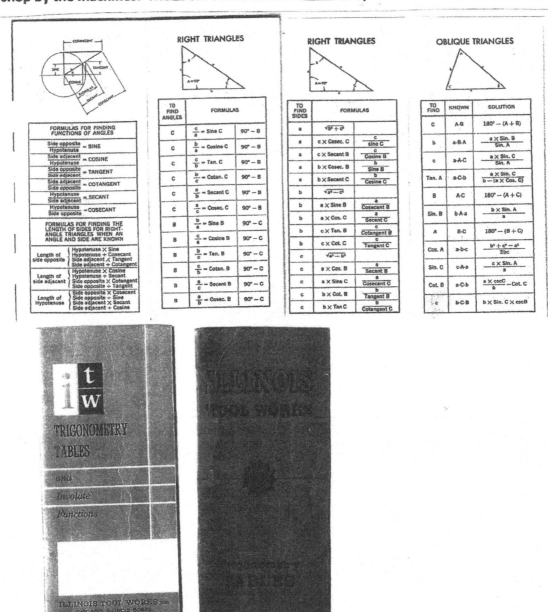

BC –MATH

The "BC" stands for "before calculators." The calculator boom in the mid-70s allowed people to complete math problems without the old methods of using pencils to add, subtract, multiply, and divide by pushing buttons and writing down the answer. It was a game-changer. I obtained a small pocket size trigonometric handbook (3 x 5) for the students to use and remember buying 100 for $25 and giving each student a book.

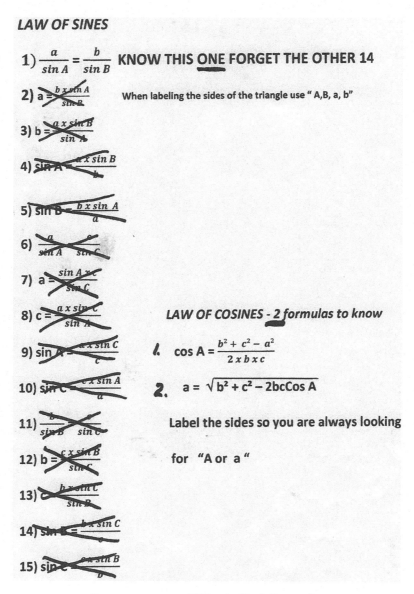

Insert courtest of Illinois Tool Company

There were ten pages of formulas and 50 or pages of values for angles. You multiplied or divided two 3 or 4 place decimal numbers look in the tables for the corresponding angle or the equivalent amount of the given angle, and use that number in a multiplication or division operation to find the answer. That was time-consuming. When we had calculators, I would, first, make the students work out a couple of problems, both ways to understand how the calculator saves time. It was stressed this quicker way was not a guarantee there would be no mistakes. Because the problem could be solved faster, a check step was to be part of the presentation. "Because everyone will know enough to become careless."

3 – 4 – 5 TRIANGLE

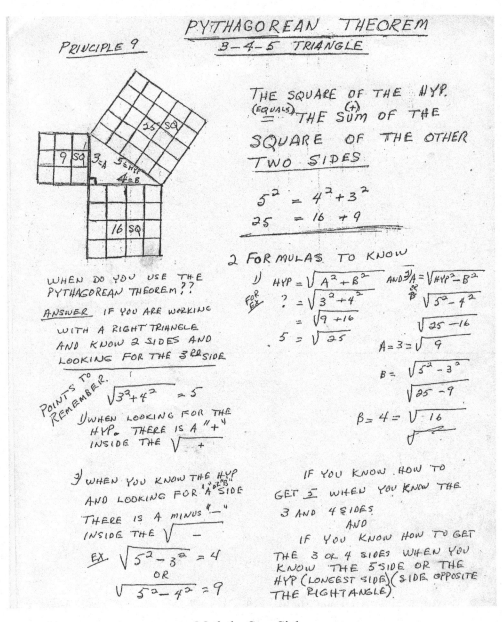

Made by Stan Sipka

One triangle I used for introduction to Trigonometry was the 3 - 4 – 5 triangle. This simple set of numbers helped with the Pythagorean Theorem (PT) and the Sine (sin), Cosine (cos), and Tangent (tan) formulas. The textbooks use A or B or C or "a – b – c) and show formulas for each letter. I found out using one capital letter (I use A) and 3 - 4 – 5 a person can minimize the number of formulas needed. When the PT was introduced, the letters were used but changed to the three numbers. Remember $3^2 + 4^2 = a$ or $A(5^2)$ or $9 + 16 = 25$; $5^2 - 3^2 = a$ or $A(4^2)$ or $25 – 9 = 16$ and $5^2 - 4^2 = a$ or $A(3^2)$ or $25 – 16 = 9$. With Sine, Cosine and Tangent use one letter. With the quickness of the calculators, the other three trig formulas Cosecant, Secant, and Cotangent, are not introduced in the beginning. Know, Sin, Cos, and Tan like they are your middle names.

SIX STEPS TO SOLVE TRIG PROBLEMS

Another idea presented was six steps in solving trig problems. There were keywords in each step to help obtain the answer. They are: 1) sketch the triangle, 2) label what you know, 3) determine what you are looking for – angle or side, 4) pick an angle to work with or look for, 5) label the sides opp, adj and hyp, 6) pick a formula that has the two sides given. These steps are on the specials sheets handed out in the beginning to show the few steps needed to solve a trig problem.

A check step was to be listed to avoid a wrong answer. Another formula in the set of 3 for each function would be the check step. As a result, two formulas out of the three would be used in each problem. If the answer was wrong and no check step, there would be 2 marked wrong.

When three formulas were introduced, the sample triangles had sides of 3 – 4 – 5 and the angles of that triangle. Simple numbers were involved.

POLAR TO RECT (P→R) & RECT. TO POLAR (R→P)

The TI calculator we used had this feature that could solve trig problems in minimal keystrokes. When p→r and r→p were introduced later, the students questioned why these weren't presented earlier? The reply was, "you have to understand what is present in the problem to use these routines." We used the completed three beginning trig assignments again using p→r and r→p to rework the problems. It was great to recheck the answers.

TEACHING TRIG TO A ROCK

I taught second-year math class in the apprenticeship program at the Akron Machining Institute in Norton, Ohio. As I greeted the students the first day, one man walks in, tells me that he can't learn math, so I should not be disappointed if he doesn't learn any math. He said, "I'm as dumb as a rock, and I won't cause any trouble." He starts to sit in the back row, but I tell him he has to sit near the front because the back row is for visitors who come to observe my performance. I ask him if I can call him "Rocky?" and he agrees. The class is once a week for 4 hours and 18 weeks. These groups of adults were great to work with, and we covered a lot of math. I tried to make them feel this would help them gain confidence, become more valuable to the company, earn more money, and not waste their time. I have handouts with steps to work problems in beginning algebra, trig, and geometry related to the machining industry. We covered the trig problem using Sine, Cosine, and Tangent formulas and the law of Sines and Cosines too. I also require a way to set-up any trig problem, and these guys did everything I asked them to do.

We are in week 16 with two more weeks to go; I mention it's time for a 10-minute break. As the guys and Rocky stand up to leave, a fellow student asks Rocky what formula did he used for problem number 6. Rocky looked at the problem, looks at the guy, and proceeded to tell him the one law of cosines by heart. He knew the formula like he knew his name. I asked him to repeat the law of cosines; he did without any hesitation. "You learned this formula, and you are as dumb as a rock?" I asked. He said even a rock could learn because of the way you present the math. Other guys also agreed with Rocky. That's what makes teaching worthwhile, and I felt good going home that evening. I stressed that I didn't want to waste their time with no effort on my part. I do check each problem and know they have family responsibilities and work long hours.

There were a few complaints because these guys felt they were benefitting from the math class even though they had homework assigned each week. One man told me all this homework interfered with his sex life. I replied I don't know what to say about that; other guys had all kinds of suggestions. One was to find a woman who knows how to do trig problems. I believe these guys felt this would help them in their companies.

MY REFERENCE SHEET OR CHEAT SHEET

The reference or cheat sheet's rule was no part of the sheet is to be seen when inside the cover of the calculator. Early in a story, a lady used a full sheet of paper for notes that folded into a small 3 x 5-inch sheet to fit inside her old style TI calculator, no part was visible when the calculator was covered.

The official name of my helping sheet was "Reference Sheet," but the students like "Cheat Sheet" better. I'm not sure when I came up with the idea, but it helped the students. I stressed it's impossible to know the hundreds of formulas used in shops and the world of work, so know a few and how to rearrange the unknown values in a few, you know. Since I assigned many trig problems, I figured a small handy sheet for trig formulas could help. I would stress to look at the problem, try to determine what to use, *THEN* check the sheet. Eventually, you will select the correct one because you would learn what's given, what you are looking for (angle or side), and what to use. The sheet would be the back-up source. As time went by, I added other formulas but in simple forms. (a copy of the sheet)

I'll explain each one (sample sheet)

180° rule = no. of degrees in a triangle

90° rule = sum of the number of degrees in a right angle (90)triangle

(N-2) x180° = no. of degrees in any polygon

MM=EE = product of the means=product of extremes (proportion)

$$\text{hyp} = \sqrt{a^2 + b^2} \qquad a = \sqrt{hyp^2 - b^2} \qquad \text{(PT)}$$

$$\text{Sine}° = \frac{opp}{hyp} \; ; \; opp = \text{hyp x Sine}°; \; opp = \frac{opp}{sine°}$$

$$\text{Cos}° = \frac{adj}{hyp} \; ; \; adj = \text{hyp x Cos}° \; ; \; hyp = \frac{adj}{cos°}$$

$$\text{Tan}° = \frac{opp}{adj} \; ; \; opp = \text{adj x Tan}° \; ; \; adj = \frac{opp}{tan°}$$

Law of sines (2 ways)

Law of Cosines #1 looking for a side

#2 looking for an angle

180 Rule; 90 Rule
(N-2) x180=Total Degrees
MxM=EE

$\text{Hyp} = \sqrt{a^2+b^2} \qquad a = \sqrt{Hyp^2-b^2}$

$\text{Sin} = \frac{Opp}{Hyp} \quad \text{Opp} = \text{Hyp} \cdot \text{Sin} \quad \text{Hyp} = \frac{Opp}{Sin}$

$\text{Cos} = \frac{Adj}{Hyp} \quad \text{Adj} = \text{Hyp} \cdot \text{Cos} \quad \text{Hyp} = \frac{Adj}{Cos}$

$\text{Tan} = \frac{Opp}{Adj} \quad \text{Opp} = \text{Adj} \cdot \text{Tan} \quad \text{Adj} = \frac{Opp}{Tan}$

$\frac{a}{Sin \angle A} = \frac{b}{Sin \angle B} \quad a \cdot Sin \angle B = b \cdot Sin \angle A$

Law of Cosines

① $a = \sqrt{b^2 + c^2 - 2bc \cdot Cos \angle A}$

② $Cos \angle A = \frac{b^2+c^2-a^2}{2bc}$

$\frac{\text{Lg. Dia.- Part Dia.}}{\text{Lg. Dia.- Small Dia.}} = \frac{\text{Part Length}}{\text{Total Length}}$

$\frac{\text{S Gear T}}{\text{L Gear T}} = \frac{\text{L Gear RPM}}{\text{S Gear RPM}}$

Circumference = πD

$\frac{\text{Arc Length}}{\text{Circumference}} = \frac{\text{Central} \angle}{360}$

Polar-Rectangular Functions for TI-36X

Adj.	Hyp.
X≈Y	X≈Y
Opp.	D.D.
3rd	2nd
R►P = Hyp.	P►R = Adj.
X≈Y = D.D.	X≈Y = Opp.

Printed in U.S.A. by

Made by Stan Sipka

Proportion - taper per inch
Proportion - RPM's (Inverse proportion)
Circumference of a circle
Proportion-find arc length and angles
NOTE = students use the other side
Polar to→ Rect and Rect to→ Polar
for other formulas and notes
This P to→ R and R to→ P

We used the 3, 4, 5 triangles to understand the PT and Sin, Cos, and Tan problems and to explain the $P \Rightarrow R$ and $R \Rightarrow P$ routine. One Sample problem we are given 3 (opp side) and 4 (adj side) sides of a right triangle and need to find the Hypotenuse (the hyp is 5) and both angles. Remember, we know the two angles are 36.86989765° and 53.13010235° (note the sum of these two angles equal 90 degrees). I write the steps in a vertical sequence to show each is separate and then go to the next step. We all had a TI 36X calculator so that the sequence would work. Other SI calculator may have this feature, but the procedure may be different.

Rectangle to Polar <u>You have the 4 and 3 sides looking for the angle</u>

- enter 4,
- 2nd function key
- enter 3 (opp side)
- 2nd function key then R⇒P The display will show "5", the Hyp
- 2nd function key then ⇔ The display will show 53.130....° the angle of the adj side
- enter the X ⇔ Y (obtaining the third angle)
- enter "-" (subtraction 53.130.. becomes -53.130)
- enter "+ 90 (you are going to add 90 to a – 53.130... to obtain the 3rd angle.)
- enter = and you will see the 3rd angle of 36.8698...

This procedure is quick, and it's suitable for checking answers. The reverse is also fast where you have the hyp and one angle and have to find a side or sides. I demonstrate this by asking a student to give me two sides, and I will tell him the hyp and the two angles in less than 30 seconds, and tell them my numbers and they check the "long" way. After the guys work a few problems, they want to know why I didn't show them this before. I tell them this sequence doesn't work with every problem but will work with certain information, and they must look at what is given, and maybe this can be used. I use the book to show the problems in the three assignments that allow one of these two to be used instead of us doing the problem the long way – Sin, Cos, or Tan. The term opposite and adjacent means "X" and "Y" or rectangular coordinates, and the hyp and radius are the same, and angles are polar coordinates. I mentioned if they get good at this, they can impress their friends or win a bet.

I remembered a gimmick to remember what sides are used in each formula

Opp ---------O------- Oscar   • $\sin° = \dfrac{opp}{hyp}$

Hyp ---------H------- had

Adj ---------A------ a

• $\text{cosine} = \dfrac{adj}{hyp}$

Hyp --------H------- heap

Opp --- -----O------ of

• $\text{tangent} = \dfrac{opp}{adj}$

Adj --------A------- apples

"Oscar had a heap of apples" was the way to associate what two sides went with each trig formula. I had a few guys tell me other versions that helped them learn. I forgot those versions!

I learned ways to help the guys attack a trig problem, show their work, and check the answer. As they begin working, the foreman may not trust the new guy with solving a dimension because a wrong answer could mean scrap, not 5 points off a grade.

SPECIAL HANDOUT FOR TRIG

I also made up a sheet for the trig problems that included the six steps, formulas, and squares. I wanted the students to do a problem in as few detailed steps and check their answers. At first, some guys would complain, but they realized this method was quick and prevented mistakes. On the top left side of the handout were my six steps to solve trig problems. After a couple of assignments, these steps became automatic. On the top right were the three basic formulas: Sin, Cos, and Tan. I didn't list Cosine, Secant, or Cotangent because they were used less with the calculator. The squares were there and too small for some students. Each problem was to be solved in three steps, plus a check step. The calculator did the math, and the student listed the answers. Listing a problem in an orderly fashion was important if another person did the same problem and got a different answer. A couple of times, I changed one dimension slightly on a couple of questions. The answers were announced and then asked who had the correct answers? Those who had different answers were busy checking their work, and speaking out their answer is correct. I would say check out the work and see where the difference occurred. I would have to apologize for this nasty assignment.

We selected the math workbook, "Mathematics for the Machining Technology," from the Delmar Company when we entered the new building in 1970. That book was used every year in high school, in the adult programs and apprentice programs. I knew the book by heart, which problems were wrong, and how to correct those problems. In the early 1970s, there was no reference to calculators, but later editions had sections related to calculators and metric measuring systems. Each year I was able to improve my handouts regarding the problems which allowed more to be completed; and realized that many formulas could be reduced, but steps had to be understood. One example was the drawings for a triangle had capital letters -A, B, C - to represent the angles and lower case letters the sides – a, b, c-. Each of the three-letter has three formulas to know. My instruction was to use just one letter, like "A" for the angle you were looking for and not "B" or "C." List, the unknown with the same letter, when sketching the triangle. Forget the other two letters. Know only the formula for finding "A." There were six steps to solve a trig problem:

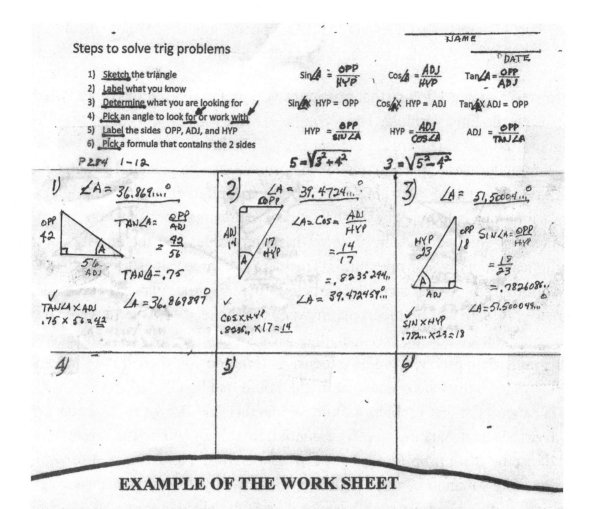

EXAMPLE OF THE WORK SHEET

The above shows how I try to simplify trig problems. The 6 steps on the top left indicates what I feel is quick and easy way to arrive at the answer. On the right are the basic 3 formulas and 2 others related to the basic 3. Each formula contains 3 values – 2 numbers and 1 angle. Each can be used. There is also the 2 Pythagorean formulas that can be used if the student feels this is a better way to arrive at the answer. The squares are to contain the work. The sheet is used to find one answer, graded and returned to be used for finding all the dimensions plus a check step. It's stressed to use one letter in each problem. I use the letter – "A, a". Another item that is stressed is sketch the triangle as it appears on the drawing or assignment. Don't reposition it to your favorite position.

Made by Stan Sipka

The six steps to solve a trig problem are:

1. <u>sketch</u> the triangle.
2. "<u>label</u> what you know." (List the information)
3. "<u>determine</u> what you are looking for (an angle? or side?)"
4. "<u>pick</u> an angle or side to look for" (pick only one)

5. "label your sides OPP, ADJ, HYP (opposite, adjacent hypotenuse)
6. "pick a formula that contains 2 of the sides. (o & h, or a & h, or o & a)

In step 5, you are to use that one letter you prefer and not the other two. So, it's always the same formula. The formulas for sine (opp / hyp), cosine (adj / hyp) tangent (opp an/ adj) were on the handouts. The handout had the formulas on top, and under were nine squares for the problems to be placed. In each square was to be a sketch of the triangle and only one capital letter (for the angle) and words like "opp, adj, hyp"(for the three sides). Below that formula, you substitute numbers for the two sides in place of the letter values and the answer (=) to a multiplication or division operations. There are just three things for each triangle. I also required a check step placed below to verify the answer. The students were told if there was an incorrect answer and no check step, there were be two wrong answers. The rule was "calculate twice, machine once." A mistake on a job from a math problem can be expensive. Imagine you owned the shop and a worker made a mistake because of math, would that be OK?

The details of that problem should be together and shown in the square, not all over the sheet. Writing steps is essential, imagine you and the foreman both did the same math problem and got different answers, and you're sure you are correct. The foreman can see your work and how you got your answer. Your detailed work is also important because if you tell the foreman, "you're wrong!" he might think you are a wise guy and be on his "???? list." You then show him your "problem development" (PD) he then can view his and your work and see where the difference occurred.

One example of PD, happen in the adult program where problems required several steps to find the answer. The student was to list his steps and the solution. The first answer will be needed to work another, and this done several times. If the final answer was wrong, it would be easy to back-track the steps to see where the error occurred. I marked a problem wrong, and no work showing how that answer was obtained. The student told me the problem was right but had no way to show his work, so he took the next guy's paper and walked through the other guy's steps to show me why his problem was correct. The complaining student got to the end and noticed a different right answer. The student stopped, looked, and walked away. After that, his assignments were detailed.

Classes were able to work on triangles other than a right triangle. Again the student was encouraged to use one letter (I told them I always use "A") when they sketch the triangle. There is one law of sine and two laws of cosine formulas. Using one letter, you only need three formulas. Again I wanted the students to use the six steps and the handouts with the squares. Here the student would use both formulas, one to get the answer and the other to check the answer. All three were on the handout and "cheat-sheet," and that is why "Rocky" knew them by heart. The students knew the formulas were on the handout but were told to do the six steps and determine or guess what formula to use based on the information on the sketch, then look at the cheat sheet as back up. If their choice matched what was listed, do the math calculations with the calculator for the answer and then the check step. I argued that the companies want the workers to work a problem quickly and to check the answer because a calculator helps the worker do both. Calculators save a lot of time, but this quickness could lead to simple mistakes like hitting the wrong keys and not spotting the error. The students range from just out of high school to grandfathers, men, and women.

At the open house, for the adult evening class, a mother comes in and tells me her son would sit at the table doing his math and could be heard cursing. He didn't like my demand to write the problem my way, why not just the answers? The mother told him he should quit if he were not learning anything; the kid continued and did use the system. I told his mother to start a cuss jar.

Our book had a variety of geometric principles and trig problems. I had used and embellished over the years; in fact, I also had a couple from the Ford Motor Apprentice program. The first three trig assignments were in the book. All problems were to be placed on the handout that had nine squares, one for each triangle. The reason for the small space was each problem needs 3 or 4 steps, and it's easy to follow the results.

The sample sheet has three examples. The numbers obtained from the math operations,

$(+, -, x, \div, \sqrt{}, x°)$ from the calculator, are placed in the space.

The first assignment had 12 triangles, all looking for the angle. The second assignment had ten triangles looking for one or both sides. The third assignment had eight triangles to looking for angles and sides. These 30 problems were placed on these sheets, along with a check step and the PT. Yes, some were placed on the back, but the simple steps were used for all problems. It was three steps to the answer and one step to check the answer. These three assignments were used again when we introduced polar to rect., and rect. to polar.

The next set of problems side dimensions were the unknown. One sample is included where you see a before and after to help you to construct lines needed to understand the triangles to be solved. On my handouts, you can see clues as to how to break down the shape to obtain the triangle(s). Letters were used to identify tangent points, intersections, and clues to where the triangles appear. Knowledge of geometric principles was valuable. The book would list a principle and have sample problems illustrating that

THE PYTHAGOREAN THEOREM (PT)

The Theorem or formula is part of the cheat sheet. It starts by listing $a^2 + b^2 = c^2$; when talking about this, I mentioned we would use $3^2 + 4^2 = 5^2$ instead of $a^2 + b^2 = c^2$. A person will understand this formula with numbers $3^2 + 4^2 = 5^2$ and $5^2 - 3^2 = 4^2$ and $5^2 - 4^2 = 3^2$. In trig 3, 4 and 5 help learning sine, cosine, and tangent right angle trig problems. In the $3 - 4 - 5$ triangle, we would use 3 for the opposite side (opp), 4 for the adjacent side (adj), and 5 for the hypotenuse (hyp) to find angles and sides. A check step was required, too, because it's easy to include a wrong number and not be aware and assume the answer is correct. With a check step, the formula will be used twice.

I remember this theorem when I saw the movie "Wizard of Oz" when the straw man received his brain near the end of the movie. He said several things he just learned and one of them was "$a^2 + b^2 = c^2$" I learned the Pythagorean Theorem from the Nuns at St Hedwig's grade school. The seventh and eighth grades were in the same room, and one nun taught both classes. Both classes had 6 or 7 students, so it was almost like a private school. This nun was strict and controlled the students. If that nun were teaching today and doing her favorite discipline activities, she would be arrested for student brutality. Those hits over the knuckles with a wooden ruler or pulling the short hair around the ears can produce fear of women in black dresses. I'm just kidding; there were times when I deserved the hair being pulled and the ruler. That's what the parents of those days thought was suitable for their child and children. Those two years introduced me to the PT and I, received a lot of practice using the PT, including how to pronounce the word Pythagorean.

 One day in an adult machining class, a student mentioned his mother, a math teacher, told her son to correct me with the pronunciation of Pythagorean. I stopped and listened to her version (path-a-gorean). I mentioned his mother might be correct, but I don't want the nun mad at me if I use your mom's version. YOU DON'T MESS WITH A NUN!.

30 + 10 = DOES NOT EQUAL 40!

10° + 30° = DOES NOT EQUAL = 40° (using a sine bar)

Here's a drawing to describe why 10° + 30° does not equal 40° with a sine bar setup. This happen to two of us working side by side machining cavities and cores. The quarter of a circle represents 90° with the 0° position on the horizontal (X axis) line. Lines are drawn to represent 2 adjacent angles: 1° & 2°, 44° & 45°, 88° & 89°. There is a difference of 1 degree between each. The sine function represents the vertical (opposite) distance. On the drawing the vertical distances are listed to 8 decimal places. If you subtract the following : sine 2° - sine 1° and sine 45° - 44° and 89° - 88° the differences are NOT the same even though the difference between numbers is the same -- one degree. That's why we didn't machine the required 40° The angled that was machined was **42.349..°** or **42° 21'** not 40°

Sin 2° = .034899497   Sin 45° = .707106787   Sin 89° = .999847695
- Sin 1° = .017452406   - Sin 44° = .69465837   - Sin 88° = .999390827
    .017447091   .012448411   .000456868

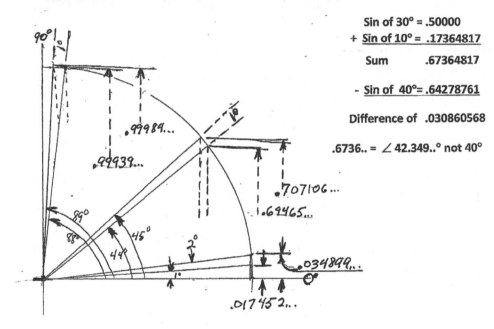

Sin of 30° = .50000
+ Sin of 10° = .17364817

Sum   .67364817

- Sin of 40°= .64278761

Difference of .030860568

.6736.. = ∠ 42.349..° not 40°

A sine bar is a tool used to machine angles to exact angle requirements. A sine plate is larger and can be clamped to a base and allows the work to be clamped to the plate.

The above statement would make everyone want to correct me in my addition. I experienced that 30+10 does not equal 40 while working at Main Mold & Machine while attending KSU. Two of us were working on a job; I was machining the cavities, and Mitchell machining the cores. The parts required a matched machined surface of 40 degrees. We were to use a sine bar to obtain the 40 degrees. The procedure is to figure the required height to set under the end of the sine bar to obtain a 40-degree angle. Mitch had two blocks he had used many times for these two angles – 10° and 30° height blocks. We both set the two blocks under the bar and machined the surfaces. We finish and place the cavity and core together and the 40° surfaces "DID NOT MATCH!!" Mitch and I look at each other and wonder what we or one of us did wrong. A foreman also can't figure out why the two mating surfaces aren't touching. Mr. Donavan walked by, looks at the problem, sees our setup, with the two blocks that should give us a 40-degree angle, and said you must not put a 30, and 10° blocks on each other because the total degree is more than 40°. We both learned something that day, and I said I would tell every student that 30 + 10 doesn't 40.

Here's why 10+ 30 doesn't = 40. The sine of 10° = .17364….; sine of 30° = .50000…. If you place the two on top of each, you get a distance of .67364…. Now the sine of 40° = .64278…. When I present this information, I ask the students to determine what angle did Mitch and I machine? If you find the angle, you would see we had an angle of 43.34° or 43° 20'.

While I'm writing the numbers above, I also had to explain to the students that the two angles listed above are both being used in industry, and you must be careful what measuring system you are using. The inch system we have and still uses degrees, minutes, and seconds (DMS). The metric measuring system uses degrees and decimal parts of a degree (DD).

SLIDE RULES (SR)

My introduction to SR was in my High School's Drafting class, where each student used a small rule for a couple of days working simple math problems. You would see pictures of engineers using slide rules, and it looked like a valuable tool. As the calculator burst on the scene, the slide rules fell out of importance because a faster device was now available. I have an expensive slide rule that I use for demonstration and can show the guys progress by holding an SL and calculator next to each other. The calculators we used had logarithm features, and I would make assignments they had to use the logarithm keys to solve problems. In algebra, we spent time learning exponents and radical operations because of their inclusion in the formulas we use. At Ferriot Machine Company, a guy would use logs to solve trig problems because he didn't want the guys copying his work.

LOGARITHMS AND EXPONENTS

Rules for exponents: (and Logs too!)

When adding and subtracting the same values with exponents === YOU DO NOTHING ex. $2^2 + 2^3$ DO NOTHING or $2^3 - 2^2 = $ <u>DO NOTHING</u>

When multiplying common values with exponents ==== YOU ADD THE EXPONENTS ex. $2^2 \times 2^3 = 2^{2+3} = 2^5$ <u>ADD EXPONENTS</u>

When you divide common values with exponents = YOU SUBTRACT THE EXPONENTS, ex. $\dfrac{2^4}{2^3} = 2^{4-3} = 2^1 = 2$ <u>SUBTRACT EXPONENTS</u>

When you take a root of a value ====== YOU DIVIDE THE EXPONENTS ex. $\sqrt[2]{4^8} = 4^{\frac{8}{2}} = 4^4$ OR $\sqrt[2]{2^5} = 2^{5 \div 2} = 2^3$ <u>DIVIDE EXPONENTS</u>

When you take a value to an indicated power ==== YOU MULTIPLY THE EXPONENTS ex. $\left(4^2\right)^3 = 4^{2 \times 3} = 4^6$ <u>MULTIPLY EXPONENTS</u>

EXPONENTS When you have a zero (0) exponent === <u>the value is one</u>, ex.. $456^\circ = 1$, $A^\circ = 1$, $\dfrac{4^3}{4^3} = 4^{3-3} = 4^0 = 1$ <u>VALUE IS ONE</u>

EXPONENTS When you have a negative exponent = $A^{-2} == \dfrac{1}{A^2}$

$$\frac{A \cdot A \cdot A}{A \cdot A \cdot A \cdot A \cdot A} = \frac{A^3}{A^5} = A^{3-5} = A^{-2} \text{ OR } \frac{1}{A^2}$$

EXPONENTS An exponent can be a mixed number, fraction or decimal, == ex. $A^{2.3}$ $A^{\frac{3}{4}}$ A^{612}

EXPONENTS Change a fractional exponent to a radical root or radical to a fractional exponent. Ex. $8^{\frac{2}{3}} = \sqrt[3]{8^2} = 4$ or $\sqrt[2]{5^3} = 5^{\frac{3}{2}}$ $\sqrt[2]{25^1} = 25^{\frac{1}{2}}$

RATIO AND PROPORTION

Ratio is the comparison between two like quantities by division. Both terms must be expressed in the same unit of measure and reduced to the lowest terms. Ratios are shown in two ways

- A colon is between the two terms, such as 3: 4. The ratio is read as 3 is to 4.
- With a division sign separating the two numbers $3 \div 4$ or $\frac{3}{4}$.

PROPORTION is the comparison of two ratios and expressed in two ways.

- 3 : 4 :: 6 : 8, which is read as 3 is to 4 as 6 is to 8.

- $\frac{3}{4} = \frac{6}{8}$ write in fraction form

A proportion consists of 4 terms. The first and last are called *extremes* in the above example, 3 and 8 are extremes. And the second and third are called *means*, 4 and 6 are the means. You can see the product of the means = the product of the extremes. If the problem is written as two fractions, you can see you cross multiply. I have this on the cheat sheet as MM=EE. To express the formula in simple terms, you "cross multiply the two given and divide by the single value.

The above is a direct proportion. There is also an inverse proportion that can be used in the shop. The best example of inverse proportion is gears and RPMs (revolutions per minute). Imagine we have a 40 tooth gear meshed with a 20 tooth gear. A motor is driving the 40 tooth gear at 400 RPMs; you see a 40 : 20 ratio. In direct proportion, the RPMs of the 20 tooth gear would be 200. That is not possible because one turn of the 40 tooth gear will turn the 20 tooth gear two times. The formula would be, small gear : large gear:: the large gear RPMs: small gear RPMs, 20 : 40 :: 200 : X(small gear RPMs). Using the MM=EE formula, we would multiply 40 X 200 and, by 20. The result would be 800 divided by 20 = 400 RPMs for the small gear. The unit had a variety of direct and indirect problems.

We would return to ratio and proportion when we begin trig and understand the formulas. Every trig formula, sine, cosine, and tangent is a proportion problem.

Sine would be sin∠A : 1 :: Opp. : Hyp. In trig, you will see, sin∠A = opp. divided by hyp. Cosine, tangent, cotangent, secant, and cosecant are the same.

ALGEBRA FOR MACHINING INDUSTRY

We started with the basic math then advanced to algebra. My philosophy was to work with as few formulas as possible and know how to rearrange these formulas. I had special handouts to help the students with problems in the book. Having the ability to rearrange formulas, you don't need to memorize hundreds of formulas, just a few that you can rearrange. The following are the procedures for solving equations consisting of combined operation:

- work with parentheses
- combine values on both sides and combine terms
- use "+" addition and "-"subtraction to arrange unknown terms on one side and known terms on the other side
- combine like terms
- if needed use the multiply and division
- lastly, apply the power and root operations

Each student is required to write in abbreviations what they used to arrive at the next step. It was stressed, when you view the problem, look at every feature of the problem like exponents, radical signs, multiplication, and division, and addition and subtraction. Think of the sequence based on what you see and the rules listed above. LOOK AND THINK! It was also mentioned when you learn these steps, you will have to think the opposite when you work problems where you rearrange literal values. Today everyone has experienced a math problem on Facebook, where there are numbers and different signs of operations and challenging a reader to solve the "simple" problem.

The first weeks of senior math start with working combined operation problems. The given problem was to be listed, the next step was to be listed under the given problem, and only one operation completed. (Yes, more than one thing can be done but, until confidence is built do one thing at a time) Eventually, the features in the problem would disappear until the final answer – a cone. The guy had to know the order of operations and arrive at the answer.

The student also lists his keystrokes on the calculator to check his work going from start to finish <u>vertically.</u> Both indicate the correct problem. I called this "Problem Development" or PD. Students were cautioned that certain features had to be keyed in a certain way. One step was written under the previous step; there was a vertical line of numbers and letters with the answer to the last item. I said I don't just want the answer.

Included are five problems and the vertical listing of the keystrokes to help the student to check work or arrive at an answer. I gave all the answers, and the guys were to list the sequence used with their calculators to get their answers. Certain arrangements have to be understood.

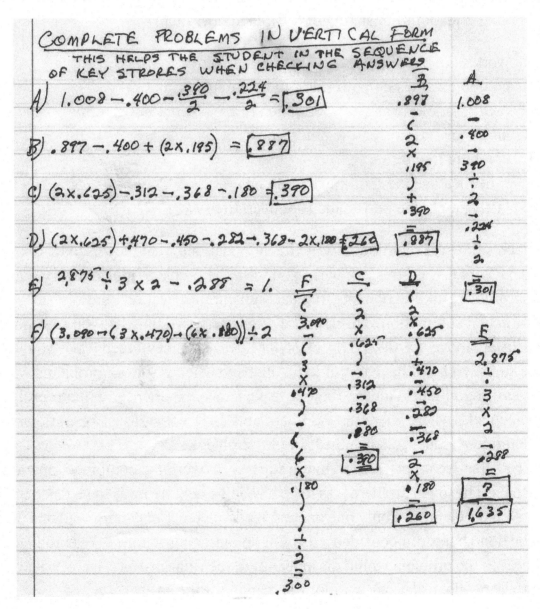

Insert by Stan Sipka

COMMUNICATION IS IMPORTANT

Tell me without a sketch or hand movements some object in another place in your house. They all remembered times when they could not understand someone's verbal directions. I told them an example of how to keep from making mistakes when you are given verbal instructions. Write down what you are told to do. A former student came to visit and said he was going to quit because the foreman was always yelling at him. He was to prepare stock for machining and would use saws to cut and deliver the pieces to the workers in the shop. He would be instructed to cut "seven pieces 10 inches long". He did and was told he cut the wrong sizes. It was to be "ten pieces 7 inches long". I suggested he have a pencil and note pad handy, and when told number and sizes, write down what he heard and repeat the numbers back to the foreman. Communicating is important.

THE OTHER KINDS OF PROBLEMS

The next section is where you rearrange a formula to arrive at the new formula. The students are shown the pages of formulas in the Machinist and pocket handbook they may need. If you can rearrange formulas, you can forget 90% of those listed. The following is the Order of Operation involving rearranging of equations:

- Grouping symbols ( ), parentheses; ÷ division bar, $\sqrt{}$ radical symbols

- $\sqrt{}$ $x°$ *Roots and Powers*

- "x" Multiplication and, "÷ division
- "+" Addition and "-" subtraction

One handout had several arrangements starting with simple to hard. The beginning required one operation to others that needed many steps.

1. Provide simple numbers to the original problem like:"a+ b= c."
2. Use "5 for a" and "2 for b"; therefore, "c would be 7".
3. Rearrange the formula for "a" and "b."
4. It should look like "a = c − b" and "b = c − a."
5. To check if this rearranging is correct, substitute "5 and 2 and 7."

6. The rearrangement is correct. Each problem is more involved, but the same rule applies to substitute numbers for the letters in the original formula, arrive at an answer, and use it when you arrive at the new rearranged formula. If "5 + 2 = 7," you have repositioned the formula correctly.

When the student does one step at a time, he will find the last problem is one of the two laws of cosine and how it changes to the other law of cosine; thus, they learn the two law of cosine formula

Another level of learning is to list <u>how a problem was solved</u>. The student was to indicate what was done to rearrange the given formula using abbreviated words and symbols followed each changed line.

$(6.12 \times 3)^2 \div (2^2 + 16 - 12)$ given
$(18.36)^2 \div (2^2 + 16 - 12)$ (mult. 6.12 x 3)
$(337.0896) \div (2^2 + 16 - 12)$ (sq. 2)
$(337.0896) \div (4 + 16 - 12)$ (sq 2)
$(337.0896) \div (20 - 12)$ (+ 4 +16)
$337.0896 \div 8 = \underline{42.1362}$ ($\div$ 8 into 337.0896)

The student could do two operations at the same time, but if there were some concerns, just do one step at a time. The hard part is for the student to be patient and do one thing at a time. Be careful because a mistake on a job could cost money, not a lower grade on an assignment. It was stated, when you believe you are good enough, hurry and do multiple steps, mistakes happen. There's a saying, "you will know enough to become careless!"

NOTE – THERE WERE 4 MORE PROBLEMS ON THE BACK

Rearranging Formulas
Show development

NAME

1) Solve for B, C

$$A = \frac{B}{C}$$

$B = 10$
$C = 2$
$A = 5$

$CA = B \quad (\times BSC)$

$C = \frac{B}{A} \quad (\div BSA)$

$2 = \frac{10}{5} \checkmark$

2) Solve for B, C, D

$D = 20; C = 2, D = 4, A = 14$

$$A = \frac{B}{C} + D$$

$A - D = \frac{B}{C} \quad (-D \; BS)$

$C(A-D) = B \quad (\times C \; BS)$

$C = \frac{B}{(A-D)} \quad (\div (A-D) BS)$

$D = A - \frac{B}{C} \quad (-\frac{B}{C} \; BS)$

$4 = 14 - \frac{20}{2} \checkmark$

3) Solve for B, C, D, E

$$A = \frac{B}{C} - \frac{D}{E}$$

$A + \frac{D}{E} = \frac{B}{C} \quad (+\frac{D}{E} BS)$

$C(A + \frac{D}{E}) = B \quad (\times C \; BS)$

$C = \frac{B}{(A+\frac{D}{E})} \quad (\div (A+\frac{D}{E}) BS)$

$\frac{D}{E} + A = \frac{B}{C} \quad (+\frac{D}{E} BS)$

$\frac{D}{E} = \frac{B}{C} - A \quad (-A \; BS)$

$D = (\frac{B}{C} - A) \quad (\times E \; BS)$

$\frac{D}{\frac{B}{C} - A} = E \quad (\div (\frac{B}{C} - A) BS)$

4) Solve for B, C, D

$$A = \frac{2B}{3C} + 4D$$

$A - 4D = \frac{2B}{3C}$

$3C(A-4D) = 2B$

$\frac{3C(A-4D)}{2} = B$

$3C(A-4D) = 2B$

$\frac{3C(A-4D)}{2} = 2B$

$3C(A-4D) = 2B$

$C = \frac{2B}{3(A-4D)}$

$A - \frac{2B}{3C} = 4D$

$\frac{A - \frac{2B}{3C}}{4} = D$

5) Solve for B, C, D

$$A = \frac{B}{C+D}$$

$A(C+D) = B$

$C+D = \frac{B}{A}$

$C = \frac{B}{A} - D$

$D = \frac{B}{A} - C$

6) Solve for B, C, D

$$A = \frac{B-D}{C}$$

$CA = B-D$

$CA + D = B$

$D = B - CA$

$CA + D = B$

$CA = B - D$

$C = \frac{B-D}{A}$

7) Solve for a

$$\cos \angle A = \frac{c^2 + b^2 - a^2}{2 \cdot c \cdot b}$$

$2 \cdot c \cdot b \cdot \cos \angle A = c^2 + b^2 - a^2$

$a^2 \cdot 2 \cdot c \cdot b \cdot \cos \angle A = c^2 + b^2$

$a^2 = c^2 + b^2 - 2 \cdot c \cdot b \cdot \cos \angle A$

$a = \sqrt{c^2 + b^2 - 2 \cdot c \cdot b \cdot \cos \angle A}$

(*the law of cosines*)

GEOMETRY AND TRIG FOR THE MACHINING INDUSTRY

In the 1970s and 1980s, Numerical Control (NC) was typical. But, the rapid transition to Computer Numerical Control (CNC) evolved, and companies were producing more with fewer workers because knowledge was feeding this growth. The old NC control units were the size of a large home refrigerator that used paper tape with punched holes to control movement. Today the control units are like small microwave units or computer screens. Knowing geometric principles was a critical catalyst for this growth. The part description is typed into a particular program that transfers the data into the motion of cutters, tables, and machine features so that there is continuous movement at high feed and speed rates. When you see a spindle turning at 20,000 RPM's and the table moving 200 inches a minute, you can understand there is little or no heat from friction and notice the surface is almost free of marks that have to be benched to part standards. The compressed air is to blow the chips away. These features are present now and will improve and become more efficient. I'm a guy from the 1960s-80s and speechless when I see what is being done now. Can I learn how to run one of these machines where you don't turn handles just push keys on a keyboard? When you turn a handle you feel, see, hear and sometimes get burnt by the chip, now you see and hear the cutting looking through a break-proof window or a mirror, and watch information flashing on a screen.

I present the units from our textbook and add extra features collected over the years. If you were in my first classes, you would not have seen what is presented now. I mentioned, "teaching was an education," and I learned from my teaching and transfer that knowledge to the students. I will include a few examples of my other problems and challenge those reading this to work the problems. Many times the instructions were "DO NOT DO SPECIFIC PROBLEMS BECAUSE THEY ARE DIFFICULT." Those requests were almost a sure guarantee those problems are worked. I know that it is sneaky because I was told this many times.

GEOMETRIC & TRIG ADVANCE PROBLEMS

"Before and After" problems illustrated how geometric principles were used to solve dimensions. The before view is given, but lines and numbers have to be added to see details needed to explain how to obtain the dimension(s). Steps appear to be worked, which adds to other steps requiring calculations. It's essential to work and list these steps in a way that shows problem development. Listing details and steps also can be helpful if you and another person working the problem have answers that don't match. Backtracking can show where and who had a different answer on the way to a final answer.

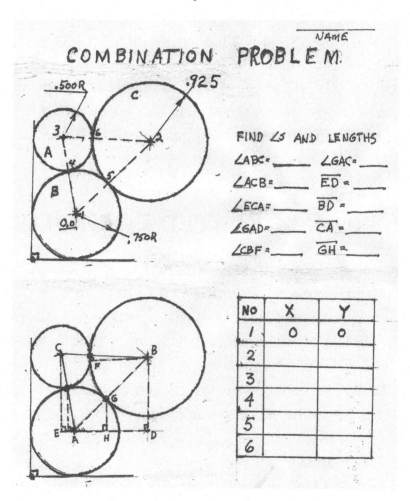

BINARY NUMBERS

I include problems in the binary number system because it is essential to know how easy it is to understand. I'm sure people will disagree, but having a basic knowledge of this will help us understand how computers work. The TI calculators had features dealing with binary as well as the textbook. I would show samples of NC paper tapes used to control NC machines and try to "read" the tape. We tried writing numbers and using the calculators to see the conversions in both directions. House numbers, the grade they wanted, their grandparents' ages (guess) were put in binary numbers for practice. The calculator was used to show how fast and slow the TI was by working easy and involved operations. When you push the number 7 key, the calculator knows binary number 7 and combined with other numbers or operations computes answers, and returns to numbers we recognize. The time it took to complete the involved math problem was because of the capacity of the TI. To demonstrate speed, we multiply a three place number and a one place number and see the answer quickly. Next, we take a large number ex. 234^{23} and notice the few seconds needed to arrive at an answer. We talked about "pixels" regarding screens on doors and televisions and each function related to the picture on the screen. Our latest textbook had a unit on binary and binary-decimal systems. The binary-decimal is used to control CNC machines.

CLASSROOM RELATED INFORMATION

Both the junior and senior classes had one period of related instruction in a classroom. The junior class was introduced to basic mathematics, blueprint reading, and shop procedures. The seniors were involved with advanced machine operations and the use of attachments that required time in the classroom to introduce the material. One example was the introduction of the dividing head for milling of the angular surfaces on the tap wrench. The attachments and math involved were started in the classroom and then in the shop on the unit. The dividing head allows machining of multiple equally spaced sides; an example is a simple gear. This attachment was used when we machined a ¾ hexagon on the end of the threaded shaft of the grinder vice and the sloped surfaces on the tap wrench. Instead of showing each one, we had a related class when the first boy was ready to machine the nut or sides. It was mentioned that that attachment required understanding of fractions and mixed numbers and not decimal numbers due to the nature of different angles or number of sides.

One example of what can be done with a dividing head is to make a drum-like those in music boxes. Short pins are located along a cylinder at planed locations when the pins meet a leaf of metal, causing it to bend and vibrate for a distinct sound.

MATERIALS

We also had classroom discussions when we were doing heat treating, case hardening, and shrink fitting. The students were introduced to the characteristics of water, oil, and air-hardening steels. I had several samples of steel and used the grinders to notice the sparks from the different steels. The steel we received from Akromold for the vise was P-20 - pre-harden steel, and we discussed this material and considerations when machining this steel. It was stressed that the worker couldn't change the material; he just has to understand how to machine what he was given. Cast iron was one topic for several sessions and how to recognized and machine CI. The guys were told to ask questions at their job site and even take notes if there were a lot of steps to follow and know what they were machining.

TOOL AND CUTTER GRINDER

We required each student to sharpen end mill cutters on the tool and cutter grinder. We didn't expect to sharpen all our end mills because the sharpening process is complicated. The guys were to understand how the cutter produced a chip and the required angles. We had an air bearing cylinder where the cylinder would float on compressed air to allow the person to drag the cutter over the guide with no effort. We used glass wax to clean the cylinder and avoid touching the surface because a fingerprint would interfere with the cylinder floating.

We arranged to have our cutters sharpened by an outside company because this requires skills a person must accumulate over time. We had high-speed steel cutters no carbide cutters up to 1987

SHRINK FITS

Shrink fits was another method of fitting parts together. We would try to fit the stationary handle of the tap wrench to the body using this procedure. The diameter of the solid end of the handle would not enter the hole. The coefficient of heat expansion was introduced, and data was found in the Machinist's Handbook. We had no trouble heating the body to expand the hole end but had trouble cooling the end of the handle. We would take the handle to the Home Economics

Kitchen, and they would place it in the freezer section of their refrigerator. We did get a little shrinkage. Dry ice would have been better cooling the piece, but that was out of the question. We had to hurry with the handle from the Home Ec. Area and slide the end into (hopefully) in the body. Some fit, and some didn't, but this was an experience for everyone. If the fit didn't work, we would pin the two together and bench the pin, so it's not visible. That was another experience that required benching. My experience with heat treating at Sackmann's and bench work at other companies was transferred to these guys.

FILE HARD

I learned at Sackmann's how to check pieces that were hardened or not harden with a worn metal file, run it over a piece of steel to see if it is hard or soft. A file is extremely hard, and if the worn file is moved over a piece of steel and can remove a sliver of the steel, the steel is not hardened but soft. If the part is hard, the file will slide over and not remove any metal. This test was used after the student harden his 1x2x3 blocks. We also mentioned a hardened piece of steel would sound different if the part is struck (lightly) with a hammer. We would show this by hitting two pieces, one harden and one soft.

Another demonstration of how a file can be used to check hardness is the spark test. We would touch a file to a revolving grinding wheel and notice the spark pattern and then touch a regular piece of steel. The patterns were different.

"YOU "MISSPELLED" YOUR NAME"

I wanted the student to place his name on everything he made. The procedure was to machine a ¼ wide slot 1/64 deep as long as his name. The guy was to write down his last name, count each letter, and add one letter space before and after his name. The length of the slot would depend on the number of letters in the name. The student was to stamp his name in the slot. He was the find the center, stamp the letters from the center to the right. Next, stamp the letters from the center to the left. This way, the name would be centered. More than one student would misspell his name when he would go from the center to the beginning of his name. If he misspelled the name, he would machine the slot deeper and stamp the name again.

We also positioned the guy, so if he hit the stamp off-center, it would fly out of his hand and not hit anyone just a wall, and we had several marks on the wall. Most of the guys were afraid of hitting their hand with the hammer, a few did and were told it was a good thing we didn't have a cuss jar because they would have contributed a few coins.

BENCH GRINDERS

A bench grinder is a typical machine found in basement and garage shops and used in the early days of employment. It's like a drill press. We had two floor models and considered these a part of a young man's experience. The seniors had to sharpen different lathe tool bits and twist drills. The first thing stressed was safety. One question I would ask the student the first day of class was, "What machines are dangerous?" Students would point to this one or that one, but I would say,

> "None of those machines are dangerous as they stand
> there. But as soon as someone works that machine, it
> can be dangerous and hurt you or those close to you".

I also stressed a routine called "walk-around" each should do when they start to work on a machine. Walk all the way around, looking for items that can be a hazard. There were things I stressed about grinders too. Using a bench grinder would be a machine a new worker use for preparing stock for the other workers. Every time we had to change wheels, there was an hour of instruction about this procedure. The critical first step was to turn off the power to the machine. We would change both wheels for balance. Next, check the new wheels to see if they were OK and not cracked by applying the "ring test" to the wheels. As we would place a sample wheel on a wooden dowel and tap it with a piece of metal, we would hear a sharp ping sound, but when we tested our marked cracked wheel, there was a dull sound. The guys would notice this, and many would look to see the crack but couldn't find the break. Next, replacing wheels required essential steps. Surfaces were wiped clean, and care was taken, putting the wheel on the spindle. Tightening the wheel was important – not too much and not too little, just enough. The side guards and the front guard must be on before the machine is turned on. There was also a spinning by hand to make sure the wheel didn't touch the front guard. The wall switch was turned on; the guys were told not to stand in line with the wheel as one jogs the start and stop switch to check if there is any wobble. Next, the wheel is allowed to run and ready to be dressed. You cover your mouth and nose; hold the wheel dresser firmly; position your feet, and move the dresser across the surface of the wheel to remove any out of roundness. Lastly, the front wheel guards are placed close to the wheel. We had two different wheels because each had features needed for various procedures.

SPECIAL INSERT - METRIC AND INCHES

I developed the following seven pages when I presented 4 three hour classes for a local company who had to convert their workforce to the metric measuring system. Their design department was in Germany and would not use the inch system on the drawings. The local division had to convert to the metric system.

In 1965, the metric measurement system was introduced to take over the inch -foot system gradually. The teachers had work sessions about the idea that this system would become the system for all quickly. That didn't happen, but there were subtle changes included in our daily lives. The following article describes several changes.

Those in school in the 1990s and beyond most likely had experience with the metric system. Those "older folks" may have had more encounters with the inch system. Eventually, the metric system will be the system the unborn will experience.

METRIC AND INCH MADE EASY

Metric and Inch made easy is a presentation in 3 parts to help people understand how the two measuring systems compare. The first part is a simple way to compare sizes in both modes. When you see a metric dimension, what would be the equivalent size in the inch system and vice versa? The second and third parts will go into more detail with both measuring systems.

WHY WE HAVE BOTH SYSTEMS

Welcome to learning how to compare metric and inch measuring systems. Since the mid-twentieth century, there were many attempts to convert the United States to the world standard "metric." In 1866 The United States Congress authorized HR 596, which allows the use of the metric system of weights and measures as our standard, and in 1875 the United States became a charter member of the "The Treaty of Paris." a worldwide organization's attempt to make the metric system the standard. Communications being like they were in those days, the word didn't get around, and the companies and workers stayed with what they used and knew. The workers used the system they felt comfortable with, and that system created a period of tremendous productivity in the late 1890s and early 1900s standards for innovations and production. But, in the 1960s, other countries in Europe and far West began to advance their production and started to equal and pass our country in productivity. America was losing out while the other countries were progressing as foreign companies and American companies combined, or were purchased by international companies. An example is an Ohio company combined with a German Company, and all design is being done in Germany. They use the metric system in Germany, and the manufacturing of the products is done in Ohio. The Ohio Company had to retrain their workers to think and learn metric and use metric measuring tools. With two different measuring systems used in manufacturing, there were glitches in product developments. Since the USA is the only developed country using the inch system, it was thought to begin a transition to the metric system.

This orderly transition started in the mid-1960s and was met with stiff opposition from industry. We began to see duel speedometers in cars, math problems in math books with answers in inches with metric answers in parenthesis. Soon we had the automotive industry change how to determine engine sizes from cubic inch engines to liters. Industry didn't change quickly, and when President George Bush (Senior) left office, he issued another directive regarding the change to using metric. Industry again said the cost to change was too high and proceeded to change in small steps. President Clinton also pushes the issue for a quicker transition, and there were some changes, but still, opposition to incorporate metrics was intense. As America began to reinvent their production capability in the 1990s, it began to see the need to work with metric and include this system. This incorporation requires the workers to adapt. It is safe to say the new workers can adjust to the metric system quicker than the older workers. They feel confident in their old way, but when they see how simple the metric system is, they will feel more satisfied because they can work in both measuring methods.

BASIC METRIC TO INCH CONVERSION "25 RULE"

The inch system has words, "inch, foot or feet, yard, and mile." and common fractions like ½, 5/8, and mixed numbers 2 ¾, 12 1/64, and decimal numbers or fractions like .500, .375 4.125. Most individuals can spread their fingers to approximate the asked for size because he or she has used this system all their life. If that person was asked to show the distance of a metric dimension, could they do the same with their fingers? This exercise is to help learn how to be very close to understanding the metric equivalent size.

First, there is a standard that states 25.4 MMS equals 1 inch. KNOW THESE NUMBERS

In our exercise, we will drop the .4 and rewrite the above statement as 25mms = 1 inch; we must stress this for you to understand or be able to <u>compare</u> metric sizes to inch sizes. *In <u>any</u> <u>serious</u> <u>conversion,</u> <u>the</u> 25.4 <u>must</u> <u>be</u> <u>used</u>*.

25mms = 1 inch
50mms = 2 inches
75mms= 3 inches
150mms = 6 inches, you should see a pattern here that for every 25mms we have one inch (for estimation sake).

If you see a dimension like 38mms, what would the approximate size be in the inch system??

You would notice you have at least 25 mm, so the size is at lease 1inch, and there is 13mms more (38mms-25mms = 13mms). You will then make a fraction of 13/25, and you should see a 1/2 addition to the 1 inch. Therefore 38mms would be ABOUT 1 and ½ inches.

Another example would be 106mms, what would that be in inches? You see 100mms, so that would mean 4 inches for sure and a remainder of 6mms. So 6 /25 (figure 6 divided by 24 not 25) would be about ¼ inch. So 106mms would be ABOUT 4 and 1/4 inches.

Going the other way from inches to metric, use the 25mms=1 inch rule again. You have a 3.750 or 3 3/4 inch dimension. What would that size be in MMS? You have 3 inches or 75 MMS for sure. The fraction of 3/4 would mean ¾ times 24 (it should be 25, but we substitue24) or 18 more MMS. So, three 3/4inches would be ABOUT 93mms (75 + 18).

Example #2 you have a dimension of 5.625 or 5 5/8. Five inches you have 125mms (5 x 25 = 125). The fraction 5/8 can be converted to 15/24 or roughly 15 more MMS. The approximate size would be 140mms (125 + 15 = 140mms). Let's see how close our estimate answer would be 5.625 x 25.4 = 142.875 actual MMS. So, our guess would be off 2.875 MMS.

REMEMBER THE 25 RULE WHEN YOU TRY TO COMPARE METRIC TO INCH AND INCH TO METRIC DIMENSIONS. You are using the "25 rule."

Another offshoot of the 25 rule is the .040 rule. When you hear or see a dimension in millimeters, remember .040. We know that 25.4mms equals one inch. One mm divided by 25.4 (1/25.4 = .03937...). Here's the trick! Take the number .03937 and change it to .040 or .04. This change is minimal, and again we are using .040 to help compare sizes of inches to MMS. This change is very close, and again we are using .040 to help compare the different measuring systems. You are using a metric wrench, and it is marked 18mms. What would be that be close to in inches? 18mms x .04 = .720. Your ¾ wrench could fit, but just be careful the wrench could slip.

Another example:

On a drawing, there is a dimension of .5mms. What is that in inches? Take .5mms X .04, and your answer is .020.

Remember, use .040 when you want to find the inch size of a small or large metric dimension, ex. 3mms drill X .04 = .120 Ex

Ex#2 112mms. = What is the approximate size in inches 112mms X .04 = 4.48 inches. The actual dimension would be 4.410. Again you are approximating

MORE WORK WITH BOTH SYSTEM PART 2

You now have experienced the "25 RULE" and "0.040 rule", we will try more problems to realize how you can work with the two systems. In this section, we will find how the metric sizes can be remembered in everyday objects. We will also show the terms used in the metric system like millimeters, centimeters, decimeters, and meters compare to the inch, foot, yard, and mile.

FIRST The millimeter (mm) is the smallest size commonly used in measuring the metric system. One mm is equivalent to .03937 inches. (How .03937 was obtained was just explained). If you take 13 sheets of paper and squeeze them together, you are holding one mm. A sheet of paper is about .003 thick, and 13 sheets would equal one mm. (13 x .003)

1 millimeter (mm) ---------------------- Ex -- 13 sheets of paper held together
10 millimeters = 1 centimeter
1 centimeter (cm) ---------------------- Ex -- small fingernail width on your hand
10 centimeter = 1 decimeter
1 decimeter (dm) ------------------------- Ex – an ordinary cigarette
10 decimeter = 1 meter -------------------- Ex – a yardstick
1 kilometer = 1000 meters ---------- Ex -- one mile (one kilometer is .62 miles)

REMEMBER THESE COMPARISONS

Think of one milli as 1/10 of one cent or penny -------------------------(.001)
Therefore 10 mils = one cent (centimeter)------------------------(penny .01)
Therefore 10 cents or 10 pennies = one dime (decimeter) -----(dime .10)
Therefore 10 decimeters or 10 dimes = one dollar (meter)----------($1.00)
MILLI

This term is used when there are requests for additional money from numerous organizations during a local election in your area. Example: There is a request from the local school district for four mills levy (.004) on the ballot at the next election. They are asking for .004 parts of one dollar of property value. Think of .004 as 4/10's of one penny

COMPARING SYSTEMS WITH NUMBERS PART 3

In this part, we will delve into numbers and how to work with each system. In the inch system, we should be comfortable with our calculations. We will see inches as the common term, and when lengths exceed 72, those inches dimensions are listed in feet and inches. We have been talking about millimeters, and other metric size terms are listed and will now work with more exact numbers.

We know that there are 25.4mms in one inch. Another number to know is how big in inches is one mm? We would divide 25.4 into 1.000 (1/25.4) and obtain a quotient of .03937…. This five place number is used even though there is a remainder.

We have standard tables used to determine the exact size in the other system. We also include some everyday items we use or see in our daily life to help us understand the meter

One mm = .03937inches (hold 13 sheets of paper)

10mms = one cm = 0.3937inches (the small fingernail width)

100mms = 10cms =one dm = 3.937inches (a regular cigarette)

1000mms = 100cms =10dms = one Meter = 39.37inches (a 36 inch yardstick)

All this is to help adjust to visualizing sizes in the metric measuring system.

If you have to convert a metric dimension to the exact inch dimension or if this conversion is reversed, you have to multiply one way and divide the other way. It is recommended to use 25.4 as the constant in converting. If you use .03937, there are more numbers involved and more chances for mistakes.

Remember, 25.4mms equals 1 inch, and 50.8mms equals 2 inches.

Rule #1 if given an inch dimension <u>MULTIPLY</u> by 25.4 to obtain the metric equivalent.

EX. 3.750 inches =???MMS =95.25mms (3.750 x 25.4 = 95.25mms)

Rule #2 if given an mm dimension <u>DIVIDE</u> the mm by 25.4 to obtain the inch equivalent

EX. Given 95.25mms =??? Inches (95.25 divided by 25.4 = 3.75)

NOTE!!! <u>CHECK</u>+<u>CHECK</u>+<u>CHECK</u> = We used 3.75 and obtained 95.25 and then used 95.25 to obtain 3.75. If you machine to a wrong dimension, there could be a scrap problem. There is a saying that is appropriate that you "FIGURE TWICE (or check your answer) AND MACHINE ONCE." Also, imagine you own the company.

Additional information #1

The most common dimension in the inch system is a three-place number. In the metric system, the common dimension is a two-place dimension. A four-place inch dimension is equivalent to a three-place metric dimension.

Additional information #2 *Angles are different in both systems*

In the inch system, angular dimensions are listed as degrees and minutes (sometimes seconds too). In the metric system, the angles are listed as degrees and decimal parts of a degree (D.D) Example: inch = 35 degrees 30 minute or

35° 30′. the metric = 35.5° degrees. NOTE there is a .5 in the metric dimension, whereas the inch dimension has "30". Be aware of this difference.

We are at the end of this presentation, and we hope you have benefited from reading this attempt to help people understand the comparison of the two measuring systems. In time the metric system will be used as much as the inch system was used in the early 1900s. Everyone agrees that working with units of 10 is better than 12 inches = one foot. Keep your 6-inch scales and micrometers in good shape because, in time, they will be considered valuable antiques.

If anyone wants to read more about the evolvement of the measuring systems check out the website www.cutsmart.com/pages/articles/METRIC VS ENGLISH SYSTEM OF MEASURE

PART 3 – YOU HAVE HOMEWORK!

The title list three parts. This section will show what I did with and for the students. The seniors in the vocational machine trades at Cuyahoga Falls High School were my main concern. The adult machining classes were next in importance and last the junior high school students. The material presented in the last years was more involved than in the beginning years. As I said, teaching was an education. I wanted to make it easy for a person to understand a concept, so I kept looking for that magic word or phrase to help understand the assignment. If I could see a puzzled look on their face, I would want to explain it from another direction.

Part 3 will have more handouts and worksheets that were developed over time. There will be examples of theory, blueprint reading, shop math, and jobs the students made. If someone considers this as a homework assignment, remember the students had workbooks with the answers. The book was titled "MATHEMATICS FOR MACHINE TECHNOLOGY" Delmar Publishing Company Inc. editions 2 – 3 - 4, by Robert D. Smith.

RELATED CLASS MATERIAL

The junior and senior classes had a period of related instruction each day for the school or 180 days. Both instructors believed this time was valuable because the student needs to understand there is more to our trade than just working on a machine. I can remember times when both classes would take a few more minutes in the related room to complete an important assignment. We stressed machine theory, blueprint reading, and shop math. There were other things experienced too. Metric measurement was becoming the standard, so we had to include that system also.

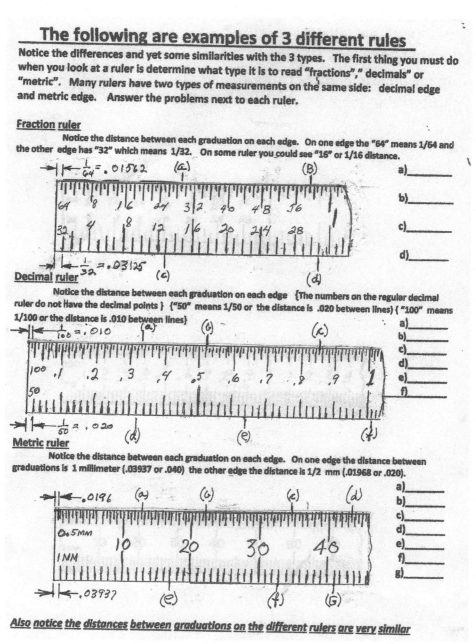

Insert by Stan Sipka

I remember Mr. Gruber; the junior class instructor would teach the guys how to shake hands when they meet a person interviewing them for a job. I remembered telling guys not to be the first guy at the time clock every day. Another statement was to remember your company expects you to help them make money and will pay you in return.

Several copies of homework will be presented representing machines, math, blueprint reading, and general topics.

1. Procedure for the lathe test piece
2. Matching Quiz Units 40,42and 43
3. Int. to Geometric Figures Units 40 and 41
4. Math Matching Par
5. Law of Sines (Watch Out)

All inserts by Stan Sipka

PROCEDURE FOR LATHE TEST PIECE

____ 1. Check stock for size.

____ 2. Position in three jaw chuck
Hold enough stock in chuck to machine 2 1/2 inch to
1.000 diameter

____ 3. Machine stock to 1.000 dia approximately 2 1/2 long
R.P.M.'s_____   feed rate _____

____ 4. Machine 7/8 dia === Layout distance on lathe
rough machine to .890 to .900 dia to 1/16 of length.

____ 5. Finish .875 dia to exact length
Note = use the travel dial to determine length
Feed rate should be reduced. rate is _____
Note == Need square shoulders

____ 6. Machine 5/8 dia === Layout distance on lathe
rough machine to .640 to .650 to 1/16 of length.

____ 7. Finish .625 dia. to exact length.
Feed rate _____   Note == Need square shoulders

____ 8. Remove from lathe, layout 4.000 length and 3/4 dia
length.

____ 9. Position in 3 jaw chuck. Hold on .875 dia

____ 10. Face stock to 4.000 length. Measure from should of
.875 dia.

____ 11. Rough 3/4 dia to .765 to .775 to 1/16 of length

____ 12. Finish 3/4 dia to .750 and exact length.
feed rate _____   Note == Remember square shoulders

____ 13. Rough and finish .500 dia the same way the other dia
have been machined.   Note == need square shoulders

____ 14 Remove, inspect, remove burrs and graded.

1.000 dia _____   1.250 length _____

.875 dia _____   .875 length _____   _____
                                                        grade
.750 dia _____   .750 length _____
                                                        _____
.625 dia _____   .625 length _____   date
                                                        finished
.500 dia _____   .500 length _____

Burrs _____   square corners (4)(3)(2)(1)

Matching Quiz Units 40, 42, and 43

Match items in column B with those in column A

Column A	Column B
____ When 2 angles are added together = 90 degrees	A) Right
____ When 2 angles added together = 180 degrees	B) polygon
____ A line that intersects (cuts)2 or more lines	C) parallel lines
____ A triangle that has one 90 angle	D) D.D.
____ A Triangle that has 3 angles each 60 degrees	E) transversal
____ A Triangle that has 2 sides the same length	F) DMS
____ A angle that is 180 degrees	G) plane geometry
____ A angle less than 90 degrees	H) complementary
____ Two lines that do not touch	J) acute
____ The "point" where lines meet to form an angle	K) straight line
____ Unit of angular measure - metric system	L) scalene
____ Lines that meet or intersect at 90 degrees	M) perpendicular
____ The branch of math that deals with points, lines an figures	N) equilateral
____ A triangle that has 3 unequal angles and length of sides none of	O) vertex
which is 90 degrees.	Q) Axioms
	S) isosceles

UNIT 40 and 41 INTRODUCTION TO GEOMETIC FIGURES

PLANE GEOMETRY – is that branch of math that deals with points, lines and various figures that are made of combinations of points and lines.

AXIOMS - are basic statements which are assumed to be true.

Ex. A) The whole is equal to the sum of the whole

Ex. B) Only a straight line can be drawn between two points

Ex. C) Two straight can only intersect at one point only

POINT – Has no size or form, it has location only. (a teacher I had in high school had one) the end view of a line.

 LINE - Means a straight line

PARALLEL LINES Two or more straight lines that do not meet. SYMBOL "II'

 Ex. AB II CD

PERPENDICULAR LINES - lines that meet or intersect at a right angle 90° SYMBOL   __|__

OBLIQUE LINES – all the other lines that meet or intersect

ANGLE – A figure which consists of two lines that meet at a point called – VERTEX.   Units of measure are 1) degrees, minutes, seconds (DMS) and in the (2) metric system degrees and decimal degrees (DD)

UNIT 41   (super important to know)

COMPLEMENTARY ANGLES Two angles are complementary when their sum equals 90°

SUPPLEMENTARY ANGLES – Two angles are supplementary when their sum is 180°

Name _____

Date _____

Instructions: Match items in Column I with those in column II. Some items can be used more than once, while some have no answer. If there is a blank, place the letter "Z" to indicate none of the above. If there is a "#", place the actual value of the answer instead one of the letters.

COLUMN I

A. thousands
B. radical sign
C. divison
D. addition
E. power and roots
F. index of the root
G. term
H. like
J. parenthesis
K. X and ÷
L. reciprocal

M. + and -
N. literal value
O. sum
P. multiplication
Q. product
R. ✳ and -
S. signs of grouping
T. difference

Z. none of the above

COLUMN II

1. What is the name of the answers to:
   addition problems- - - -(   )
   subtraction problems- - -(   )
   multiplication problems- - - - -(   )
2. List the order of operation in the correct order
   1st - - - -(   )
   2nd - - - -(   )
   3rd - - - -(   )
   4th - - - -(   )
3. An algebraic expression separated by a "+" or "-" sign - - - - - - - - - - - - - - - - - - -(   )
4. List two signs of grouping - - - - - - - - -(   )(   )
5. The number of MM's in one inch - - - - - (#   )
6. 5/6 & 6/5 ; 6/5 is the ??? of 5/6 - - - - -(   )
7. The number value of a term - - - - - - - - - - -(   )
8. What principle of Equality would be used to solve the following:
   A) 7A = 42 - - - - - - - - - - - - - - - - - - - (   )
   B) $^A/_7$ = 6 - - - - - - - - - - - - - - - - - - - (   )
9. $\sqrt[x]{}$ "x" is ??? - - - - - - (   )

10. SOLVE -

            ← EXPONENT

$$312.45^{\circ}$$
$$\times \quad 10$$

LAW OF SINES (WATCH OUT!)

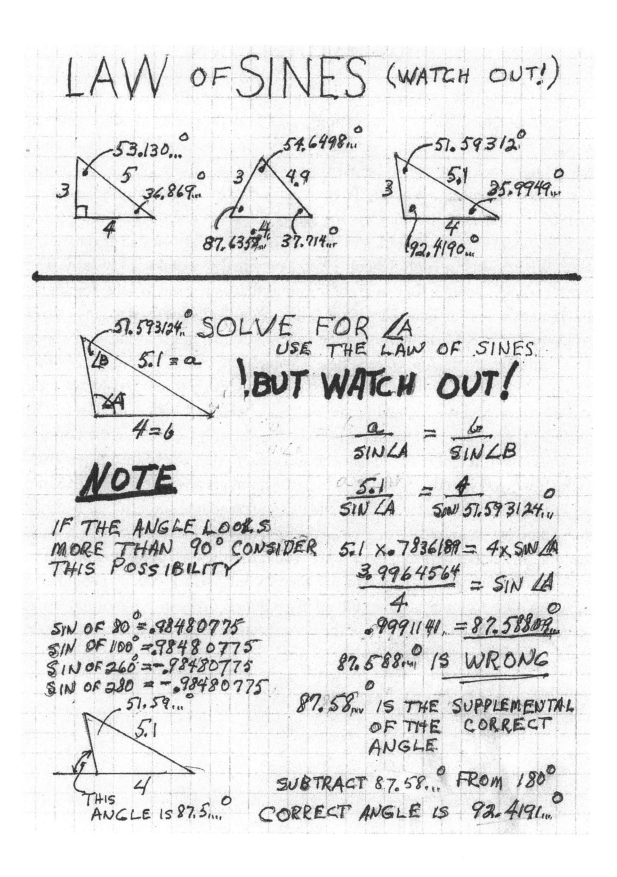

SOLVE FOR ∠A

USE THE LAW OF SINES.

!BUT WATCH OUT!

<u>NOTE</u>

IF THE ANGLE LOOKS
MORE THAN 90° CONSIDER
THIS POSSIBILITY

SIN OF 80° = .98480775
SIN OF 100° = .98480775
SIN OF 260° = -.98480775
SIN OF 280° = -.98480775

$$\frac{a}{\sin \angle A} = \frac{b}{\sin \angle B}$$

$$\frac{5.1}{\sin \angle A} = \frac{4}{\sin 51.593124...°}$$

$5.1 \times .7836189 = 4 \times \sin \angle A$

$$\frac{3.9964564}{4} = \sin \angle A$$

$.9991141... = 87.5880...°$

87.588...° IS <u>WRONG</u>

87.58...° IS THE SUPPLEMENTAL
OF THE CORRECT
ANGLE

SUBTRACT 87.58...° FROM 180°
CORRECT ANGLE IS 92.4191...°

THIS
ANGLE IS 87.5...°

SHOP MATHEMATICS

BC MATH – We will begin by showing how a trig problem was solved BC (before calculators). There were be three pages from the pocket handbook copied to show how to find a length or angle dimension. The Machinist's Handbook was a large book that was to be part of a toolbox, but the book was too large, so a small reference book with "Trigonometry Tables" and formulas was used. In 1967, I purchased 100 booklets for $25 or .25 cents each. I gave most away free to students young and old, still, have a few new bright orange covers never used. When I was in High School, 1952, I obtained one and used it daily. The front few pages contain four pages of formulas that were used to solve for angles and dimensions. Illustrated here is the last page of the tables used to solve a trig problem. You see 44° at the top of the page and down the left side, you notice 0 – 60 minutes. At the top, you see Sine, Cosine, Tan, Cotan, Secant, and Cosec. You would look at the top of the page if using angles up to 44° 59'. NOW, look at the bottom; you see 45° and up the right side, you will notice another 0 – 60 seconds. Lastly, you will see the same six trig formulas names on the bottom, BUT each is different than the name at the top. If you were to turn pages back to the front, you would see (at the bottom) the numbers advance to 89° 60' at the beginning. The educated workers would use any one of the six formulas because many problems required a 4 or 5 place decimal divided into another 4 or 5 place decimal. Instead of division, the worker would use the formula where he would multiply the numbers. If you would use Sine formula and divide, you could also use the cosec formula but multiply. This reduced division for multiplication operations. Sin and Cosec and Cos and Secant can be used for the same problem.

Sample problem: #1

You have the opposite side as .501 and the adjacent side as .508. You use the (tan) tangent formula. It's .501 divided by .508 = .986220...

You would open the book and look for the tan column and .98622. You would end up on the page, locate the tan column and move your finger down until you find .98622 or the closest number. This number falls between two numbers. Take the number on top = 44° and 36' (.98613) 37' (.98671). If you had to determine the number of seconds you would (*means find the value*) have to INTERPOLATE. You would find *in second* the exact number of seconds.

A second example: #2

M	Sine	Cosine	Tan.	Cotan.	Secant	Cosec.	M
			TAN ↓44°				
0	.69466	.71934	.96569	1.0355	1.3902	1.4395	60
1	.69487	.71914	.96625	.0349	.3905	.4391	59
2	.69508	.71893	.96681	.0343	.3909	.4387	58
3	.69528	.71873	.96738	.0337	.3913	.4382	57
4	.69549	.71853	.96794	.0331	.3917	.4378	56
5	.69570	.71833	.96850	1.0325	1.3921	1.4374	55
6	.69591	.71813	.96907	.0319	.3925	.4370	54
7	.69612	.71792	.96963	.0313	.3929	.4365	53
8	.69633	.71772	.97020	.0307	.3933	.4361	52
9	.69654	.71752	.97076	.0301	.3937	.4357	51
10	.69675	.71732	.97133	1.0295	1.3941	1.4352	50
11	.69696	.71711	.97189	.0289	.3945	.4348	49
12	.69716	.71691	.97246	.0283	.3949	.4344	48
13	.69737	.71671	.97302	.0277	.3953	.4339	47
14	.69758	.71650	.97359	.0271	.3957	.4335	46
15	.69779	.71630	.97416	1.0265	1.3960	1.4331	45
16	.69800	.71610	.97472	.0259	.3964	.4327	44
17	.69821	.71589	.97529	.0253	.3968	.4322	43
18	.69841	.71569	.97586	.0247	.3972	.4318	42
19	.69862	.71549	.97643	.0241	.3976	.4314	41
20	.69883	.71529	.97700	1.0235	1.3980	1.4310	40
21	.69904	.71508	.97756	.0229	.3984	.4305	39
22	.69925	.71488	.97813	.0223	.3988	.4301	38
23	.69945	.71468	.97870	.0218	.3992	.4297	37
24	.69966	.71447	.97927	.0212	.3996	.4292	36
25	.69987	.71427	.97984	1.0206	1.4000	1.4288	35
26	.70008	.71406	.98041	.0200	.4004	.4284	34
27	.70029	.71386	.98098	.0194	.4008	.4280	33
28	.70049	.71366	.98155	.0188	.4012	.4276	32
29	.70070	.71345	.98212	.0182	.4016	.4271	31
30	.70091	.71325	.98270	1.0176	1.4020	1.4267	30
31	.70112	.71305	.98327	.0170	.4024	.4263	29
32	.70132	.71284	.98384	.0164	.4028	.4259	28
33	.70153	.71264	.98441	.0158	.4032	.4254	27
34	.70174	.71243	.98499	.0152	.4036	.4250	26
35	.70194	.71223	.98556	1.0146	1.4040	1.4246	25
36	.70215	.71203	.98613	.0141	.4044	.4242	24
37	.70236	.71182	.98671	.0135	.4048	.4238	23
38	.70257	.71162	.98728	.0129	.4052	.4233	22
39	.70277	.71141	.98786	.0123	.4056	.4229	21
40	.70298	.71121	.98843	1.0117	1.4060	1.4225	20
41	.70319	.71100	.98901	.0111	.4065	.4221	19
42	.70339	.71080	.98958	.0105	.4069	.4217	18
43	.70360	.71059	.99016	.0099	.4073	.4212	17
44	.70381	.71039	.99073	.0093	.4077	.4208	16
45	.70401	.71018	.99131	1.0088	1.4081	1.4204	15
46	.70422	.70998	.99189	.0082	.4085	.4200	14
47	.70443	.70977	.99246	.0076	.4089	.4196	13
48	.70463	.70957	.99304	.0070	.4093	.4192	12
49	.70484	.70936	.99362	.0064	.4097	.4188	11
50	.70505	.70916	.99420	1.0058	1.4101	1.4183	10
51	.70525	.70895	.99478	.0052	.4105	.4179	9
52	.70546	.70875	.99536	.0047	.4109	.4175	8
53	.70566	.70854	.99593	.0041	.4113	.4171	7
54	.70587	.70834	.99651	.0035	.4117	.4167	6
55	.70608	.70813	.99709	1.0029	1.4122	1.4163	5
56	.70628	.70793	.99767	.0023	.4126	.4159	4
57	.70649	.70772	.99826	.0017	.4130	.4154	3
58	.70669	.70752	.99884	.0012	.4134	.4150	2
59	.70690	.70731	.99942	.0006	.4138	.4146	1
60	.70711	.70711	1.0000	1.0000	1.4142	1.4142	0
M	Cosine	Sine	Cotan.	Tan.	Cosec.	Secant	M
			45° ↑ TAN				

Opp side is .508 and Adj side is .501 . We use the tan formula and take .508 divided by .501 = 1.01397... You start at the top in the tan column and go down and notice 1.01397 is not in the top down column. At the bottom there is a tan column but not above the top "tan" notation. Move up the column and find 1.01397 or numbers close to this. You find 1.0135 (23) and 1.0141(24) not 1.01397. You started up the tan column from the bottom and you have 45° you reach the two numbers above and under now move to the right column to determine the seconds. If you needed seconds you again would INTERPOLATE. Congratulations you just solve 2 trig problems the BC way. Wasn't that fun?

Courtesy of the Illinois Tool Works Company

NOW MATH "WC" WITH CALCULATORS

"MATHEMATICS FOR MACHINE TECHNOLOGY EDITIONS 1, 2 AND 3" from the Delmar Publishers Inc. by Robert D. Smith, was the workbook we use from 1967 to the last year of our high school vocational and adult apprentice classes. I knew every problem and developed problems to enhance those in the book. Preparing this section, I wanted better examples for the students to experience. The 3rd edition had a unit on "Introduction to Electronic Calculators" for the first time. We worked on 1) Linear Measurement, 2) Fundamentals of Algebra, 3) Fundamentals of Plane Geometry,4) Trigonometry. We touched on Numerical control and binary. The plan is to show examples of what the students received as assignments. A few students complained about the homework, but most did what was expected. You could see the guys gain confidence in talking about these seemingly impossible problems.

We progressed after a few days into "Combined Operations of Decimal Factions." I realized tons of formulas could be reduced if a person knows how to rearrange the terms in the formulas. So, I made up sheets that help the person see what is to be done in changing from one step to another on their way to an answer. Patience is to become each student's middle name. There is an example of how I convey this idea to the students. This book has excellent examples to reinforce the concept. There's one sketch "stamped steel plate,"

My response was you could see just one thing or operation you have done, and you're not bothered with numbers before and after to distract you. I was always saying do one thing at a time like the saying, "the hurrier you go the behinder you get!

BLUEPRINT READING

VISUALIZATION, SKETCHING, AND VERBAL SKILLS

The word "BLUE" in blueprint reading is not used now because new copying machines don't require the time-consuming method used when you saw white lines on blue paper. How did they produce white lines on blue paper? The draftsman (draftsperson now) would draw the object with ink on special chemical treated white paper. The completed drawing was rolled up and placed in a cylindrical tube. The base of the tube had a reservoir of ammonia; the fumes would rise up the cylinder and react with the paper turning the paper blue except where there were the black inked lines; those lines would provide the white lines. The high school drafting teacher made my class sign our names on this paper and place the sheet in the tube to allow us to get a good whiff of the ammonia used to obtain the blue color on the distinctive white paper. Learn that smell well. Each student received a copy with the class names to keep as a souvenir.

BluePrint Reading was the title of workbooks we used, "Beginning" in the junior year and "intermediate" in the senior year.

The assignments stressed learning how to see the job – visualization. In the machining industry, the worker works from drawings and has to "see" the job completed. We used workbooks and special handouts to provide different levels of learning. Mr. Gruber, the junior class teacher, spent time on the beginning textbook and sketching techniques. I was to advance those skills with advanced textbook worksheets and drawings from industry.

The exercises included orthographic and isometric drawings, missing lines, and or views assignments. Students experience drawing isometric views first using isometric graph paper and then without. The instruction was to use a pencil draw light lines when corrected, darken the lines. Understandably, the lines would not be perfectly straight, but this would be a sketch. It could be better to draw what you may have to explain, and would say a picture can be worth a thousand words. Another request was to print and words in CAPITAL letters.

Awareness of verbal descriptions was critical because, in the shop, verbal instruction is typical and could lead to mistakes.

THE RED BRICK - I did use this story to illustrate verbal instruction. A teacher placed an ordinary red brick on the desk, hands out a sheet of paper, and indicates the assignment was to write about this red brick. The teacher begins to work at her desk, allowing time to write. After a few minutes, she notices most are sitting there done. As she walks around, she sees very few words on the papers and comments on why so little on so many papers. She then mentions things she can think of and could write about, which would describe the brick. Color, has anyone seen different colored bricks? Next, where or how bricks are used? For houses, buildings, fireplaces, stacked under a car while working on the car, even used as paperweights. Why are there holes in the bricks and different size bricks? She then asked the students to try to add some words to the assignment. More was written after the teacher presented suggestions.

The students would understand they knew a lot about the brick after they were made aware of their experiences. I would ask what we could write about, how about - toilet paper. This request produced a lot of comments.

NOTE this – red brick assignment - was an example of something learned after teaching for years. It helped convey the communication skills needed by those working. I wished I knew this the first day of teaching.

ASSIGNMENTS FROM THE BOOK

There are several examples of assignments from the workbook and missing lines and views and surface identification. The list should include;

1. BPR Matching Units part2 Unit 1 – 2
2. Quiz
3. Quiz – BPR – Line Identification
4. 508
5. 1925

MATCHING BLUE PRINT READING - PART 2 UNIT 1−2 _____

Instructions: Match items in Column I with those in Column II. Some items can be used more than once, while some have no answer. If there is a blank, place the letter "Z" to indicate none of the above.

COLUMN I

A) projection lines

B) 3rd angle

C) interpreting
D) simple symmetrical

E) complexity
F) half

G) 1st angle
H) visualizing

J) revolved
K) top view

L) front
M) aligned

N) full section
O) shape

P) views

Q) removed

R) broken-out

S) metric
T) tolerance

U) interference
half view
X) X (times)
Y) Y
Z) none of the above

COLUMN II

1) The process of forming a mental picture of an object ---------( )

2) The ??? and ??? of the object determine the number and arrangement of the views. ------------------------------( )—( )

3) These lines show the relationship of points and surfaces in one view to those in the other views ----------------------------------( )

4) Holes of equal size may be identified by specifying the number of features required by the letter ----------------------------------( )

5) Visualizing requires a worker knowledge of how the individual ??? are obtained through ??? ------------------------------( )—( )

6) The difference between and 1st and 3rd angle projection is the relative position of views in relation to ??? view. -----------( )

7) In drawing what type of object (regarding section views) can the cutting plane line be omitted? --------------------------------( )

8) Practice in projecting lines in their imaginary position helps to develop skill in ???? drawings? ------------------------------( )

9) One advantage of this section view is that it shows both the interior and exterior of the same object ------------------------( )

10) These section show the cross-section shapes of spokes and ribs-- ( )

11) This section is taken out of it's normal rotated position in relation to standard views--( )

12) This section is at times enlarged to show better details-( )

13) This section isolates only one area for clarification ------( )

QUIZ — BPR
_____ NAME

1) WHY IS GEOMETRIC TOLERANGING BEING USED OR BECOMING SOMETHING A PERSON SCHOULD BE INFORMED OF?

2) WHAT IS MEANT BY:
   a) CONCENTRICITY

   b) PERPENDICULARITY

3) WHAT IS ONE PURPOSE OF BUTTRESS THREADS?

4) WHAT IS ONE PURPOSE OF WORM THREADS?

5) WHEN IS THE PITCH AND LEAD:
   a) THE SAME?

   b) DIFFERENT?

6) WHAT IS THE CREST AND ROOT OF A THREAD?
   a) CREST?   b) ROOT?

7) WHAT FEATURE OF PIPE THREADS ALLOWS THE THREADS TO BE USED WITH NATURAL GAS FUEL LINES?

8) HOW ARE DIFFERENT TYPES OF STEEL IDENTIFIED?

9) WHAT ELEMENT MAKES THE BIGGEST DIFFERENCE IN THE QUALITY OR CHARACTERISTIC OF STEEL?

10) LIST THE CORRECT GEOMETRIC SYMBOL FOR THE FOLLOWING: PLACE THE SYMBOL NEXT TO THE WORD.
   a) ____ PERPENDICULARITY   b) ____ TOTAL RUNOUT

   c) ____ STRAIGHTNESS   d) ____ FLATNESS

   e) ____ PARALLELISM   f) ____ CONCENTRICITY   G) ____ ANGLARITY

QUIZ   LINE INDENTIFICATION

_____ 1) ————— — — — —

_____ 2)  ———— — — — —

_____ 3) INDICATES INFORMATION OFF THE
        VIEWS

_____ 4)  ———— — — — —→

_____ 5) HEAVY LINES THAT MAY HAVE
        ARROWS ON THE ENDS

_____ 6) 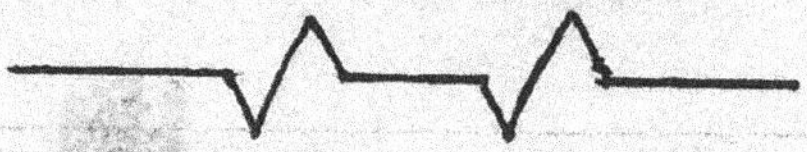 ⟋\⟋\⟋_____

_____ 7)  ————————➤

_____ 8) REPRESENTS THE EDGES
        OF AN OBJECT

_____ 9) LINE THAT SHOWS ALTERNATE
        POSITIONS

_____ 10) LINES THAT INDICATES THE
        CENTER OF ARCS

_____ 11) LINES THAT ESTABLISH THE RELATIONSHIP OF
        DETAILS IN ONE VIEW WITH CORRESPONDING DETAILS
        IN OTHER VIEWS

_____ 12) (FREEHAND DRAWN LINE) ‿‿‿‿‿‿‿

_____ 13) LINE TO ELIMENATE DRAWING REPEATING DETAILS
        OR ALTERNATING POSITION (GEAR TEETH)

A) OBJECT

B) HIDDEN

C) CENTER

D) EXTENSION

E) DIMENSION

F) PROJECTION

G) CUTTING
   PLANE

H) BREAK

J) PHANTOM

K) LEADER

L) BROKEN
   DIMENSION

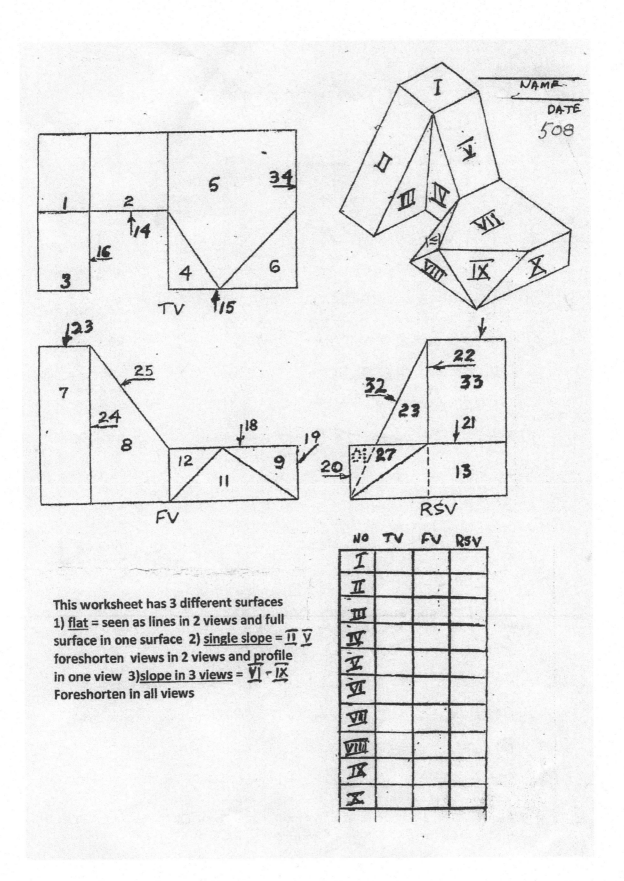

This worksheet has 3 different surfaces
1) **flat** = seen as lines in 2 views and full
surface in one surface 2) **single slope** = $\overline{II}$ $\overline{V}$
foreshorten views in 2 views and profile
in one view 3)**slope in 3 views** = $\overline{VI}$ - $\overline{IX}$
Foreshorten in all views

NO	TV	FV	RSV
I			
II			
III			
IV			
V			
VI			
VII			
VIII			
IX			
X			

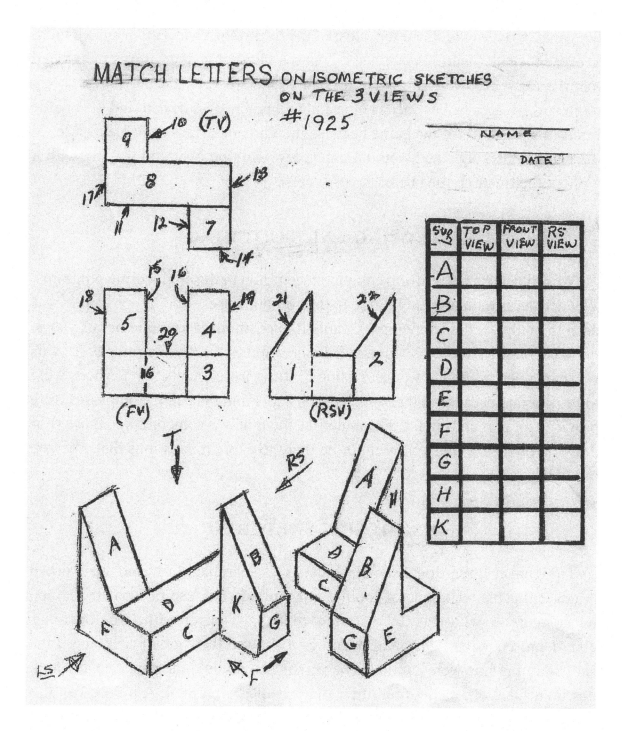

I also used the family's "Superfection Game" on occasion in middle school, high school, and adult classes. It was a different example of visualization in Blue Print Reading. I didn't make everyone try the 2-minute game. It did create excitement as the time ticked down the students would try to help the student to use this or that one to complete the pair. At two minutes, the base would pop up, and several students did arrange the 16 pairs. It was noted if a student repeated the game, most would do better. Most of the time, those watched arranged more because they saw features that helped put the blocks together. It was mentioned that the two parts were of different colors. One student said he wanted to try tomorrow because he has one at home and will practice "if he can find it!" I never forced a student to try the game because it could embarrass him. I would leave the game on the table and would notice a few walking over and playing with it without the timer on the one or two minutes.

DRAWING AND SKETCHING

We did not use the drafting equipment common to the engineering programs. Wood rulers, regular pencils, inexpensive compasses, and graph paper was used to complete the "drawing." Details like positioning and number of views, dimensioning location, using capital letters, and notes were stressed. All this was explained as though we were using drafting instruments. Dimensions were to be accurate because of the ¼ inch graph paper and the ruler. Compasses were provided for arcs and circles. The underline thought was someone would use your drawing or sketch, and you will not be there to explain questions that a person might have.

ISOMETRIC SKETCHING

Drawing a three-dimensional object is a desirable skill, and we worked at acquiring the technique of fooling one's mind. The use of isometric graph paper made drawing easy. We started with graph paper with large openings and then used paper with small openings. I showed the trick of checking if the six beginning line were parallel. The person should hold the paper up and look down each set of 3 beginning lines; they should be parallel. A person can use ordinary paper to draw the 3D drawing if they understand this simple way to start a drawing.

The following sheets were used for a couple of assignments. One sheet presented earlier was a major part of the isometric drawings. Other assignments showed the three views, and the student was to draw the isometric for a grade. Next, the student was to draw the isometrics with the help of a special "master" sheet with darken lines; plain white paper is placed over the master and trace the lines. This way, the master was used several times. The objects were more detailed and complex and included how to draw isometric circles.

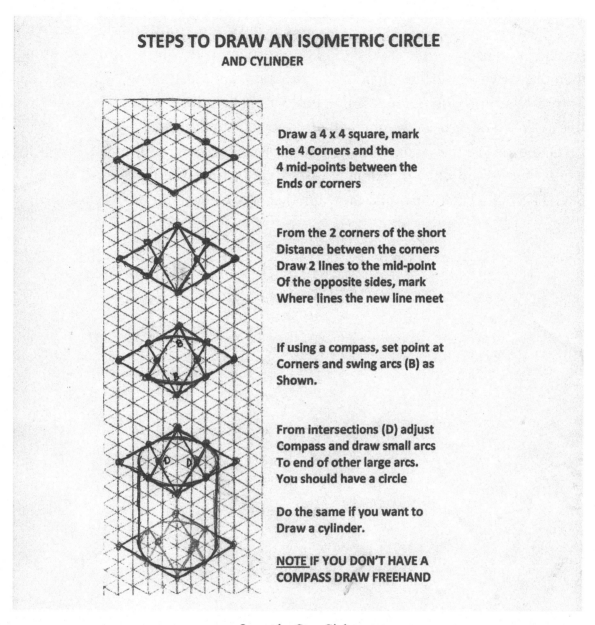

STEPS TO DRAW AN ISOMETRIC CIRCLE
AND CYLINDER

Draw a 4 x 4 square, mark the 4 Corners and the 4 mid-points between the Ends or corners

From the 2 corners of the short Distance between the corners Draw 2 lines to the mid-point Of the opposite sides, mark Where lines the new line meet

If using a compass, set point at Corners and swing arcs (B) as Shown.

From intersections (D) adjust Compass and draw small arcs To end of other large arcs. You should have a circle

Do the same if you want to Draw a cylinder.

NOTE IF YOU DON'T HAVE A COMPASS DRAW FREEHAND

Insert by Stan Sipka

We will start with a clock face;

1. From the center of the clock draw a line (no. 1) down to the six o'clock position (this is the thickness from top to bottom)
2. From the center, draw a line to the two o'clock position (no. 2)(this is the width from front to back)

3. From the center, draw a line to 10 o'clock position (no. 3) (this is the length from the right side to the left side).

Those three lines will help start the three views, top, front, and right side with additional lines. Continue by drawing two vertical lines (line 1)– top to bottom, then draw two lines (line 2) from front to back and, last, draw two lines (line 3) from the right side to the left side three units long for the length. These first lines were to be light in weight and, after corrected, darken.

One example was used to show how to change one's view of the object by words. We would draw a rectangle, 4x5x6 units, and write TOP, FRONT and RIGHT SIDE. Then we would draw another block but write BOTTOM,

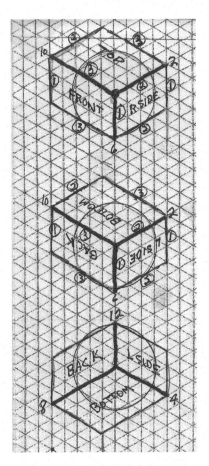

Insert by Stan Sipka

BACK, AND LEFT SIDE in reverse. The comment was, "it's upside down now!" I had several simple blocks with the six names, and you could see the guys and girls twisting the blocks. These types of exercises were given to the 6th and 7th graders, and they enjoyed the activity. I used those helpful comments with

intricate shapes "don't do this one or that one because they are too difficult." It was sneaky!

The class had a few assignments dealing with isometric circles and lettering. I asked many if they ever had to draw this way?; "no" was the common answer. I feel they enjoyed drawing something in three dimensions. I had examples of assemblies of motors that showed the inside of items. The saying "a picture is worth a thousand words" was mentioned as new skills were introduced. One drawing was a simple four by five by six rectangular block with the top, front, and right side drawn. We then cut features out by verbal instruction.

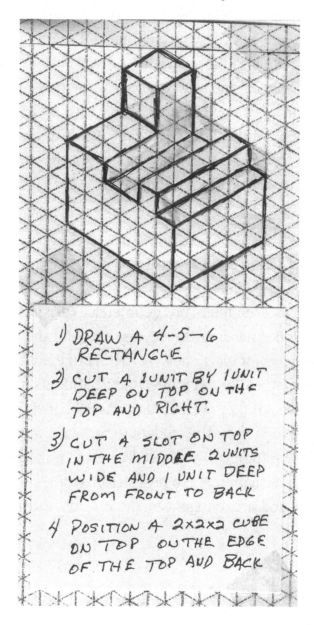

1) DRAW A 4-5-6 RECTANGLE

2) CUT A 1 UNIT BY 1 UNIT DEEP ON TOP ON THE TOP AND RIGHT.

3) CUT A SLOT ON TOP IN THE MIDDLE 2 UNITS WIDE AND 1 UNIT DEEP FROM FRONT TO BACK

4 POSITION A 2x2x2 CUBE ON TOP ON THE EDGE OF THE TOP AND BACK

An example, there is a step on top, running from front to back, on the edge of the right side. It is one unit in from the right side and one unit down from the top. Another addition to the block was, add a one by one by one cube on top at the corner of the left side and backside. These assignments kept them busy, and many enjoyed there drawing.

Two bits of advice 1)was to twist the pencil as they draw a line. That will keep the point sharp and be concerned 2) about the pressure being used to draw the line.

On many handouts, I would make wooden blocks to help the individual see the object on paper. It's a 3'D block viewed in 2 dimensions. I commented on how the person that drew the block used the technique of shading to help make it look 3'D. A circle was drawn, and I asked, what do you see? A circle, I would then draw on the circle three holes and shade the circle and make it look like a bowling ball. I would ask again what you see. Of course, I would hear a "bowling ball."

The last assignment would be the student would pick out 3 – 4 pieces of scrap wood and glue the pieces together but caution them they had to draw the object too. Needless, to say we did get some wild shapes from the middle school students

GEOMETRIC CONSTRUCTION

Our textbook had a chapter on geometric construction, and we had assignments. I remember hearing the saying drawing the shape will help you understand geometric principals, how to determine dimensions like angles and distances. There were 24 exercises - six handouts with four individual construction problems. All they were to use was a 12-inch ruler and a compass.

I added a special exercise for the student to draw an angle (for example) 25.5 degrees. A trig problem (tangent) was used to determine the opposite side and establish a point on a vertical line. No protractor was to be used. The advanced problems had circles and arcs tangent to the outside and inside of circles and lines.

GEOMETRIC EXAMPLES

Our text has sections dealing with the different principles of geometric construction. Here is one of the last examples. The second example is not in the unit, but I thought it can be useful in ~~layout~~ templates.

DRAW A ¾ RADIUS TANGENT TO LINE <u>AB</u> AND ARC "A"

1) Construct a ¾ line (line CD) parallel to line <u>AB</u>
2) Draw an arc (arc B) (3 – ¾ = 2 ¼) from PT "A"
3) Mark intersection of line CD and arc B PT "B"
4) From PT "B" draw a perpendicular line to line <u>AB</u>, mark intersection PT "C"
5) Draw a line from Center of arc A thru PT "B" to intersect arc A, PT"D"
6) Draw ¾ arc from PT "D" to PT "C"

DRAW A 25.5° ANGLE FROM POINT "A" (note 25.5° not 25° 50')

1) Draw line 4 + inches long, mark PT "A" ½ from left end
2) From PT "A" measure down 2.000 inches mark as PT "B"
3) From PT"B" draw a perpendicular line up from PT "B"
4) Calculate the opposite side of 25.5° with a 2 inch (adj side) use tangent= .95395..
5) Measure up on line and mark PT "C" .95395 as close as possible
6) Draw line from PT"A" to PT "C"   angle is 25.5°

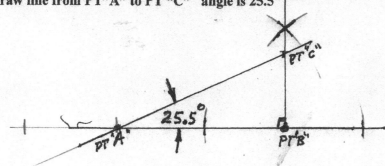

VOCATIONAL CERTIFICATE

STATE DEPARTMENT OF EDUCATION

DIVISION OF VOCATIONAL EDUCATION

CERTIFICATE OF COMPLETION

This Certifies That

ED QUINN

has satisfactorily completed 1228 hours of Skill and Related Vocational Instruction as provided by the board of education for the occupation of **Machine Trades**

In Testimony Whereof, this Certificate is issued by the State Division of Vocational Education and the **Cuyahoga Falls** Board of Education this 7th day of June 19 74.

_____
State Superintendent of Public Instruction

_____
Director Vocational Education

_____
Superintendent

_____
Instructors

This certificate verifies that the student has completed a vocational program in accordance with the State Plan for Vocational Education, including a minimum of 80% attendance and satisfactory grades and skill achievement.

COMMENTS:

MACHINES	SENIOR HOURS
VERT. MILL	136
HOR. MILL	21
LATHE	126
SHAPER	8
BENCH	11
BENCH GRINDER	19
SURFACE GRINDER	194
TOOL & CUTTER GRINDER	30
RADIAL DRILL PRESS	46
HOURS PRESENT	591
HOURS ABSENT	45

_____
Instructor(s)

Insert provided by the Ohio Dept of Education Vocational division

The Vocational Department of Ohio developed a certificate a student could show an employer regarding his experiences in the vocational program. A sample is included. We had a real-time clock and timecard that allowed the student to log his time on the various machines. Hours were listed daily regarding machine operations and machines. The time on each machine was typed on the back of the student's certificate to show the employer. To indicate the hours were to show an employer, the individual did have time and experience on machining equipment. All the time, we stressed precision and close-fitting components of each job because the industry expects quality and quantity. Companies plan for a period where the new worker adapts to the shop procedures and is not an asset. Our program was designed to reduce the time a new worker was considered a liability

THINGS THAT THE STUDENT MADE

On the first day for the seniors, the guys perform "machine orientation," procedures to review what the individual knows about our different machines. There were sheets for each group of machines, such as lathe, milling machines, grinders, and drill presses. The student walks through using the worksheet to review the machine functions like starting and stopping the machine, setting R.P.M.s, feed rates, graduations on dials, lubrication requirements, and other basic features.

The students spent three periods in the shop each school day and one period in a classroom for related instruction. The student would have 540 hours on machines each year (180 days x 3 hours = 540) or 1080 hours for two years. Both instructors designed jobs that were similar to those of industry and would stress quality before quantity in our program. With practice, the quantity would develop.

LARGE TAP WRENCH

THE TAP WRENCH

The large tap wrench was an important project for the class. This design was what former student recommended. This one is rusty but those made were highly polished. There was much effort in fitting the solid jaw (on the left) so there was no   ight seemed. Each student had to use the dividing dead on the milling machine to machine the angles and used radius gages to bench radius on the edges. We would tell the student the surface should be so smooth that if a fly landed on it, if would slip off and break his leg. We also tried to shrink fit on a few. A left and right thread had to be made also. When the body was placed in the lathe. It was to be indicated within plus or minus .003. It was 18 plus inches long

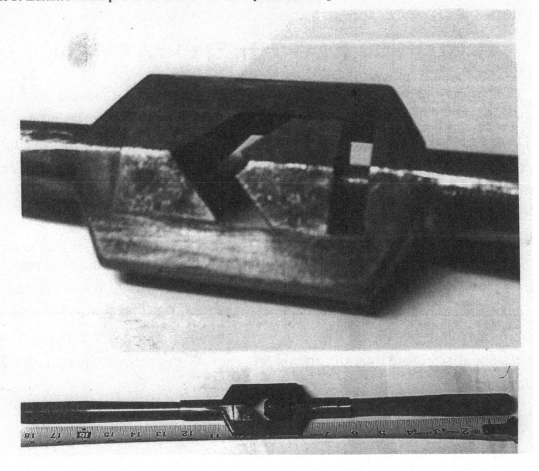

A student suggested we make a larger tap wrench after he returned and commented on the small tap wrench we were making was OK, but he needed a larger one like the one in the tool room. We copied the dimension, and the Vocational Drafting senior class made drawings. We required the surface finish to show no machine marks. The students did appreciate the appearance of their wrench because it looked like a store-bought tap wrench. We have included a picture of the larger size wrench, which required a lot of fitting. At the end of the square pocket, a v-shaped insert was fastened. If the wrench was held up to the light, no light should be seen between the insert and pocket. We used a combination of gage blocks to determine the inside dimension of the slot, and that number was used to grind the insert to size. Benching or fitting was needed until it was OK. Once a student said his wrench was to be checked regarding the light requirement, but he wanted to hold the wrench while I looked at the end and fit. Usually, I hold the wrench and look with the ceiling light as a background. I insisted on keeping it and looked close; I could see a film of grease between the insert and body. I mentioned this "grease problem," and the student said he didn't know how the grease got there. They laughed, and many mentioned that it was a good idea.

We used the dividing head on the body to produce the angles on both sides, then time to bench radii on the edges and remove all machine marks. When the student complained about the hard work on the finish, we would show the store-bought wrench. I told them one shop foreman in charge of mold finishing said he wants the finish so smooth that if a fly landed on the surface, he would slip off and break a leg. The wrench in the picture is rusty, is old, and has been used a lot by the former student.

V - BLOCK

Thanks to Mike Nelson for his v-block

We wanted each student to make a V-block and had several different designs. We would heat treat and then grind the blocks square and parallel. The grinding process is usually a final operation, and the required dimensions are important and would require a lot of indicating to obtain close tolerances. The guys would use angle plates and tissue paper to clamp the blocks to help maintain sides that would be square and parallel. When we had 2 or 3 sets, we would heat treat the blocks in our furnace and temper them in the other furnace. We used oil hardening steel, and that was an experience. We had guys who were afraid of immersing 1500 degrees, red hot steel in a barrel of oil because some were worried about the oil flashing (igniting into a flame). Flashing would happen if the steel at 1500 degrees is kept in the same place in the oil, or above the surface, the surface would erupt into a flame. I demonstrated how to stand sideways so my face would not be over the barrel; how to move the steel deep with circular movements into the oil until the pulsating stopped. We would talk about safety regarding this and had plans ready to implement. One student said he planned to run out of the building, then yell for help outside the building.

THE GRINDERS' VISE

The main project, a grinder's vise, was the senior exam. Many seniors didn't complete their vise because they were working and spent their last weeks on the job. Several photos are showing the parts and one assembled. The material was (P-20) pre harden steel donated by Akromold Company. All I had to do was to call Mr. Don Hatherill, plant supervisor, and tell him how many guys were making the vise, travel to the plant after school in my car, and pick up the pieces. There was no paperwork or waiting for school board approval. We stressed precision in machining to a thousandth of an inch. This precision would be expected of the students on the job in the industry.

THE GRINDER VICE

The vice was 3 x 4 x 7 and able to stand on 5 surfaces. The top picture shows the first vice design, The bottom picture shows the last design. Changes were made from comments from students. The screw diameter was increased and double lead Threads which means It would open and close quicker. The end was a 3/4 hexagon to allow a wrench to be used. The grinding ensured the sides were parallel and square. The middle picture shows the parts needed to complete the vice. When a student finished his vice I felt as good as he did looking at the job well done.

Thanks again to Akromold for the steel

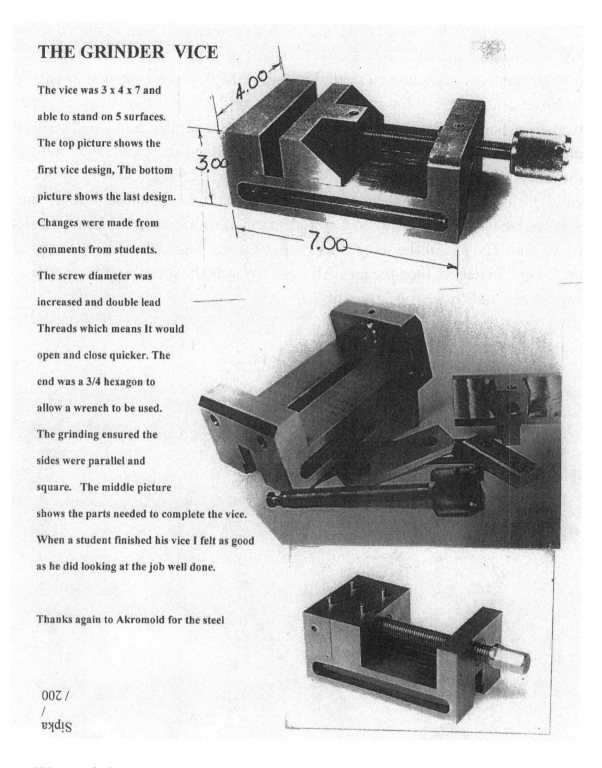

We used the paper that one would use if they were to roll a cigarette. The paper was close to .001 thousandths of an inch, and we use the strips of paper to determine how close dimensions were to the required sizes and how pieces fit together. For example, on the vise, we required two pieces of paper under the loose jaw and the vise body when the sliding jaw was fastened to the vise body.

The jaw should slide but not wobble. Another requirement was when the loose jaw was against the solid jaw, four little strips of paper were placed top right, bottom right, and the same on the left was to be held, and no paper slips should slide out as the loose jaw was forced into the solid jaw. All four strips of paper were to be held firmly. The vise was to be square and parallel so it could be used on the sides and bottom when grinding to close dimensions. In the beginning, the screw was a single lead thread, but students said it took too long to open and close the loose jaw, so we changed to a double lead thread for a faster movement. The double lead thread required the student machine a special bushing that fits in the end. The end of the screw was changed when we machined a ¾ hexagon on the end to help tighten the jaw. All I can say was the jobs the students made were theirs and "industrial strength."

RUSS'S VICE

(picture) Russ's complete job one pictures before description 1)

There are photos of one extraordinary job done by a student. One time the class schedule had one instructor teach the same class for the junior and senior years. The time I had the class for both years was 1969-1970 and 1970 – 1971. Russ had time to complete all the extra parts to this project. Besides making the vise, this young man wanted to make a 10-inch sine plate than a base unit that fits under the vise and attached to the sine plate in 3 different places. I drilled holes in the top of the sine plate at Martz Mold and Machine Company during a tour. I had worked there and figured this could show how an NC machine works. Next, he calibrated the base unit in degrees and added a Vernier scale that could set 15 minutes of a degree. The last feature was brackets attached to the side of the sine plate and a base plate so the whole unit could be fastened to a machine table. There was a high degree of precision in all these parts. A lot of cigarette paper was used.

Russ was present in 1971 when we made the first coasters with the student's name at the bottom of the coaster.

1 X 2 X 3 BLOCKS

Thank Larry Dudek for is blocks

A person on any machine should be aware of controlling position – know where the tool is in relationship to the finish dimension. The operator must know how much to remove to obtain the finish dimension, how many rough cuts and depth of finish cut should be taken to remove the material quickly because time is money to the company. On a lathe, the stock rotates, and the cutter moves. On a milling machine, the cutter rotates, and the stock moves. We would use the job of 1 x 2 x 3 blocks to understand control positioning. We had a job-grade sheet that listed the operations and a line for a grade for each procedure. The student then went to the next operation. The job was a rectangle 1 x 2 x 3 inches with six holes through the 1-inch dimension. The stock was 1.25 x 2.25 x 3.5 to begin machining. We used the extra stock to practice machining slots to learn how to control position. We did not lay out the slots. An example: machine a slot .750 wide .125 deep 3 inches long in the middle of the 2inch + 3inch surface with no layout lines. The graduated dials, micrometers, pencil, and paper were used to obtain the first grade. Another practice exercise for a grade, and then the main objective was started – to machine 1 x 2 x 3 blocks.

The six holes were to be drilled again by understanding the graduations on the dials on the machine tables. We calculated X and Y coordinates for each hole from a corner and listed the operations to be used to perform on the six holes. The student was to use a ½ inch round rod in the machine spindle, touch the side against the solid jaw, using the tissue paper to touch the surface and setting the graduated dial to zero. Another surface 90 degrees from the first edge is touched-off and dial set to zero. We can now move the drills using the numbers from our calculating from "X" zero and "Y" zero. The graduated dials on the longitude movement (X dimension, left to right) and cross-movement (Y dimension, in and out). The same procedure was used when we obtained two Digital Read Out Systems (DRO's).

All six holes are center drilled and checked visually with a six-inch ruler, then drilled with a ½ inch diameter drill through the piece and finish by countersinking the holes. Next, they were to remove the block, turn the block over and countersink the holes on the other side using the coordinates from the first side. The holes could have been drilled quicker, but the work of figuring coordinates is "Controlling Position."

First, the stock was to be 1.015, 2.015, and 3.015 to allow for heat treatment and grinding to dimensions of 1.000 +/-.002 and 2.000 +/- .002 and 3.000 +-.002

and be square and parallel. Each step was graded and placed on the procedure sheet.

I wish to thank Mr. Larry Dudack for letting me use his blocks for the picture.

PROCEDURE SHEET FOR 1-2-3 BLOCKS

_____   _____

                                 Name   date

PART 1) Machine all 6 sides on both blocks

PART 2) Machine slots   a) from Right – Left and b) front to back

        A) Calculate and layout slots
        B) Use ½ dia cutter zero out the cutter, set vertical dial to zero
        C) Raise table .025 per cut and machine to a depth of .275
        D) Begin to machine sides, mark dials for each cut and record on paper
        E) Machine with conventional table movement (no climb mill)
        F) Determine the amount to cut to arrive at the rough dimension
        G) Finish cut depth and move to finish sizes on both sides <u>DO NOT REMOVE FROM VISE -</u> ASK TO BE GRADED

_____

  Grade

PART 3) Obtain dimensions for the second cut from front to back. Repeat steps A-H

_____

  Grade

PART 4) Machine both blocks to 1.020 , 2.020, 3.020 +/- .003.

_____

  Grade

PART 5) Grind to 1.000, 2.000, 3.000 +/- .002 square and parallel

_____

  Grade

FINAL GRADE _____   **Date** _____

COMMENTS

(picture of procedure sheet for 1 – 2- 3 blocks)

BALL VISE

This project won the North Eastern VICA contest (Vocational Clubs of America) in 1970 and the Ohio State VICA contest, which allowed the student and teacher, Mr. Gruber, to travel to Chicago to compete on the national level. This project was added after my ball vise was used in the class to help with students finishing their jobs. I bought it when I worked at Sackmanns in the 1950s. The ball sits in a leather ring, and the person can file or work on the item and rotate the piece 360 degrees and swing the bottom half of the ball forward or backward to see the object better. The drafting class drew  the drawings. There were several difficult parts to be made, and the student was successful. The screw had a right and left-hand threads, as well as each moveable jaw, had the matching threads. Both threads were "chased" or machined and not made by using a thread die. Holding the bottom sphere required a specialized lathe attachment called "Tracing Attachment," which needed a template to be made that was to produce the bottom half sphere. All the students were aware of how this attachment worked and was told it could be a standard attachment they might use in the machining industry. Several parts required planning the sequence of machining operations. The alignment of the two jaws and the screw that moved the jaws was critical. The student was efficient in his completing the vise. We made one more ball vise.

BORING BAR ASSEMBLY

The boring bar assembly (BBA) was used to produced holes too large for standard twist drills. We use it when the student would machine a large fastener that required internal and external threads. The Vocational Drafting Class produced a drawing from our unit. Our BBA was used when the main body was bored out to size. The indexing head was used on the vertical milling machine to produce the three different diameter holes.

TURRET TOOL HOLDER

Thanks to G. Carver and unknow student for the use of the turret tool holders

The turret tool holder required work on lathes, milling machines, and surface grinders. Most of the handle was machined using the lathe's tracing attachment. The other end needed a cam design to lock the holder in place when in use. This feature required using files and templates. The square top and the inside cylinder required eight round holes that allow the top to be positioned eight different ways while on the lathe. The dividing attachment was used for this detail for the two parts of the holder. Use of precision indicating devices were used though out the job.

One thing that was done to allow the top to be rotated and locked quickly was to make a spring. We had the correct music wire, and I knew how to wind the spring on the lathe, which I learned in high school in1952. I mentioned my instructor, Mr. Alex Musser, in High School, told us he learned this in the 1920s. He would say he as old as dirt. I guess I can say the same thing.

I wish to thank Mr. G.Carver for using his turret tool holder. I do not know the young man who made the other holder.

One more thing, the drawing on the cover of this book shows the body of this job. Someone used this drawing.

VOCATIONAL CLUBS OF AMERICA (VICA)

Cuyahoga Falls Vocational programs belonged to the Vocational Clubs of America or VICA, which held annual contests among different trade classes and schools in Ohio and the United States. The drawings and the ball vice were taken to the state contest in Columbus and was awarded first prize and was to represent Ohio in the National VICA contest in Chicago, Illinois. I was teaching the junior class, and Mr. Bob Gruber, the senior instructor, went along with the student. I'm not sure of the results, but I do know that was the last year they had a contest where a project was graded. In 1972 the VICA contests were statewide and were at facilities where the student would work on 4 or 5 procedures in his trade area and then be evaluated, no trips to another competition for the winners.

Ohio State also required a written test to evaluate the standard skills for that trade area. We always scored high in all the sections in both the Junior and Senior classes.

EPILOGUE

MY REQUEST TO HUSBANDS

The lost of my wife was devastating. I wanted to relive the last few years and show her how important she was to me. I can't do that now. I would like to suggest husbands have a habit of giving her a ever-so gentle kiss on the cheek or forehead. If she wants to know what's that for? Tell her "it's because you are here!"

HOW DID MY PERSONALITY DEVELOP?

The letters ONCUE describe me. The ON stands for original nature, which means my parents, Helen and Steve Sipka (my dad was – Stanley, but he liked Steve). Living on Mustill Street with four sisters and being the oldest made me think I had some responsibility for them. I remember a time when my friends from Hower came to visit and found out I had pretty sisters; they would ask me to fix them up with Rita, who was the oldest. A couple of guys said they would keep visiting after they graduate because of my sisters. They would tell my mom they would want to visit me. I would kid them that I know too much about them and would watch out for my sisters. I did think my sisters were pretty.

When I worked in the bowling alley, I didn't mind giving my mom the money for help with expenses.

The "C" stands for CULTURE, which is to me North Hill in Akron. It could have been other places, but the houses on Otto and Mustill Streets showed me what life was like in my neighborhood. My world was a few blocks and diversified surroundings. We had two dumps to visit and look for treasures. We played our neighborhood baseball games on a field on the edge of the one dump. The home plate was positioned against a hill, so foul balls were easy to find. We drank water from a well next to a shack. The ragged looking man would come out and use his ladle, dip it in the barrel and help us quench our thirst. On beggers night, we went to houses and didn't worry about what was given to us beggars. Our area was mixed, and we heard and were to respect the parents of our friends. It was easy to do that.

The UE stands for UNIQUE EXPERIENCES. There were many moments, good and bad, that influenced me. I often think about moments that changed my life. For example:

1. Going to St. Hedwigs Grade School
2. Going to Hower Vocational High School,
3. The blind date with Joanne and our time together
4. My quitting Sackmann
5. Finding a job at Main Mold
6. My walkthrough Van Dusen Hall because it was raining and seeing the room full of machines like Hower Vocational High School.
7. Student teaching at Sill Middle School
8. My dad dying early
9. Many others

THINGS ARE DIFFERENT NOW

My experiences in the metal machining industry are ancient compared to what is done today. I viewed a video of a process called Stereo Lithography in 1971 and thought it was going to be the next big time saver. Nothing happened until the last five years when it resurfaced as "3D Printing." Now, 3D Printing units come in all sizes and are own by families for fun and serious projects.

There are numerous videoes of machining centers completing the job in minutes with little participation from the operator. No measuring, just watching the screen or the cutting through the window. The need for a machinist is still present, but the term operator is used today.

I visited Akromold or Prospect recently and didn't recognize the main bay. I saw two old Bridgeport vertical milling machines covered with dust. Years ago, there were 8 to 10 Bridgeports busy with individuals working. The machines today are enclosed in metal walls with a glass window to watch the cutting. There is no turning of handles to control position; all movements are controlled by the information typed into a keyboard. The screen is showing the numbers, which indicates movements and operations. Where there were 100 workers, you will find 30 doing more than those 100. Not that the 30 are superhuman, but the computer controls the machine. Plans will be to reduce the need for those 30 workers in the future.

Imagine a stream of water, the thickness of a wooden toothpick, cutting through a 1-inch thick piece of steel. Waterjet cutting is another process that is becoming incorporated in manufacturing. I watched an operation cut a complicated opening six times in a piece of steel. CNC controlled the cut, and the piece was 1-inch thick. We have seen high-pressure washing units cleaning sides on houses, sidewalks, and roofs. Imagine the pressure needed to cut a piece of steel. There is pinpoint accuracy, and little removal of burrs and heat-treated steel is not changed. Safety is important; the stream of water is like a knife. I stayed there asking questions of the operator and was fascinated by water cutting steel. Thus, another time-saver and reduction of workforce.

The average person can buy a unit that cuts like the water jet but uses routers. These machines are becoming typical in school shops. The instructor must attend classes because the operations are different. It's set it up, type in the program, and watch the machine complete the job. Just know-how to stop the machine if there's a problem.

There have been plans to have a driver-less large truck on interstate highways and no engineers on trains. I imagine older people will be concerned there is no human element for those moments when a human needs to act. How about a wage for not working or a 24-hour workweek. Being old allows me to compare what was, to what is, and what might be. The Ford Motor Company production line of the early 1900s showed men side-by-side producing a car every few minutes. Now you see robots all working to produce the modern-day "Model A" faster. "All different shades of black," as Henry Ford would say.

ALL GOOD THINGS COME TO AN END!

Yes! ALL GOOD THINGS COME TO AN END, some come quick and some last a long time. The 61 years of marriage and the two years before marriage with Joanne was a long time, and it was GOOD for me. The hardest thing for me is I can't touch her. This book is a form of grieving for me. I think she is looking over my shoulder, making comments. I'm beginning to see the end where I'll place that last period in this bucket list item. Then it will be another item but less demanding than this one. Now it's thinking about the last period. It will look like an ordinary period but will be the most significant of all the letters, words, and punctuation. It's tiny and final.

I read over every page and made changes. The trick is not to read anymore. The easy part was to write what you see and read; the hard part is to organize the material into a book. People have asked me why did I write this? My answer is like that person who was asked why he climbed that mountain? His answer was, "because it was there!" My answer would be the same. Other questions were, who do I want to read this? Who is your audience? How many books do you want?; I don't know how many, at least two, one for me and one for someone else. I believe part of my contract with the publishing company includes five books. It's another bucket list item that challenged me like the bevel stain glass window; it was a challenge too, and it turned out to be a beautiful daily enjoyed sight. The amount will be more than two because two friends said they want to buy one, so I will need four books. The more people I tell about this project, the more indicate they would like one. Will I hear comments like those I received from the window? When I held the two-foot by four-foot window up, I was the happiest person around, and I remember that feeling; the thrill of success, especially after my mother-in-law, said it was beautiful. I will imagine Joanne will tell me her opinion because she is still with me. That will be the only one that matters.

The virus is making me stay in to be safe. I'm in that age group that is vulnerable. My daughters are watching over me and want me around for a while. So, working on this book fills my day. Soon the weather will be nice, the daylight longer, grass to mow, and tomatoes to plant.

Joanne and I and my family want to thank you for taking the time to read and view what has been presented. The picture shows my Family, who has to take care of me now. They are adults now, and their birthday gifts are greatly reduced. It used to be $5 per year now it's $20 or less. On my 80th birthday, I told them that would mean my present would be 400 dollars ($5 x 80) they said it would be more like .25 cents per year or 20 dollars. I told them .25 cents per year would be the standard now.

It's a good feeling to see this coming to an end as Joanne, and I sit on our chairs, under the umbrella, holding hands watching the ocean and waiting for high tide. We always would walk a little way into the Ocean and kiss at least once a day. It was like that first kiss years and years ago. I have to be good and get to heaven because that's where she's watching me and still helping me. Thank you, Joanne. I love you.

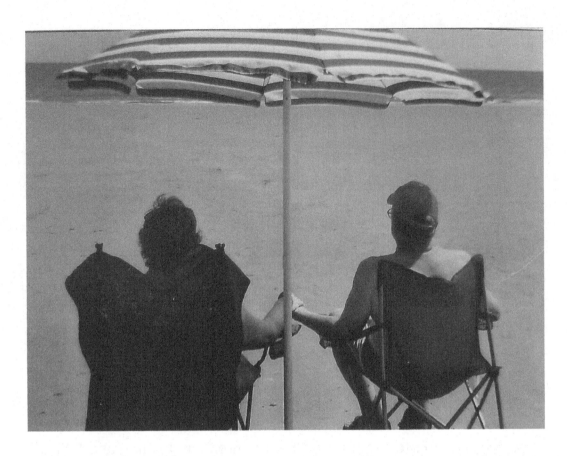

The final period arrived on October 11, Friday, 2019, when our three daughters, me and Joanne, held hands for the last time (<u>THE</u> <u>FINAL</u> <u>PERIOD</u>).

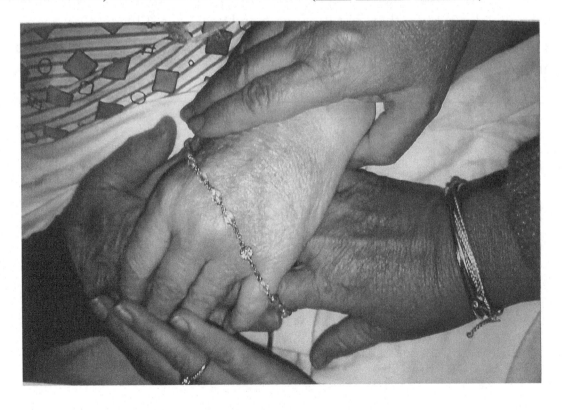

Printed in the United States
By Bookmasters